The Politics of
The Atlantic Alliance

The Politics of
The Atlantic Alliance

ALVIN J. COTTRELL

JAMES E. DOUGHERTY

FREDERICK A. PRAEGER, *Publisher*

New York · London

FREDERICK A. PRAEGER, PUBLISHER
64 UNIVERSITY PLACE, NEW YORK 3, N.Y., U.S.A.
77-79 CHARLOTTE STREET, LONDON W.1, ENGLAND

Published in the United States of America in 1964
by Frederick A. Praeger, Inc., Publisher

Published in the United Kingdom in 1964
by The Pall Mall Press, Ltd., London and Dunmow
under the title:
THE ATLANTIC ALLIANCE—A Short Political Guide

All rights reserved

© Alvin J. Cottrell and James E. Dougherty, 1964
Library of Congress Catalog Card Number: 64-13494

Printed in the United States of America

CONTENTS

TO JOY AND MARIA

PREFACE

The authors of this short political guide have been keenly interested in the fortunes of NATO for over a decade, that is, since their graduate days at the University of Pennsylvania. The decision to write this book was undertaken after Hans Kohn, Professor Emeritus of the City College of New York —one of the outstanding leaders in the field of Atlantic Community studies—suggested that the publishers commission Dr Alvin J. Cottrell, of the Institute for Defense Analyses, to prepare a survey of the political lines along which the North Atlantic Alliance has evolved since its formation. Dr Cottrell then enlisted Dr James E. Dougherty, his former colleague at the Foreign Policy Research Institute of the University of Pennsylvania, to collaborate with him on the work.

It became apparent at a very early planning stage that a guide to the politics of NATO could not be focused exclusively upon things purely political, i.e., upon political history, or a description of political institutions, processes and issues. To a great extent, the politics of the Western Alliance since 1949 have been intimately bound up with problems of military strategy and economic integration. Political, military and economic factors form a seamless web; the inclusion of all three subjects within the scope of the book was unavoidable. The authors also thought that a chapter on Soviet views of NATO would serve a highly useful purpose by adding a perspective that is only too often overlooked in treatments of this sort. As for the actual division of labour, Dr Cottrell wrote Chapters 2 and 3. Dr Dougherty wrote Chapters 4 and 5. The opening and concluding chapters are the product of joint efforts.

Most of the writing was completed when the Alliance began to pass through its "time of troubles" in December, 1962—the cancellation of Skybolt, the Nassau Agreement for a NATO Polaris deterrent, President de Gaulle's veto of Britain's application for entry into the EEC and the complex diplomatic aftermath of that event. The rapid unfolding of significant new developments constitutes, of course, one of the major occupational hazards of those who have the temerity to write books on international affairs. There is a temptation to fasten excessively upon the latest crisis and to accord it a disproportionate amount of attention. Such a temptation was particularly strong early in 1963, when NATO was beset by a crisis which was undoubtedly more profound than the one it experienced at the time of Suez— more profound because it pertained to the very structural core of the Alliance and not merely to a disagreement over policy towards a geographic area that lay outside the territory covered by the Treaty.

The authors, however, instead of entering the maelstrom of current polemic debate, tried to place the crisis of early 1963 in a proper perspective. They considered the possibility of devoting a special chapter to the implications for NATO of President de Gaulle's policies—his determination to press towards an independent national nuclear deterrent (*force de dissuasion*), his decision to suspend the Brussels negotiations, his efforts to establish French leadership within the European Community and to establish a special relationship with West Germany which would offset the influence of *les Anglo-Saxons* within NATO, and to bring about something approaching an equilibrium between Europe and America within the Western coalition. Certainly President de Gaulle's policies—not only these but others which are more obscure and harder to evaluate—are fraught with potentially grave consequences for the future of NATO. But at the present stage of the transatlantic diplomatic encounter, the prevailing arguments depend in great measure upon political speculation rather than upon the kind of settled facts with which the scholar prefers to deal. It was decided, therefore, that it might be safer not to write a special chapter on NATO's latest upheaval, but simply to treat its specific aspects in the appropriate chapters on military, economic and political questions, and in the Conclusions. De Gaulle's policies, after all, represent one statesman's reactions to the whole pattern of intra-Alliance problems discussed throughout the book. France is but one member of the Alliance. Even if de Gaulle spoke for all of France (which he does not), he could not by himself determine the fate of the Alliance. He himself must accept facts, bend before countervailing pressures, and accommodate to new situations as they emerge. The authors do not presume to judge whether he is right or wrong in what he is trying to do for France, or even whether his policies are good or bad for NATO. They are primarily interested here in analysing the persistent problems confronting the Alliance and in sketching with broad strokes the major direction in which it is moving. Deriving some modest comfort from the fact that the Suez crisis, which imposed such serious strains at the time, could be handled dispassionately seven years later within the space of a few pages, the authors both hope and believe that this latest crisis, too, shall pass.

Although the authors by necessity worked in close co-operation, each owes specific debts of gratitude. Dr Cottrell would like to thank the following colleagues in the Institute for Defense Analyses for their critical comments at various stages of the draft: Mr James E. King, Jr., Dr John K. Moriarty, Mr John Ponturo and Mrs Anne Jonas. Dr Cottrell is particularly indebted to Col. Frederick J. Yeager for his thorough critique of Chapter 2 on the USSR and NATO and for making available to him his extensive research on the same subject.

Dr Dougherty wishes to acknowledge that much of what he has contributed to this book represents, as it were, a "spin-off" of a research-writing project on the Atlantic Community in which he has participated during the last four years at the Foreign Policy Research Institute of the University of Pennsylvania, under the Directorship of Professor Robert Strausz-Hupé. This project was supported by a grant from the A. W. Mellon Educational and Charitable Trust, and culminated in a book, *Building the Atlantic World*, by Robert Strausz-Hupé, James E. Dougherty, William R. Kintner and others, published by Harper and Row in 1963. During those years, Dr Dougherty's understanding of the problems of NATO has been enhanced immeasurably as a result of discussions with the following: Dr Robert Strausz-Hupé, Dr William R. Kintner, Dr Hans Kohn, Dr Norman Palmer, Dr Arthur P. Whitaker, Dr Stefan T. Possony and Dr William Y. Elliott, all fellow Associates within the Foreign Policy Research Institute; Mr Robert C. Herber, Mr Robert P. Pfaltzgraff, Jr., Mr Gerhart Mally and Mr Herbert Folpe, all members of the Institute staff; Mr Francis P. Hoeber, of the Stanford Research Institute, who helped to cast a great deal of light upon the economics of NATO; Brig. General Donald Bennett, of the NATO Standing Group; Colonel F. O. Miksche, of France; Dr Kurt Birrenbach, member of the Bundestag of the German Federal Republic; Mr Frederick W. Mulley, Labour MP and Vice-President of the Assembly of the Western European Union; Mr Timothy Stanley of the Council of Foreign Relations; Dr Malcolm W. Hoag, of the Rand Corporation; General Richard Stilwell, Commandant of Cadets, US Military

Academy; Mr Jeremy Blanchett, of the US Arms Control and Disarmament Agency; and other officials of the Departments of State and Defense and other governmental agencies who would doubtless prefer to remain anonymous but who nevertheless have given generously of their time and their insights.

The authors wish especially to thank Walter F. Hahn who has collaborated with them on a number of previous writings on NATO policy and strategy. He participated in the drafting of the military section of a study written for the US Senate Foreign Relations Committee in 1959 which formed a partial basis for Chapter 3 of this book.

Both authors join in expressing appreciation to the hardy people who were instrumental in the "logistics" of preparing the manuscript—particularly Mrs Geraldine Kuzner, Miss Giulia Gibbons, Mrs Vera Driver, Miss Eleanor Walters and Mrs Elvera Marschhausen.

Finally, the authors would like very much to thank the following publications and organisations for permitting them to quote copyrighted materials: *Current History* for granting Dr Cottrell permission to use portions of two of his articles which appeared in the April and September, 1960 issues of that journal; the Doubleday Co. and the Institute of American Strategy for permission to use portions of one of Dr Cottrell's chapters which appeared in *American Strategy in the Nuclear Age* which was published for the Institute of American Strategy by Doubleday in 1959; the Foreign Policy Research Institute for permission to quote freely from *Orbis*; the Council on Foreign Relations for permission to quote extensively from several issues of *Foreign Affairs*, and from various Council books, especially Henry A. Kissinger, *Nuclear Weapons and Foreign Policy* (Harper, 1957) and Ben T. Moore, *NATO and the Future of Europe* (Harper, 1958); Yale University Press for permission to quote from *The Yale Review*.

Chapter 1

THE NORTH ATLANTIC TREATY ORGANISATION

NATO was the West's response to a number of ominous postwar moves by the Soviet Union which seemed to foreshadow an imminent communist military thrust into Western Europe. By 1948, Poland, Bulgaria, Hungary and Roumania had been completely incorporated into the Soviet empire. Turkey and Iran were under persistent Soviet pressure, and Greece had been the victim of a communist guerrilla attack which was finally defeated by the Greek armed forces bolstered by American military assistance sent under the Truman Doctrine. The communist insurrection in Greece was also severely weakened by Yugoslavia's defection from the Soviet bloc. But perhaps the most significant catalyst of the alliance was the forcible overthrow of the Czecho-Slovakian government, in 1948, by an internal communist revolt, backed by the Red Army. As Paul-Henri Spaak of Belgium has said: "The determining factor in international politics after the Second World War was the *coup d'état* in Prague. The replacement of a democratic, progressive regime by a totalitarian government dominated by a communist minority deserves a singularly important place in postwar history. The tragedy of Czecho-Slovakia was the bolt of lightning which roused the West. After 1948,

everyone in Western Europe and in the New World understood that the Western nations, for their own safety, had to
unite and make clear to Soviet Russia that Prague was the
last act of Soviet imperialism on the European continent
which we would tolerate."[1]

The Second World War had left Europe with its morale
shattered, its economy ruined, and its defences weak. Many
Europeans, apprehensive about the rapid withdrawal of
United States forces and precipitous demobilisation, feared a
Soviet thrust westward toward the Atlantic. Several Western
analysts have expressed doubts that the Soviet ever intended
to launch a military attack on Western Europe. Still, whatever the actual Soviet intentions were, in the late 1940s the
Europeans found themselves face to face with a potentially
aggressive power, and it was rather unnerving to many of
them to read about Maurice Thorez telling the French
National Assembly that the French people would welcome
Soviet forces as an army of liberation, and Palmiro Togliatti
uttering similar sentiments in parliament at Rome. After all,
Thorez and Togliatti controlled large, disciplined and
aggressive communist parties.

The United States previously had taken energetic action
to buttress Europe with an imaginative programme of
economic aid—the Marshall Plan. But the swallowing up of
Czecho-Slovakia and the Berlin blockade made it obvious
that economic aid, although indispensable, would not by
itself suffice to deter Soviet aggression. The US government
realised that Sovietisation of the entire European continent
would: (1) contaminate the wellspring of Western culture;
(2) endanger the survival of free political institutions everywhere, including the United States; (3) render Europe's
colonies, bases and spheres of influence throughout the
world vulnerable to communist takeover; (4) place the grow-

[1] "The Atlantic Community and NATO," *Orbis*, Vol. I
(Winter, 1958), p. 411.

ing productive potential of Western Europe at the disposal of the Soviet Union's aggressive policies and (5) greatly reduce the defence-in-depth capabilities of the United States, by depriving its air, ground and naval forces of access to the eastern coast of the Atlantic Ocean.

Clearly, the defence of Western Europe was now in the United States' national interest. It had become an essential element of the national strategy of the United States, and this demanded a profound transformation of the American attitude towards world affairs. Since the time of Washington's Farewell Address and the Monroe Doctrine, the principle of non-involvement in the "balance of power" politics of Europe had been deeply ingrained in the minds of the American people. The United States, it is true, had intervened twice in world wars originating in Europe, to maintain the freedom of the Atlantic Ocean, to help preserve constitutional democratic regimes and to prevent an absolutist power from establishing hegemony over the Continent. But in the absence of an overt aggressive act, it seemed unlikely that American public opinion would support a policy that would involve the United States in long-range military commitments overseas. Nevertheless, the American government, backed by responsible public opinion, quickly recognised that henceforth freedom in Europe and North America would be inextricably bound together. They were able to convince the nation that isolation from European affairs, which had been the traditional American attitude, had to be abandoned in favour of a new concept: full commitment to the Atlantic Community. The United States Senate adopted a resolution authorising the government to enter into regional defence arrangements that would be of benefit to the national security. Before long, the treaty formalising the North Atlantic Alliance was signed. In it, the United States and the other signatories pledged themselves to regard an attack upon one as an attack upon all. Thus, on 4 April,

1949, occurred one of the major diplomatic revolutions of history.

In forming NATO, the United States and the European allies sought to prevent the absorption of Western Europe into the Soviet Empire. As NATO grew in strength, a new and different challenge arose, in addition to the basic military threat, *viz.* the possibility of its neutralisation as a result of Soviet psychological-diplomatic strategy (see Chapter 3). If Western Europe were neutralised by Soviet pressure, the region's vast resources might eventually be denied to the free world. Meanwhile, to the extent that the Soviets have refrained from direct military aggression, NATO deserves to be called successful.

It may be argued that the case for NATO's success has not yet been proved because there is no tangible evidence that the Soviets ever planned a direct military assault on Western Europe. It must always be borne in mind, however, that what the Soviets do or do not do is intimately related to the West's own behaviour. Some of the greatest achievements in history tend to be minimised precisely because they headed off spectacular developments; in politics, as in medicine, prevention is always less dramatic than the cure. Suffice it to say that NATO, backed by the United States' strategic nuclear power operating at first from a ring of bases round the Soviet heartland of communism and more recently from bases in the US and Polaris submarines at sea as well, has, throughout the postwar period, provided a formidable deterrent to a potential Soviet thrust to the English Channel.

NATO's Importance for the West

It would be an error, however, to view NATO's value to the West as little more than that of a formal military alliance for the declared purpose of defending Western Europe. As vital as this objective may be to the security of the free world, it is by no means the only one. No one has argued the case for NATO's over-all importance to the West more eloquently than the former Secretary of State, Dean G. Acheson.

Speaking before an audience of US Reserve Officers at the National War College in July, 1959, Mr Acheson pointed out that the United States alone could not possibly cope with the formidable problems confronting it in all areas of the globe. There are today, on this side of the Iron and Bamboo Curtains, he argued, two great centres of power: the United States and Western Europe. If the United States, as the leader of the Western world, is to prevent the further shift of power eastward to the communist bloc and to deal successfully with proliferating problems of awakening continents, then it can do so only in co-operation with Western Europe. It is not, as Mr Acheson was careful to explain, that Americans consider Europeans superior as a people to those inhabiting the under-developed nations of Asia, Africa and Latin America. The problem, he said, is rather one of priorities: if the newly emerging nations are to be helped, as they must be, first priority has to be given to the effective organisation of the primary resources of the Western world —the resources of Western Europe and North America. Since Mr Acheson was one of the principal architects of NATO, it is worth quoting at length from a statement in which he reflected on the significance of the Alliance in the world today: "The indispensable collaborator of the United States in providing security and opportunity for the free world is Western Europe. Geography, history, population, resources and technology all combine to make this so. Working together these two areas have twice the population and three times the productive capacity of the Soviet Union, an ample base for military defence and economic development. But if the Soviet Union should be able to control the production of Europe, our problems would soon be beyond our capacity to deal with them.

"It is all too easy to lose sight of this vital truth, or never see it at all. We are, and should be, deeply concerned with social, political and economic development in Latin America, Asia and Africa. In all of these areas revolutionary movements are pressing hard for change and improvement. In many of them independence has been wrested from weakened colonial powers by people wholly incompetent to manage their own affairs and, therefore, in desperate need of disinterested help and instruction.

"It is often said, sometimes within the United States government itself, that our interests in the alliance with Europe and in the underdeveloped areas are competing and conflicting. This is the opposite of the truth; only the North American-Western European connection makes possible the development of Latin-American, Asian and African countries in security and in an environment which leaves them freedom of choice to develop in their own way. In some cases memories of a colonial past feed suspicion; in others, the liquidation of remaining colonial relations may bring conflict and brutalities. Both only obscure an essential truth.

"The essential truth is that the hope of the whole free world, developed and undeveloped nations alike, lies in the ever closer association and economic growth of Western Europe and North America. For in that economic growth —impossible without common institutions to harmonise economies which deeply affect one another—lie expanding capabilities to deal with the needs of growing populations at home, the export of capital goods for development abroad and the provision for military defence."[2]

The primacy of Europe in the United States' foreign policy was one of the major reasons which prompted the

[2] "Fifty Years After," *The Yale Review*, Vol. 51 (Autumn, 1961), pp. 7-8. Cf. also Mr Acheson's article, "The Premises of American Policy," *Orbis*, Vol. III (Autumn, 1959).

decision of the Truman Administration to oppose the extension of the Korean War into Manchuria. President Truman and his advisers believed, rightly or wrongly, that such a policy would inevitably lead to US over-involvement in Asia at the expense of and to the detriment of the nation's commitments in Western Europe.

Domination of Western Europe by the Russians would almost certainly turn the tide of the protracted world conflict irreversibly against the West. For, as Henry A. Kissinger, Associate Director of Harvard's Center of International Affairs, has stated trenchantly: "If Eurasia were to be dominated by a hostile power or group of powers, we would confront an overpowering threat. And the key to Eurasia is Western Europe because its loss would bring with it the loss of the Middle East and the upheaval of Africa. Were this to happen, the strategic advantage in all-out war would shift to the USSR. If the United States were ever confined to 'Fortress America', or even if Soviet expansion went far enough to sap our allies' will to resist, the western hemisphere would be confronted by three-quarters of mankind and hardly less of its resources, and our continued existence would be precarious. At best we would be forced into a military effort incompatible with what is now considered the American way of life."[3]

Membership

The North Atlantic Treaty brought together the five Brussels Pact powers (i.e., the United Kingdom, France, Belgium, the Netherlands and Luxemburg) with seven other states (Canada, Denmark, Iceland, Italy, Norway, Portugal and the United States). All of the charter signatories shared democratic, parliamentary institutions of government except Portugal—a relatively mild dictatorship based upon

[3] *Nuclear Weapons and Foreign Policy*, Harper and Brothers (New York, 1957), pp. 269-270.

the principles of the corporate state. It was the US government which had suggested that Portugal be included because
of her strategic importance,[4] and the British were favourably
disposed to the idea since their oldest extant treaty of
alliance was with the Portuguese. The initial signatories
were all located in the geographic area usually regarded as
the North Atlantic civilisation basin. On 18 February, 1952,
two members from the eastern end of the Mediterranean,
the kingdom of Greece and the republic of Turkey, were
added to the NATO roster by a special protocol to the
treaty. Greece, of course, could claim to be the ancient home
of the liberal ideals cherished so highly by the Atlantic
nations; Turkey, the first non-Western state ever admitted
to the Western state system, although it was historically
outside the mainstream of Judaeo-Christian, Graeco-Roman
culture, had, nevertheless, attempted to "westernise" itself
in the twentieth century, especially under Kemal Ataturk
after the First World War. Moreover, because of their
geographical position, both countries were important to the
security of the Middle East and the Mediterranean, i.e., the
south-eastern and southern flanks of the European NATO
area. (This fact had already received expression in the
Truman Doctrine of March, 1947.) Three years later, on
5 May, 1955, the Federal Republic of Germany, which had
recently been admitted to the Western European Union (an
outgrowth of the Brussels Pact of 1948), acceded to NATO
by a special protocol.

The question arises from time to time as to the possibility
of admitting other states to NATO. There would appear to
be sound strategic reasons why Sweden, for example, ought
to be a member. It is generally recognised, however, that

---

[4] Undoubtedly the American policy-makers had in mind
the importance of the Azores as a potential air base. The
Secretary of State, Dean Acheson, has said of the base in
the Azores that it is ". . . perhaps the single most important
one we have anywhere." *Fifty Years After*, op. cit., p. 9.

Sweden serves as a sort of Scandinavian "buffer". The Western-oriented neutrality of Sweden is a *quid pro quo* for the Soviet-enforced neutrality of Finland.[5] If Sweden should adhere to NATO, the USSR would probably convert Finland into a forward military base. Conversely, if the Soviets should apply too much pressure against Finland, Sweden would have good reason to apply for entry into NATO and would undoubtedly be admitted. In the meantime, Sweden discreetly co-ordinates its armaments programmes and defence planning with those of its Scandinavian neighbours, Denmark and Norway, which are members of NATO.

Occasionally it is suggested that Spain should logically be brought into NATO, not only because the Franco regime is staunchly anti-communist but also because Spain has already entered into arrangements with the United States under which the latter maintains some of its most important naval and air bases in the European theatre. Furthermore, the argument is sometimes made that the entrance of Spain into the Alliance might help to bring about a liberalisation of the country's political institutions. Most of the democratic governments of Western Europe, however, remembering Franco's relations with Hitler and Mussolini and resenting the authoritarian character of his regime, take the position that the admission of Spain would tarnish NATO's image as a coalition of democratic nations. Despite the fact that the United States is frequently reported as favourable to the idea of Spanish membership, it does not appear likely that any serious effort will be made to bring Spain in so long as General Franco rules the country.[6]

[5] For an excellent discussion of this question see Abrahamsen, Samuel, *Sweden's Foreign Policy*, Public Affairs Press (Washington, 1957), p. 91.

[6] Other countries which have been sympathetic to Spain's admission are Portugal, West Germany, and France. Some other governments tacitly favour it. The unanimous consent required for admission of new members has been withheld by Denmark and Norway. See Whitaker, Arthur P., *Spain*

The Nature and Scope of the Alliance

NATO is essentially a defensive alliance, designed primarily to deter a military attack upon Western Europe and to provide mutual support to the members in case an attack should occur either in Europe or North America. (It was taken for granted in 1949 that the United States alone possessed sufficient strength to deter a Soviet attack upon North America, but if such an attack took place the United States would find the co-operative military action of European allies highly important.) That the Treaty was not intended to serve aggressive intentions is made clear in Article 1, where the parties undertake to refrain from the "threat or use of force in any manner inconsistent with the purposes of the United Nations."[7]

The NATO area was defined in Article 6 of the Treaty to include the territory of any of the parties in Europe or North America, the Algerian departments of France and the islands under the jurisdiction of any party in the North Atlantic area north of the Tropic of Cancer. An attack upon the vessels or aircraft of any of the parties in the North Atlantic area would also fall within the meaning of the term "armed attack" as used in the Treaty. In order to cover the possibility of an attack upon NATO member forces in Berlin and Austria (until the latter was neutralised by the Austrian

---

and Defense of the West: Ally and Liability, Harper and Bros. for the Council on Foreign Relations (New York, 1961), pp. 372-3. C. L. Sulzberger, writing in the *New York Times,* 15 April, 1963, reported that the status of "association" with NATO is under consideration for Malta after the island, which serves as an important naval headquarters and base, is granted independence by Britain. He suggested that a similar arrangement might be worked out in the case of Spain.

[7] In Article 5 of the Treaty, the allies call attention to the right of individual or collective self-defence recognised by Article 51 of the United Nations Charter.

State Treaty in 1955), the guarantee was extended to include the "occupation forces of any of the parties in Europe". When Greece and Turkey acceded to the Alliance, Greece came automatically under the category of "the parties in Europe". But Article 6 of the Treaty had to be modified to make specific mention of Turkey, which historically has not been considered a European state; this was done by Article II of the Protocol. The same article expanded the meaning of "armed attack" to include an attack "on the forces, vessels or aircraft of any of the parties, when in or over these territories or any other area in Europe in which occupation forces of any of the parties were stationed on the date when the Treaty entered into force or the Mediterranean Sea or the North Atlantic Area north of the Tropic of Cancer." Technically, the wording of the Treaty leaves the new American state of Hawaii uncovered. Alaska, however, is implicitly covered as part of the North American continent. After the Evian Accord of 1962, arrangements were made to modify the meaning of the provisions of Article 6 of the Treaty in order to take Algeria's independence into account.

If any one of the NATO members should become involved in military hostilities outside the area precisely defined by the Treaty, even though it might be against communist aggression, the other members are not obliged under the Treaty to furnish assistance. In the Korean War, the Western nations had obligations under the United Nations Charter but not under the North Atlantic Treaty. Similarly, when the British were fighting against the communist guerrillas in Malaya, and the French against the communist Viet Minh in Indo-China, their NATO partners were not obliged by the language of the Treaty to render aid, even if requested to do so (see Chapter 5). Thus if the United States should find itself confronted with an attack upon its bilateral ally, Nationalist China (i.e., the Chinese government on Formosa), by the People's Republic of China, the *casus foederis* under the Atlantic Alliance would not arise unless and until hostilities had been extended to the NATO area. In the case of Algeria, the *casus foederis* did not arise even though a territory mentioned by name in the Treaty was "under attack". (The Treaty does not lay down any stipulations concerning the source of the attack.) In a sense, Algeria may be said to be the first territory originally covered by the Treaty which was "lost" to NATO. Even though the coastal areas, which were considered legally to be departments of metropolitan France and which were cited in the language of Article 6 of the Treaty, were "under attack" from forces hostile to France, operating from political sanctuaries in Tunisia and Morocco, France's allies did not regard the Algerian hostilities as falling within the scope of the pact. Indeed, some of the members of the Alliance were obviously sympathetic to the insurgents' cause. From the beginning, France herself claimed that the Algerian rebellion was a "purely domestic matter" and refrained from formally appealing for aid under the provisions of the NATO treaty.

It is often proposed that NATO should be "globalised" in order to deter communist aggression and infiltration in the Middle East, South-east Asia, the Far East and Latin America (see Chapter 5). But expanding the scope of the Treaty to co-ordinate the policies of the Atlantic Powers *vis-à-vis* challenges hurled down in non-Western regions must remain an informal process until there should be a major re-negotiation of the Alliance. Barring such a re-negotiation it must be presumed that, from a strictly legal point of view, the intended scope of the alliance's area of deterrence does not extend beyond those regions described in the original Treaty and the subsequent Protocols.[8]

[8]An interesting problem is posed by the dual membership of Turkey in NATO and in the Central Treaty Organisation (CENTO). Although the United States is not a fully-fledged member of CENTO (being only a member of its Military Committee), there is always the possibility that if

None of the members has formally relinquished its sovereignty as states do when they enter into a federal system. Indeed, NATO even lacks those central institutions of government (such as a legislature) which usually distiguish a *confederation* from a treaty alliance. NATO possesses no central governing mechanism. Such institutional co-ordination as it does achieve is confined mainly to the military sphere. At the political level, NATO is an inter-governmental organisation in the traditional style, which takes its decisions by the rule of unanimity rather than by majority vote. According to Article 5, there is not even a firm, binding promise of action in case of attack upon a member; each party agrees only to take "such action as it deems necessary, including the use of armed force, to restore and maintain the security of the North Atlantic area." In short, unlike certain famous secret treaties of the Bismarckian era and the Axis alliances prior to the outbreak of the Second World War,[9] the North Atlantic Treaty contains no solid guarantee that the attacked nation's allies will automatically commit their full armed strength. But once this

---

the Soviet Union should attack any member of CENTO (such as Iran or Pakistan) and Turkey should, by coming to the aid of the invaded partner, incur the effects of Soviet offensive action on Turkish territory, the United States and the other members of NATO would have no alternative but to regard this as an attack within the meaning of Article 5 of the Treaty. At the time of the Turkish-Syrian border crisis in the Autumn of 1957, Mr Khrushchev hinted that it was unwise for Turkey to withdraw forces to its south-eastern border and leave its northern border unguarded. The Secretary of State, Mr Dulles, took this opportunity to remind the Soviets of the US commitment to Turkey under NATO.

[9] Article 3 of the so-called "Pact of Steel", of 1939, binding together Germany and Italy, stated: "If one of (the contracting parties) becomes involved in warlike complications with another power or powers, the other contracting party will come to its aid . . . with all its military forces on land, on sea, and in the air."

caveat regarding the degree of sovereign freedom of action retained by the NATO allies has been made, it must be recognised that the Atlantic alliance possesses an institutional solidarity very different from most of the alliances known to history. While it is undeniable that it was the common fear of Soviet aggression which gave birth to the Alliance, it is no less true, as Massimo Salvadori has pointed out, that "a common civilisation, the deep and sincere attachment to basic beliefs, values and institutions, was the unifying element around which NATO was built."[10] From the start, NATO has had something of the character of a permanent as distinct from a merely temporary alliance.[11] History is filled with instances in which politically dissimilar nations have been thrown together by strategic accident, as were the Soviet Union and the Western democracies during the Second World War. But such alliances usually dissolve, as that one did, when the *ad hoc* purposes for which they were brought into being (e.g., the defeat of a common enemy) have been achieved. But when an alliance which is founded on geographic and strategic logic is also buttressed by the existence of political, social, economic and cultural commonalities, it deserves to be called a "permanent alliance". NATO meets these qualifications and merits the designation.

Despite the freedom of action which the individual members of NATO reserve to themselves under the wording of Article 5, it is important to bear in mind, as Robert Osgood has pointed out in a scholarly study, that NATO has not "remained, as at the outset, essentially a traditional guaranty pact, simply committing its members to come to each other's assistance and calling for minimal peacetime collaboration.

[10] Salvadori, Massimo, *NATO: A Twentieth Century Community of Nations,* Van Nostrand (Princeton, 1957), p. 13.
[11] Article 13 provides that after the Treaty has been in force for twenty years (i.e., after 1969), any member may terminate its adherence upon one year's notice. Otherwise, the Treaty contains no time limit.

. . . Since the Korean War and establishment of a central command shortly afterwards, NATO has acquired the characteristics of an integrated military-political organisation, exacting unprecedented peacetime contributions and commitments."[12]

One of the most significant examples of these unprecedented commitments has been the establishment of bases and the deployment of troops by some of the principal members of the Alliance on the soil of other members. The American forces stationed in Europe, the British Army of the Rhine and the appearance of West German soldiers for training on French soil constitute impressive evidence of the high degree of peacetime military-political collaboration which has occurred under the aegis of NATO. After many years of co-operation in joint military planning and political consultation, there is reason to expect that an attack on any member of NATO would be viewed by all the members as a challenge to their vital interests, if not to their very survival and would be met swiftly with a "team response". All the members undoubtedly realise that NATO could not survive a failure on the part of the stronger partners to come to the aid of a victim ally.

The intimate collaboration which has evolved within NATO in the military sphere has been paralleled, of necessity, by co-ordination in the spheres of foreign and economic policy. The requirements of common defence furnish powerful motives for working out institutional arrangements for diplomatic and financial co-operation. NATO, as Professors Haas and Whiting have observed, has gradually been transformed from a mutual guaranty pact into a regional organisation which is beginning to have every appearance of permanency: "Alliances today surpass the scope and power of international organisations in many ways. With the emer-

[12] Osgood, Robert, *NATO: The Entangling Alliance,* University of Chicago Press (Chicago, 1962), p. 23.

gence of 'total war' and its demands upon economic, political and military planning, alliances acquire increasing responsibility in all fields of endeavour. From military planning to full regional integration is a long step, but it is an unmistakable trend in both NATO and the Soviet system. Standardisation of weapons, elimination of national economic barriers, pooling of resources and ultimately the meshing of policy, although not always successful, remain characteristic of the efforts of both major alliance systems. Despite the many obstacles hindering the achievement of these aims, they remain as evidence of the profound impact of the twentieth century upon alliances as a traditional means of foreign policy."[13]

That judgment was written in 1956. Certainly its accuracy, at least with respect to NATO, has been amply borne out by the developments of the intervening years.

ORGANISATIONAL STRUCTURE OF NATO

The North Atlantic Council

The Council is the only formal NATO organ mentioned in the Treaty. Article 9 stipulates that the members establish a Council "on which each of them shall be represented, to consider matters concerning the implementation of this Treaty." Although the Treaty does not explicitly state that the representation would be equal, this has always been understood. In fact, the term "representation" is not well chosen, for the Council is not a representative body; it is a vehicle for *executive* co-ordination. Within NATO the traditional concept of the legal equality of states prevails.

[13] Haas, Ernest B., and Whiting, Allen S., *Dynamics of International Relations*, McGraw-Hill Book Co. (New York, 1956), p. 184. In quoting Drs Haas and Whiting there is no intent on the part of the authors to suggest that there is any great similarity between NATO and the Warsaw Pact. See the comment by Kurt London in Chapter 2 below, p. 52.

Undoubtedly the four major allies (United States, Britain, France and West Germany) carry a great deal more political weight than, say, Iceland or Luxemburg. But, unlike the Charter of the United Nations, which reserves special privileges to five Powers, the NATO Treaty does not spell out any special powers (such as a veto) for the major members which are withheld from the lesser allies. The Council reaches decisions by unanimous consent.

The Council is fundamentally a meeting ground for governmental Ministers. Actually, however, it can meet at three levels: (1) the Permanent Representatives; (2) the Ministers; and (3) Heads of Government. Since the Lisbon Meeting in February, 1952, the North Atlantic Council has been a permanent body. The Permanent Representatives, who are of ambassadorial rank, meet in sessions of the Council at least once a week during the intervals between Ministers' meetings, and wield virtually the same powers of decision as do the Ministers themselves, with whom they remain in close consultation. In practice, there has been a tendency for the Permanent Representatives to handle routine affairs by themselves but to reserve the more important questions to be resolved by the Ministers at their regular semi-annual meetings, usually held in May and December, or at an extraordinary meeting. When it meets at the ministerial level, the Council's sessions may be attended by the Foreign Ministers (or their envoys), or by the Finance (or Economic) Ministers, or by the Defence Ministers, or by all of them. It is now to be expected that the Chiefs-of-Staff of the NATO countries will also participate in an advisory capacity at Council meetings. Finally, the Council can meet at the level of Heads of Government. Thus far it has done so only once, in December, 1957, when a special display of alliance solidarity was required in view of the fact that Soviet *sputnik* successes had temporarily cast a shadow of doubt over the technological superiority of the United States.

The normal residence and meeting place of the Council is Paris, but an effort is usually made to hold one of the Council's meetings in a different NATO capital each year. Since 1957, e.g., they have been convened in Copenhagen, Washington, Istanbul, Oslo, Athens and Ottawa. The Presidency of the Council rotates annually among the Foreign Ministers of the NATO countries, listed in alphabetical order. But since 1957, the working sessions of the Council, irrespective of the level at which it is meeting, are chaired by the Secretary-General of NATO. The proceedings of Council meetings are never published; only an official communiqué is issued at the end of the conference. Hence for a knowledge of the subjects debated, the public must rely upon the somewhat speculative reporting of well-informed correspondents. This has its disadvantages in the eyes of a liberal society, but it is generally recognised that the intricate details of alliance negotiations and strategic planning cannot be argued under the full glare of publicity. The confidential nature of Council deliberations makes it much easier to achieve the "frank and free discussions and a thorough exchange of views" mentioned in the communiqué of 11 May, 1955.[14] During the decade since the Lisbon Conference, the Council has held upwards of 900 meetings.

The Council is the political heart of the Alliance; the Council at work is NATO "in action". All other official NATO organs are brought into being by its decision and remain subordinate to it. Although the Treaty does not define the Council's functions in detail, perhaps it is not too much to say that this body, as the main operational instrument of NATO, is presumed capable of doing whatever is "necessary and proper" to execute the purposes for which the

[14] *American Foreign Policy 1950-1955, Basic Documents,* US Department of State Publication No. 6446, Vol. 1, p. 1658.

CHART I: PRINCIPAL COMMITTEES OF THE COUNCIL

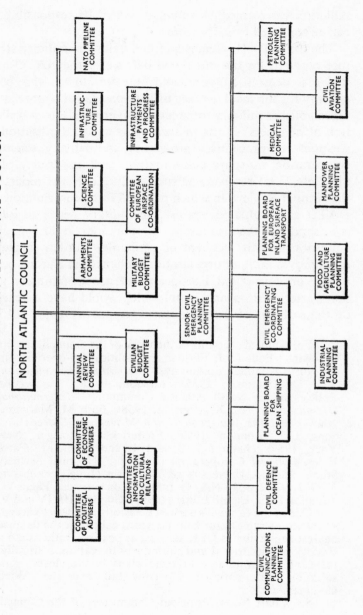

Alliance was formed. A summary list of its responsibilities can be compiled from its history.[15]

The Council: (1) creates and maintains the military structure required for the integrated defence of the NATO area under a centralised command; (2) formulates the basic strategy for the local defence of Europe against aggression;[16] (3) establishes military force levels; (4) ensures the co-ordination of members' efforts in such areas as standardisation of weapons and procedures, production and delivery, scientific co-operation, air-space co-ordination, civil emergency planning, etc.;[17] (5) receives, debates and accepts the report on the Annual Review, in which national force contributions to NATO are evaluated against the military needs of allied commanders, the resources of the individual member countries, and the concept of equitable "burden sharing"; (6) approves military organisational changes in Europe (such as the once-proposed European Defence Community and the Western European Union) which would have a bearing on the fortunes of the Alliance; (7) approves major NATO

[15] For detailed accounts of the work of the Council, see the following: Padelford, Norman J., "Political Co-operation in the North Atlantic Community," *International Organization,* Vol. IX (Summer, 1955); Lawson, Ruth, "Concerting Policies in the North Atlantic Community," *International Organization,* Vol. XII (Spring, 1958); Ball, M. Margaret, *NATO and the European Union Movement,* Stevens and Sons, Ltd. (London, 1959), Frederick A. Praeger (New York, 1959), chapters 2, 3, and 4; and Baumann, Carol Edler, *Political Co-operation in NATO,* National Security Studies Group, University of Wisconsin (June, 1960); *The NATO Handbook,* NATO Information Service, Palais de Chaillot, Paris, Eighth Edition (1960), chapters III, IV and V.

[16] One of the Council's earliest decisions, e.g., was to accept a "forward strategy" for Europe which called for the defence against aggression as far to the east as possible, rather than a strategy of withdrawal and subsequent liberation. Naturally, the Council formulates strategic plans in the closest consultation with national Chiefs-of-Staff and the Allied Commanders.

[17] See Chart No. 1, Principal Committees of the Council.

appointments such as Secretary-General and the Supreme Allied Commanders; (8) decides upon the admission of new members to NATO; (9) establishes and reviews the work of the political, cultural and economic committees which have among their tasks the carrying out of the provisions contained in Article 2 of the Treaty; (10) co-ordinates allied policy on major political questions such as German reunification, Berlin, "summit" conferences and disarmament negotiations. Finally, and most crucial of all, Article 4 stipulates that the "parties will consult together whenever, in the opinion of any of them, the territorial integrity, political independence or security of any of the parties is threatened." No matter what form this consultation might take, e.g., an international telephone conference among the Heads of Government, it would be a Council action.

From time to time, the Council has come in for criticism on several grounds. The charge is often made that, although the Council deserves a good deal of credit for the way in which it has dealt with questions arising out of the immediate security problems of Europe, it has been much less successful in co-ordinating national policies on issues outside the NATO area. Such a deficiency, however, cannot fairly be attributed to the Council as such, since the latter cannot take vigorous action beyond the scope of the purposes for which NATO was created (see Chapter 5, "The Politics of the Alliance"). It has also been suggested that, with few exceptions, the NATO governments have failed to appoint to the Council as Permanent Representatives men of political stature in their own right who could speak with authority to their peoples about the urgent problems of the Alliance.[18] Furthermore, the complaint is sometimes heard that the Council, because of its very nature as an intergovernmental institution, runs the risk of losing control over the NATO

[18] Cf. Buchan, Alastair, "The Reform of NATO," *Foreign Affairs*, Vol. 40 (January, 1962), p. 175.

military planning process to the Allied Commanders, especially the Supreme Commander, Allied Powers in Europe (SACEUR), who is, as it were, "in the thick of it" so far as defence planning is concerned.[19] Efforts were made during 1962, particularly at the Athens Council meeting, to bring about much closer consultation between the military authorities and the Minister. One effect of this was to strengthen the principle of "civilian supremacy" within the Alliance. Within recent years, the Council has intensified its scrutiny of strategic and tactical questions, and apparently has begun to discuss the "rules of engagement" by which various types of weapons would be employed under various circumstances of aggression. It is hoped that through such discussions the somewhat cumbersome character of a fifteen-nation Council can be compensated for at times of critical decision-making.

The Military Structure

The highest military authority in NATO is the Military Committee, which was created in 1949 by the Council, to which it remains ultimately responsible. The Military Committee consists of the Chiefs-of-Staff of each member country except Iceland, which is allowed civilian representation since it has no army. At the Chiefs-of-Staff level, the Military Committee meets at least twice a year. In between these meetings, work is carried on by the Permanent Military Representatives of the Chiefs-of-Staff. Although some questions must be reserved to be settled by the Chiefs-of-Staff, the Military Committee in Permanent Session (in Washington), is empowered to make the week-to-week decisions which keep the NATO military organisation operating smoothly.

The Military Committee has an executive agency to carry

[19] Cf. Buchan, Alastair, "The Reform of NATO," *Foreign Affairs*, Vol. 40 (January, 1962), p. 173.

out its decisions. This is the Standing Group, located in the Pentagon and composed of the Permanent Military Representatives of the United States, Britain and France. The Standing Group actually directs the NATO military command organisation. The Standing Group co-ordinates defence planning within the area protected by NATO forces. It is to the Standing Group that Allied Commanders are officially responsible for the execution of directives. The Standing Group is represented on the North Atlantic Council by a general officer who, with the assistance of an allied staff housed in NATO headquarters, provides liaison between the NATO political planners in the Council in Paris and the military planners in Washington. The Standing Group Representative furnishes technical military advice to the Council and transmits recommendations from the Standing Group to the Council; he also serves as the channel of authoritative communication from the Council to the Standing Group. Finally, the Standing Group supervises the Military Agency for Standardisation (London), the Advisory Group on Aeronautical Research and Development (Paris), the Communications Agencies in Europe (London and Paris) and the NATO Defence College (Paris).

The geographic area covered by the Treaty is divided among the Canada-United States Regional Planning Group, with headquarters in Washington, which is responsible for North American defence; the Channel Command, consisting of the Chiefs-of-Staff of Britain, France, Belgium and Netherlands, which is responsible for the defence of the waters around the British Isles; the Atlantic Ocean Command, headed by the Supreme Allied Commander, Atlantic (SACLANT), with headquarters at Norfolk, Virginia; and, most important of all, the European Command under the Supreme Allied Commander, Europe (SACEUR), who heads the Supreme Headquarters Allied Powers, Europe (SHAPE) in Paris. Until 1962, only SHAPE had military forces actually assigned to it in time of peace; the others

CHART 2: THE MILITARY ORGANISATION OF NATO

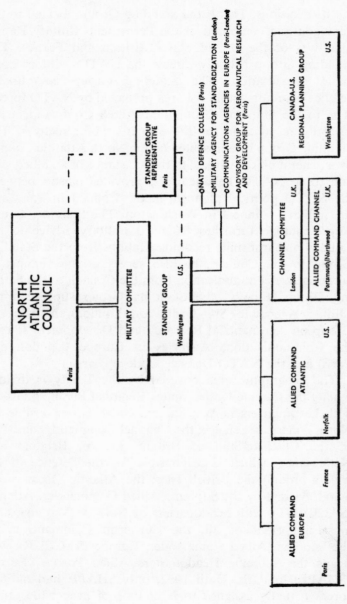

* In Washington D.C., U.S., when in Permanent Session

merely had forces earmarked for them, to be made available at some future time. But at the Athens Council meeting, the United States agreed to earmark five Polaris-type submarines to SACLANT.

The European Command covers the entire area extending from the North Cape to North Africa and from the Atlantic Ocean to the eastern border of Turkey, but excludes the United Kingdom, Portugal and Algeria. The defence of the land area of these three countries remains a national responsibility. The European Command is further subdivided into the Northern Europe Command, with headquarters at Kolsaas, Norway; the Central European Command, with headquarters at Fontainebleau, France; the Southern Europe Command, with headquarters at Naples, Italy; and the Mediterranean Command, with headquarters at Malta.[20] The entire region of the European Command is under SACEUR, aided by a Deputy SACEUR, and by Naval and Air Deputies. The post of SACEUR has always been held by American officers: General of the Army Dwight D. Eisenhower (December, 1950 – June, 1952); General Matthew B. Ridgway (June, 1952 – July, 1953); General Alfred M. Gruenther (July, 1953 – November, 1956); General Lauris Norstad (November, 1956 – January, 1963); General Lyman Lemnitzer (January, 1963 –). In time of war, SACEUR would control all land, sea and air operations in the European theatre as defined above except for strategic strike forces. In peacetime, he bears the major military responsibility for organising, training and equipping the NATO forces assigned and earmarked to his command; preparing and executing defence plans; and making recommendations to the Standing Group concerning the defence of Europe. Because of the significance of his post, SACEUR, although he receives his instructions from the Standing Group in Washington, is entitled to have direct access to the Chiefs-

[20] See Chart No. 2, The Military Organisation of NATO (from *The NATO Handbook*).

of-Staff of the NATO powers and, in certain cases, to Defence Ministers and Heads of Government.

The International Secretariat

One of the results of the Lisbon Council meeting was the creation of an international Secretariat for NATO under the direction of a Secretary-General and partly composed of civilians on short-term service 'on loan' from their governments, and partly of permanent personnel. The Secretary-General is appointed by the Council for an unspecified period. So far three persons have held the post: Lord Ismay of Britain, Paul-Henri Spaak of Belgium and Dirk Stikker of the Netherlands. The Secretary-General is responsible for organising the work of the Council and directing the international Secretariat. He presides over the Council when it is in session. Since the acceptance of the Report of the Three at the Council meeting of December, 1956, the Secretary-General has the authority to offer his "good offices" for the purpose of settling any disputes which might arise between NATO members and has actually done so, e.g., in the case of the Anglo-Greek-Turkish controversy over Cyprus. Reports from the Military Committee and the Standing Group to the Council, as well as directives from the Council to NATO's military authorities, are channelled through the Secretary-General's office.

The essential function of the Secretariat is to ensure the most efficient possible operation of the Alliance organisation. The Office of the Executive Secretary arranges the Council's work, publishes its agenda, co-ordinates the activities of the Council's committees, produces the documentation which they require, keeps records of Council meetings and sees that Council decisions are followed up. The Division of Political Affairs maintains political liaison with national NATO delegations and with international organisations (both inter-governmental and non-governmental); prepares reports on political subjects for the Council; and supervises cultural activities which are carried on in pursuance of Article 2 of the Treaty. Within the Division of Political Affairs there is also an Information Service and Press Section which seeks, through films, periodicals, radio and TV, to inform public opinion throughout the Atlantic Community concerning the aims and achievements of NATO. The Division of Economics and Finance studies economic matters which have a bearing upon the defence capabilities of the Atlantic Alliance or which otherwise might influence the well-being of the Atlantic Community. The Division of Production and Logistics seeks to promote the most efficient use of the Alliance's resources with respect to the supply and standardisation of military equipment. The Office of the Scientific Adviser keeps the Secretary-General informed on scientific matters of concern to NATO and ensures proper scientific co-operation among NATO military and civil authorities, scientific policy-makers and international scientific activities.

To carry out all the foregoing tasks, the Secretariat has a total roster of about 600 personnel, of whom about one-third are civilian "officers" with experience in the governments of the member countries. Concerning the status of the civilian personnel, Professor Ball has written: "Instead of becoming part of a permanent NATO civil service, many of the officers serve on loan from . . . their own governments for two or three years and presumably return to them after their tour of duty is over. While this creates a problem of continuity, these officers are responsible only to the Secretary-General, and do not take orders from their own governments. Most of them are paid directly from the NATO budget. . . . Only NATO nationals are eligible for appointment, and they must be cleared by their own governments before being taken on the staff."[21]

[21] Ball, op. cit. (see p. 32, note), p. 59.

Other Atlantic Community Institutions

The institutions described above comprise the principal elements in the NATO structure. In contrast to the European communities of economic integration (cf. Chapter 4), NATO has no treaty-created parliamentary assembly. Each year, however, there is an informal gathering of parliamentarians from the legislative branches of all the member countries. The first NATO Parliamentarians' Annual Conference, as it is called, was convened in 1955; the ninth one was held in Paris in November, 1963. The annual conference, which is attended by key legislators from NATO capitals, is usually addressed by the Secretary-General and by SACEUR. As an unofficial body, the Parliamentarians' Conference can make no binding decisions, but it can make recommendations to the Council which carry political weight because of the important role which the individual Parliamentarians play within their respective national legislatures. The Parliamentarians prudently refrain from undertaking actions which could be interpreted as an effort to do any of the following: to impose any form of accountability upon the Council (i.e., to establish the principle of ministerial responsibility); to interfere in the strategic planning of the military authorities; or to engage in a form of Atlantic lawmaking which would be certain to arouse the opposition of national legislative bodies.

At their Seventh Annual Conference, held in Paris in November, 1961, the NATO Parliamentarians invited the Council to submit reports on the actions taken regarding previous resolutions of the Conference. They urged the North Atlantic Council to pledge its full support to the three Western powers in the exercise of their quadripartite rights and responsibilities with respect to Berlin and Germany and *urged* the Council to continue condemning the illegal division of Berlin symbolised by the Wall. The Conference *recommended* that every possible means be employed to inform world opinion, and especially the people of the USSR, of the enslavement of twenty nations and 140 million people by Soviet and communist colonialism. The Parliamentarians also *recommended* the creation of a NATO Institute of Science and Technology, the establishment of a long-range weather forecast system for NATO and closer co-ordination of efforts towards the conversion of saline water. The Conference noted the inadequacy of present NATO and national information efforts and *urged* that they be intensified. The Conference *recommended* that the strength of the divisions committed to NATO be raised to meet the requirements called for by SACEUR and that this greater strength, once achieved, be maintained irrespective of any *détente* in the Berlin situation. Finally, it recommended the creation of truly integrated NATO commands, both as regards personnel and finance; the contribution of all member states to the Mobile Forces; and closer co-ordination of research, development and production of weapons.[22] Some of the latter recommendations on military policy might seem at first glance to constitute a form of "meddling" in the planning process. Actually, however, the Parliamentarians were merely lending their political support to measures which had long been advocated by the NATO military authorities.

During the early part of 1962, the Atlantic Convention of NATO nations, meeting in Paris, issued a formal declaration which contained a number of significant suggestions for strengthening the institutions of the Atlantic Community. The Convention was the outcome of a resolution unanimously adopted by the Third NATO Parliamentarians' Conference in November, 1957, calling upon the NATO governments to "bring about, in accordance with the constitutional

[22] Reports and Recommendations adopted by the Seventh Annual NATO Parliamentarians' Conference, Paris: The Secretariat (November, 1961).

and governmental processes of their countries, a conference composed of leading representative citizens selected on a non-partisan basis." The delegates to the Paris Convention were, for the most part, appointed under the authority of the various national legislative bodies, but instead of being officially instructed by their governments they were expected to act in accordance with their individual convictions. The Convention was attended by ninety-eight distinguished citizens, drawn from all the NATO nations in the proportions employed by the NATO Parliamentarians. Among the many recommendations embodied in the Declaration of Paris, three are worthy of note here in so far as they bear directly upon the organisational structure of NATO:

(1) The "creation at the highest political level, of a Permanent High Council, whose competence would extend to political, economic, military and cultural matters. Such a Council, assisted by a Secretariat, would not only prepare and concert policies on current questions and, in defined cases, decide them by a weighted, qualified majority vote, but would also undertake long-term planning and propose initiatives on matters of concern to the Community."[23] Sir Anthony Eden (now Lord Avon) made a similar suggestion a year earlier.[24]

(2) The development of the NATO Parliamentarians' Conference "into a consultative Atlantic Assembly, to meet at stated intervals, or upon the call of its President or otherwise, to receive reports regularly transmitted to

[23] *The Declaration of Paris,* Part I, B.1. Full text in *NATO Letter,* Vol. X (February, 1962). Whether or not the proposed High Council would be a new institution or a development of the existing Council would be left to the decision of a special commission designed to study the problem. All members of the Community would be represented on the High Council.
[24] Eden, Sir Anthony, "The Slender Margin of Safety," *Foreign Affairs,* Vol. 39 (January, 1961), p. 171.

it by the Secretaries General of other Atlantic bodies; to raise questions for and to consider, debate and review the work of all Atlantic institutions, and make recommendations to other Atlantic bodies and governments on questions of concern to the Atlantic Community."[25] It was specified that members of the Assembly would be selected by member governments in accordance with their constitutional procedures, but they would not necessarily have to be chosen from the legislative branch. In stipulated cases, Assembly recommendations could be by weighted majority vote.

(3) The "creation of a High Court of Justice, reserved to the Atlantic Community, in order to settle legal differences between members and between members and the organisations arising from the interpretation and application of treaties."[26] At the present time there is no distinctive judicial institution serving the Atlantic Community or engaged in the formulation of anything approaching an Atlantic legal code.

The Atlantic goals expressed in the Declaration of Paris were applauded widely throughout the West. Today there is substantial agreement with the assertion that "the Atlantic peoples are heir to a magnificent civilisation whose origins include the early achievements of the Near East, the classical

[25] *The Declaration of Paris,* Part I, B.2.
[26] *The Declaration of Paris,* I, B.3. An American quarterly journal commented on this recommendation as follows: "In the North Atlantic area, the preconditions for the successful operation of such a judiciary exist more abundantly than in any other region. . . . The Atlantic Community is endowed with that consensus of political, social and moral values, so lacking in the world at large, upon which legal systems depend, short of force, for their sanction. Such attitudes provide the basis for the creation of an Atlantic Court for the settlement of legal disputes which arise inevitably as political unity and economic exchanges increase." "Reflections on the Quarter," *Orbis,* Vol. VI (Spring, 1962), p. 8.

beauty of Greece, the juridical sagacity of Rome, the spiritual power of our religious traditions and the humanism of the Renaissance."[27] But a rhetorical consensus on the legacy of Western civilisation is one thing; working out practical political compromises for closer co-operation among fifteen sovereign nation-states is quite another. The Atlantic Convention of NATO which met in Paris described, in fairly general terms, the objectives which appear to be worthy of the strivings of Atlantic Community statesmen. It did not, however, attempt to draft a detailed constitutional blueprint. The delegates recognised that such an effort would be premature. The Atlantic Community, to be sure, is slowly undergoing political, economic, cultural and military integration. But because of the very characteristics of the modern nation-state system, some of the most significant aspects of this integrative process cannot easily be formalised in institutions, treaties or charters. The important fact is that the members of NATO have now amassed nearly a decade-and-a-half of experience in working together on issues of common concern. The North Atlantic Treaty itself sketches only the "bare bones" of the co-operative framework. The Alliance as a living organism has grown more by experience than by definition, more by "customs and conventions" than by the drafting of formal documents. If the Atlantic Community continues to develop more appropriate institutions, it may very well do so via an empirical, intuitive, prudently pragmatic route or, to put it differently, in a typically British way.

[27] From the Preamble to *The Declaration of Paris*.

Chapter 2

NATO, GERMANY AND THE USSR

SOVIET VIEWS OF SECURITY IN EUROPE

Traditional Concepts of Soviet Security in Europe

Russian policy towards Europe has in the past been shaped largely by traditional views of strategic factors. The topography of European Russia and north-central Europe has always confronted Russia with a defence problem of considerable dimensions. The geographic configuration of the region is largely that of a vast plain. The area encompasses the present Polish and East German states—the invasion route used by Napoleon in 1812 and by Hitler in 1941. Soviet strategists have long been preoccupied with the problem of how to secure these approaches to Russia against invasion from the West.

It may be argued that such traditional strategic considerations have lost much of their meaning with the advent of long-range nuclear striking power.[1] Yet, strategy does not

[1] Finletter, Thomas K., *Foreign Policy: The Next Phase*, Harper and Bros., for the Council on Foreign Relations (New York, 1960), p. 115. He writes: "It is true that as a matter of military tactics, modern weapons have made it unnecessary for the Russians to have a barrier between them and the

always bow to logic. Long established military doctrines
become deeply rooted in institutions of military education
and—in a form of culture lag—may continue to constitute
the warp and woof of military thought long after technological developments have modified their real significance.
A balanced assessment of the way the Soviets may have
viewed the problem of military security in Europe in the
decade immediately after the Second World War has been
made by one of England's foremost military historians.
Discussing the Soviet attitude towards eastern and central
Europe, Michael Howard has written: ". . . the territory of
eastern Europe is still of vital military significance to Russia.
From the present 'Iron Curtain' in Germany to the Russian
frontier is a distance of five or six hundred miles. This serves
as a buffer against invasion with conventional troops as well
as a springboard from which Russian troops could menace
the West; and it keeps the American bomber and missile
bases at a respectable distance from the heart of Russia."[2]

Understandably, many Western analysts have found it
difficult to see how, in the context of the present global
strategic situation, the Soviets could possibly believe that
Western policy in Europe is anything but defensive. This
scepticism has fostered the widely held notion that Soviet
accusations of Western intentions to commit aggression
against the Soviet bloc are pure propaganda and nothing else.
It is true that Soviet charges invariably have an unrealistic
ring and stand starkly at odds with the facts of the present
strategic situation. Yet, we must remember that, in the Soviet
Union, we are dealing with a mentality which is not entirely
rational, but rather with a pathology conditioned by

West; long-range weapons have made that kind of thinking
out of date. But outmoded concepts have vitality, and the
Russians apparently think of the occupied countries as a
buffer which has military value to them."

[2] *Disengagement in Europe*, Penguin Books Ltd. (London
and Baltimore, 1958), pp. 83-4.

historical experience and the peculiar thought modes of communism. George F. Kennan may have put his finger on the crux of the problem when he wrote: "In everything that can be statistically expressed—expressed, that is, in such a way as not to imply any judgment on our motivation—I believe the Soviet government to be excellently informed about us. I am sure that their information on the development of our economies, on the state of our military preparations, is absolutely first-rate. But when it comes to the analysis of our motives, I think this whole great system of intelligence-gathering breaks down seriously. I would not wish to maintain that they believe everything they say; I am sure they do not. But, I would submit that their habitual carelessness about the truth has tended to obliterate in their minds the distinction between what they do believe and what they merely find it convenient to say."

Thus, their ideological blinkers obviously distort Soviet assessment of the West's motivations. For example, viewed through Soviet eyes it may not be an exaggeration to say that the decision to rearm West Germany (despite the fact that it was a response to their own aggressive conduct) was considered by them as a provocative act—perhaps the most provocative act committed by the West thus far in the Cold War, since it has been a prime objective of Soviet foreign policy to prevent such a development.

Current Soviet Concepts of Security

There is considerable evidence that the Soviet Union now equates security with nothing less than a world socialist victory. If this be true, one could postulate that their motivation may be basically defensive[3]—in the sense that they

[3] George F. Kennan has developed this point in testimony before a Senate Committee. He stated: "I think their principal motives are defensive. I think what they have most in mind is to protect the internal integrity of their own rule

desire complete security. If the Soviets believe that their
security is endangered until their political system or
influence has been extended to embrace the entire world,
then West Germany's alliance with NATO indeed represents
to them a threat to their security, in so far as NATO's
military presence in and rearming of that nation pose an
obstacle to the achievement of their security goal, namely
global domination. In this respect the Soviets would see in
varying degree a similar threat to their security in a U.S.
alliance with, or military deployment in, any nation along
the border of the East-West confrontation, or for that matter,
anywhere else.

During the better part of the decade after the Second World
War, the Soviet view of security was probably more localised
and heavily coloured by primarily regional security considerations, i.e., how to secure the Soviet homeland against
external military attack. But since the advent of Soviet
strategic nuclear delivery power, increasingly the Soviets
have viewed their security against the longer-range consideration that Western collective security arrangements may

---

within Russia. . . . I believe they are very patient and
persistent in their purposes, but I consider that those
purposes are more defensive than is frequently supposed in
this country today. I think they have greater difficulties with
their own structure of power than many people here assume
to be the case. . . ." Senator Symington then asked Kennan
if he thought the Soviet policy of putting down the Hungarian
uprising and their rocket threats to drive the Franco-British
forces out of Suez was basically defensive and Kennan
replied (on Hungary): "Very definitely, yes." Referring to
the Middle East, he said: "I think that was designed to try
to get the Western powers out of the Middle East. But I
think the motive for wanting to get the Western powers out
of the Middle East is probably fear for the security of their
own power." In sum, Kennan argued that while their moves
are offensive they spring from a defensive psychological
motivation.—"Control and Reduction of Armaments,"
Hearings, US Senate, Part II, 9 and 10 January, 1957
(Washington, D.C.), pp. 1008-11.

block them from achieving their ultimate security goal, i.e., communist world hegemony. In short, it seems reasonable to assume that the Soviets believe their long-range delivery capabilities have solved their local security problem to the extent that they deter the West from a deliberate and premeditated military action against the Soviet Union. Thus they may now see the US alliance with Western Europe as primarily an effort which will serve to delay the final communist victory.

Mr Khrushchev himself has suggested that the old communist conception of "capitalist encirclement" requires modification; in March, 1958, he is reported to have told a French reporter: "I would like to draw your attention to the fact that at present the concept of 'capitalist encirclement' of our country itself seriously needs a more accurate definition. . . . At present it is not known who encircles whom."[4] Khrushchev may be more optimistic on this score than other members of the Soviet hierarchy. Even though some Soviet theoreticians may now think that "capitalist encirclement" is gradually being replaced by "socialist encirclement", this does not mean that the old Russian paranoia has disappeared. Writing in August, 1958, one close observer argued that " 'capitalist encirclement' remains one of the most tenacious of psychological factors and the West has made a great mistake in regarding it as a purely artificial affectation. . . . On every possible occasion, the USSR has sought to escape from 'capitalist encirclement', and this obsession is responsible for many treaties and alliances which at first glance seem to be in conflict with pure communist doctrine. It is to this we owe the Rapallo Treaty of 1922 and the treaties with China and Japan . . . the Nazi-Soviet pact on the eve of the Second World War."[5] He suggests that

---

[4] Groussard, Serge, *Le Figaro*, 19 March, 1958.
[5] Wauters, Arthur, "Four Constants of Stalinism," *Western World* (August, 1958), pp. 19-23. The author was a former Belgian ambassador to Moscow.

it is this mentality which still motivates the Soviets in seeking "disengagement", "denuclearised zones", and "liquidation of bases". However, while taking cognizance of the continuing weight of the concept of "capitalist encirclement" in Soviet motivation, one must be careful not to overstress this point. Clearly, this Soviet doctrine has indeed undergone some modification. It seems safe to assume, in retrospect, that when Stalin spoke of "capitalist encirclement" he was thinking primarily of Soviet security in Europe. Stalin was in charge of Soviet policy during a period when the strategic situation was highly unfavourable from the Soviet point of view. His policy was to counter "capitalist encirclement" by building a strong Socialist base in one country, i.e., the Soviet Union, and eventually to use that base for the purpose of spreading communist influence to other countries. The fact that the Soviets have, since Stalin's death, placed increasing emphasis on areas outside Europe is itself evidence that they now see their foreign policy and military security problem in much larger dimensions.[6] Mr Khrushchev appears to believe that Soviet power is now great enough to neutralise once and for all the last vestiges of "capitalist encirclement" by projecting Soviet power to all regions of the globe.

Thus the breaking of "capitalist encirclement", in a direct geographical sense, has given way in some measure to another key Soviet concept of world security and peace, i.e. the end of conflict between the socialist and capitalist state systems, based upon the establishment of communist world hegemony.[7] But while the old concept of "capitalist encirclement" has been downgraded considerably, the Soviets un-

[6] Cf. Rostow, W. W., *The US In the World Arena*, Harper (New York, 1960), p. 298.

[7] Charles Burton Marshall has written that Mr Khrushchev, in his important address of 6 January, 1961, "places the victory of communism in apposition to 'world peace' ", *Two Communist Manifestos*, The Washington Center of Foreign Policy Research (Washington, D.C., 1961).

doubtedly see the remnant of that encirclement in the continuing deployment of US military forces overseas, particularly in the NATO area. In short, while the Soviets may
feel confident that they have been successful in breaking
"capitalist" geographic encirclement, US strategic encirclement through NATO and other alliances, with all its political
implications, still remains a formidable political-military
obstacle to Soviet strategy and to the objective of global
hegemony.

Marshal A. Yeremenko, an important Soviet military
theorist, has written that the US overseas bases were of little
value in the purely military sense and asked rhetorically why
the United States and NATO still kept them. He suggested
the following answer: "In answering the question we leave
the military strategic field and move into the political . . .
locating their forces on foreign territory has for a long time
served as a means of spreading their influence. It is exactly
this aim which the military bases created by the United States
are serving."[8] Marshal Yeremenko's statement regarding the
political significance of the US overseas military presence
can probably be accepted to some extent at face value. The
Soviets themselves have gained considerable influence in
other countries by extending military assistance and by their
military presence, e.g. in Eastern Europe, Cuba, Egypt,
Afghanistan, Laos, Morocco, Indonesia, Communist China
and North Korea.[9] Mr Khrushchev once stated candidly that
he valued "economic aid most for political reasons and least
for economic reasons." It may be assumed that Soviet
military assistance and overseas military deployment serve

[8] *International Affairs* (Moscow, November, 1960).
[9] Cf. Dinerstein, H. S., *Military Force and Soviet Goals,* The
Rand Corporation, RM-2771 (2 June, 1961), p. iii. Dinerstein
states: "As Soviet military strength has grown in recent
years, the Soviet Union has been making political capital by
(1) demonstrating the existence of its military power; (2)
threatening to use it; and (3) selling conventional weapons to
other countries for political purposes."

similar political purposes. The Soviets maintain their hold in Eastern Europe largely by dint of their military presence; they may view the United States' position in NATO as somewhat synonomous with their own in the Warsaw Treaty Organisation, namely, in terms of the control it gives them over the policies of member countries. "As the Soviet leaders see it, NATO is an instrument for the domination of the weaker allies by the United States and to a lesser extent by the United Kingdom."[10] The fact that the Soviets draw parallels between the Warsaw Pact and NATO does not mean, of course, that these parallels are valid. The Director of George Washington University's Sino-Soviet Institute has stated: "There are superficial similarities between the 'Eastern NATO' and the Western European organisations. But NATO and WEU are voluntary regional arrangements freely arrived at by sovereign states; the Warsaw Pact merely extends 'legal' status to an already extant situation. Because the East European satellites are regarded by the Kremlin as within its security sphere, any conflict would mobilise the USSR and its East European vassals into united action under the Soviet High Command. The Warsaw pact, therefore, is not a genuine regional arrangement. Rather, it is a stratagem to tighten Soviet control while propagating bloc unity and satellite 'sovereignty' throughout the world."[11]

Bearing in mind the influence of ideology in Soviet policy, it is logical to conclude that when the Soviets charge the United States with increasing world tension by dividing the world into hostile blocs they are manifesting to some extent the traditional communist penchant for looking at the world in dialectical terms. The United States, by building up West Germany, is thwarting the final synthesis of the capitalist and

[10] Black, C. E., and Yeager, F. J., "The USSR and NATO", in *NATO and American Security*, Klaus Knorr, ed., Princeton University Press (Princeton, 1959), p. 39.
[11] London, Kurt, *The Permanent Crisis*, Walker and Co. (New York, 1962), p. 163.

the socialist state systems and thus delaying the evolution of a "peaceful", i.e., communist world.

SOVIET ATTITUDES TOWARDS GERMANY

W. Phillips Davison has written: "Ever since Prussia rose to the status of a great power, Russian rulers have been deeply concerned about their policy towards this vigorous neighbour. With the triumph of communism in Russia, this concern about relations with Germany became even more intense than it had been under the Czars."[12] Hence, no effort to assess current Soviet attitudes towards West Germany and NATO would be adequate without some reference to past Soviet-German relations and to the continuing importance of the German question in Russian foreign policy.[13]

Germany has always held a special place in the communist theories of world revolution. Because of its high level of industrialisation, Germany was once considered by Lenin as the country where the Marxist revolution would first succeed.[14] Even when these early hopes did not

---

[12] *The Berlin Blockade* (A Rand Study), Princeton University Press (Princeton, 1958), p. 20.

[13] The West German Defence Minister Strauss wrote: "There is no doubt that Germany has occupied a key position in the eyes of all bolshevik rulers since Lenin's day." Strauss, Franz-Josef, "Soviet Aims and German Unity," *Foreign Affairs*, April, 1959, p. 366.

[14] One leading Sovietologist has pointed out that the bolsheviks apparently would have preferred the revolution to have taken place first in Germany. In his own words: "It was in Russia, as it also happened, that the first possibilities opened up for seizure of power in the name of this doctrine. This was not the choice of Lenin and his associates. They would probably have preferred it had this opening appeared in Germany rather than in Russia. Germany was the original home of Marxism. It was in Germany that the preconditions for the transition from capitalism to socialism, as Marx defined them, seemed to be farthest advanced. It was Germany that had the highly developed industry and the

materialise, the bolsheviks' admiration of Germany did not wane appreciably. Imbued with a belief in the central importance of economic and technological factors, the Soviets have always been impressed with the great industrial power of Germany. These background considerations are in varying degree essential to a fuller understanding of present Soviet concern over a rearmed West Germany allied to Western Europe and the United States in NATO.

Until the emergence of communist China, little more than a decade ago, the Soviet Union had probably maintained closer relations with Germany than it had with any other nation.

From the Rapallo Treaty of 1922 between Russia and Germany (both outcast nations after the First World War) until Germany's attack on the Soviet Union in June, 1941, there were, at various times, remarkably close ties between the two nations.[15] The climactic act of collaboration was the Nazi-Soviet Non-Aggression Pact of 1939, by which the Soviet relieved Germany of the fear of attack from the East, leaving the Nazi regime free to make war on England and France in the West.

Fear of the consequences of West Germany's leadership

---

politically conscious and mature proletariat. The German Social Democratic Party was the greatest Marxist political organisation in the world, far outshadowing its weak Russian counterpart."—Kennan, George F., *Russia and the West under Lenin and Stalin,* Atlantic-Little, Brown and Co. (Boston, 1961), p. 344. In fact, Lenin himself stated: "The principal link in the chain of world revolution . . . is the German link . . . and the success of the world revolution depends more on Germany than any other country."—Lenin, "Left-Wing Childishness and Petty Bourgeois Mentality" (1918), *Selected Works* (New York), Vol. III, p. 365.

[15] For a discussion of Soviet-German collaboration during this period, see Goerlitz, Walter, *History of the German General Staff,* Frederick A. Praeger (New York, 1953), p. 228-233; Knight-Patterson, W. M., *Germany from Defeat to Conquest 1913-33,* G. Allen (London, 1945), pp. 397-403.

of NATO lies at the root of the Soviets' attitude towards the German question. A reunited Germany reconstituted on the basis of free elections and with no constraints on her foreign policy would be likely to opt, as West Germany has already done, for membership in NATO. The borders of NATO would thus be advanced eastward. One of NATO's most serious deficiencies—viz., lack of defence in depth for ground operations—would thereby be alleviated. Hence, the Soviets see their security threatened by any agreement which left a reunited Germany free to choose sides in the Cold War.[16]

Since the formation of NATO the main themes of Soviet propaganda aimed at the organisation have been as follows: NATO is a weapon of the United States for world hegemony; NATO subjects member states to American domination; NATO weakens the United Nations by circumventing it; NATO has led to the division of Europe into hostile armed camps and thus heightened international tensions; and finally, NATO has fathered the resurgence of German militarism. The charge that NATO is an instrument for the revival of German militarism has been a principal motif of Soviet propaganda against the Atlantic Alliance.

While the Soviets have certainly been aware of the propaganda possibilities of using past German aggressiveness as a weapon for stunting West Germany's rearmament and her influence in NATO,[17] there can be little doubt that the

[16] Kennan, George F., *Russia, The Atom and the West*, Harper (New York, 1958), pp. 38-9.

[17] The Soviets placed high hopes on French fears of German militarism to prevent the rearming of West Germany. The Soviet Press was jubilant when EDC (the European Defence Community) collapsed in the French Parliament on 30 August, 1954. *Pravda* stated on 10 September, 1954, that the failure of EDC "has proved that the patriotic forces of France were equal to the situation and rightly perceived in EDC a mortal threat to the security and independence of the French State"—quoted in Dallin, David J., *Soviet Foreign Policy After Stalin*, Lippincott (Philadelphia, 1961), p. 156. They have also tried to gain support for

Soviets earnestly fear a resurrection of German military and economic power and that propaganda and policy converge in Soviet strategy on this issue. The strident tone of Soviet propaganda pronouncements frequently tends to obscure this fact. The principal objective of such propaganda, however, is withdrawal of West Germany from its alliance with NATO and the United States. Perhaps to some extent the Soviet concern over a rearmed West Germany has taken on the character of an obsession—or maybe even a new tenet of communist ideology. This means that the German question is not as susceptible to the kind of traditional balance-of-power negotiations which many Western diplomatic analysts implicitly assume it to be.

The entry of West Germany into WEU and NATO was one of the greatest defeats suffered by Soviet diplomacy in the postwar period. The dissolution of NATO has been the principal target of Soviet foreign policy and propaganda since its formation. It seems clear that this objective became all the more compelling when the Russian leaders began to suspect that West Germany was to be included in the pact. It should not be difficult to imagine that the Soviets viewed West German power potential as a possible spur for a revived and powerful Western Alliance potentially superior to the Soviet bloc in all elements of power, including manpower, if communist China is excluded.

The Soviets played on two main themes in their efforts to prevent West German rearmament and membership in NATO: (1) A revival of German militarism would endanger Germany's neighbours. (2) German rearmament would make reunification impossible.

Soviet concern over German rearmament was heightened further by NATO's approval in principle of the European

---

their attitude towards West German rearmament from the smaller Scandinavian and eastern European countries who have suffered in the past from German militarism.

Defence Community (EDC) plan at the Lisbon Conference on 20 February, 1952, which called for the integration of a rearmed West Germany into NATO. At that time Moscow declared that the ruling circles in the United States were assigning West Germany the role of the main striking force in the European Army. Soviet hopes were raised when the French Parliament rejected EDC, only to be quickly dashed, however, when the WEU formula was put into effect in May, 1955. The Soviet government took one final and formidable step to prevent the implementation of the agreement to rearm West Germany and bring it into NATO when it acceded in 1955 to the Austrian State Treaty which lifted the four-power occupation of Austria and established that country as a "neutral" state in the Cold War. The significance of this step becomes clear when it is borne in mind that this has been the only major Soviet territorial concession throughout the postwar period. The Austrian State Treaty, whatever other motivation the Soviets may have had for signing it, apparently was designed to demonstrate to the German people that they could purchase reunification at the price of neutrality. As Dean Acheson has written: "When, in February, 1955, the Soviet government opened direct talks with the Austrian Chancellor it was motivated not by Austrian considerations but by concern over Western Germany. Dr Adenauer was moving steadily in discussions with the NATO powers towards becoming a member of the alliance and playing an important military role in it. The Kremlin, determined to prevent this if possible, decided to give the Germans an object lesson that the best approach to the unification of Germany and the end of the occupation of East Germany would be to pay the price which the Austrians have to pay—stay clear of alliances with the West and take a position of neutrality."[18] In short, the Austrian settlement

[18] *Sketches From the Life of Men I Have Known,* Harper (New York, 1961), pp. 181-2.

was intended to serve as a model par excellence for a potential German solution.

The Austrian settlement was concluded at a time when the West German Bundestag was debating the ratification of WEU. Even though ratification seemed a foregone conclusion, given the composition of the West German parliament, the Soviets may have believed it would take the Bundestag some time to set up the legislative machinery for rearmament, not to mention the estimate that two to three years would be required to create the West German force. The Soviets apparently thought that there would be time for the implications of the Austrian Treaty to be perceived by the Germans. But if they expected that the example of Austria would influence the Germans towards neutrality, they were badly mistaken. In any event, the Soviets made their major territorial withdrawal of the Cold War against the background of the rearmament of West Germany and its membership in NATO.

Another symptom of this concern was the formation of the Warsaw Pact. As early as November, 1954, at a conference of the heads of communist states held in Moscow, the communist leaders warned the West that they would create such an organisation if West Germany were rearmed.[19] The Pact was signed on 14 May, 1955, just nine days after the accession of the Federal Republic to NATO.[20]

In short, Soviet policy towards NATO in general, and West Germany in particular probably rests on the belief that a West Germany rearmed to its fullest potential and aligned with the United States will pose a formidable hurdle to Soviet objectives in Western Europe and the world, and that such a Germany may eventually seek to commit NATO to the

[19] Brzezinski, Zbigniew K., *The Soviet Bloc: Unity and Conflict*, Harvard University Press (Cambridge, Mass., 1960): revised edition, Frederick A. Praeger (New York, 1961), pp. 170-1.

[20] *The NATO Handbook*, The North Atlantic Treaty Organisation Information Service (Paris, 1960), p. 25.

restoration of its former position in central and eastern Europe.[21] The Soviets undoubtedly believe furthermore that the success or failure of NATO as a military alliance is, to a large extent, dependent on West Germany's continued adherence to the Pact.

The Soviets have stated frequently that West Germany is destined to become the pillar of NATO's forward strategy —this despite the fact that the US force now stationed in West Germany is clearly the best equipped and trained force within NATO.[22] Moreover, they publicly have interpreted

[21] There can be little doubt that the Soviet concern from this standpoint is closely related to fears within the Soviets' East European empire. This is particularly true in Poland. It is necessary to recall that the former German territories east of the Oder-Neisse were annexed to Poland after the Second World War. The Poles have always feared, despite Soviet guarantees of protection, that the West Germans will eventually seek to reincorporate this territory into a new Germany. As John T. Karch has written, ". . . many Poles, especially those residing in Western Territories, are sceptical about the permanency of their holdings, fearing that the area may become a pawn in international politics. However, fear of a resurgent West Germany, especially since Bonn has become a NATO power, is real and the Poles find themselves relying more upon the USSR for support."—"Oder-Neisse: Anachronism of World War II," *World Affairs,* Vol. 123 (Winter, 1960), p. 103. The Poles' concern has undoubtedly been heightened by West Germany's unwillingness to accept the Oder-Neisse line as a permanent boundary. Perhaps even more alarming is the fact that the refugees from this German territory now represent a substantial portion of the voting strength of West Germany and have called for self-determination in the area.

[22] *Current Digest of the Soviet Press* (New York) 23.10.1957, p. 15. "Party Theses on the 40th Anniversary of the Great Socialist Revolution 1917-1957." See also Nalin, Y., *Red Star,* 28 March, 1959. The writer stated: "Western Germany, in fact, after the Paris agreements of October, 1954, and her entry into NATO in the following year became the striking force of the North Atlantic Pact in Europe. Proof of the importance which the United States gives to Western Germany can be found in the appointment of the Hitlerite

the US deployment in West Germany as a protective shield behind which German militarism is being revived. While there may be some question as to whether the Soviets really assume that the West German military forces, present and projected, represent the key force in NATO,[23] they appear to believe that West Germany represents the keystone of the success or failure of the NATO alliance as an organisation for European defence.

There is yet another dimension to Soviet anxieties *vis-à-vis* Germany. The Soviets probably surmise that as the West German contribution to NATO increases in significance, as it seems destined to do, the United States will be hard put to deny the West Germans the full panoply of modern weapons. Their fear in this direction was indicated by the statement of one Soviet writer to the effect that: "NATO's leaders also intended to supply the West German Army with rocket and thermo-nuclear weapons. . . ."[24] The Soviets have placed great hopes on the possibility of eventually bringing about an American withdrawal from West Germany and a West German withdrawal from NATO. They may see their whole strategy jeopardised if the United States gives West Germany a substantial nuclear capacity. Any unilateral effort which Moscow would then make to force a settlement of the German question on its own terms would be fraught with graver risk to Soviet objectives in Europe.

It seems clear in any event that, whether the Soviets fear West Germany for purely military or other reasons, they continue to hold a healthy respect for its combined human and physical resources and the contribution these resources can make towards strengthening the NATO alliance as an impediment to Soviet goals in Europe and elsewhere. Against the US policy of encouraging West German rearmament

General Speidel as Commander of the Land Forces of NATO in Central Europe."
[23] "Party Theses on the 40th Anniversary," op. cit.
[24] "Party Theses on the 40th Anniversary," op. cit.

within NATO, the Soviets have carried on a campaign to "demilitarise", "democratise" and "unify" a "peace-loving" Germany. (In their eyes, of course, East Germany is the only "democratic" and "peace-loving" regime in German history.) In recent years, however, they have reduced their emphasis on reunification and have concentrated primarily on gaining international recognition for East Germany and on the idea of reunification as the product of the "growing together" of the two Germanies.

It seems safe to conclude that what the Soviets fear most now from West Germany, in the broad sense, is its contribution to NATO and its alliance with the United States, and not West Germany *per se*.[25] Mr Khrushchev is a good enough geopolitician to realise that a West Germany acting independently would now pose little direct threat to the USSR in a traditional military sense. The Premier himself has stated: "It should be borne in mind that if the West Germans use all the economic potential and manpower resources of their country for creating the most powerful army in West Europe, even the strength of that army would not be equal to the power of our army and those of our allies. . . ." Their main fears regarding West Germany centre on its present role as a pillar of the NATO alliance, with all its implications for Soviet strategy, and on its assumed potential role as a catalyst of general nuclear war.

The Berlin Problem

Any assessment of Soviet attitudes *vis-à-vis* the Federal Republic's membership in NATO must take into account the specific objectives of Soviet strategy in Europe, namely, to change the status of West Berlin, stabilise the East German

---

[25] Kennan, "Hearings," op. cit., p. 1017. "I do think the fear that is most prominent in the Soviet mind with regard to Germany is the association of Germany's military potential with our own. . . ."

regime, obtain Western agreement to Germany's eastern boundaries (i.e., the Oder-Neisse line), and ultimately to bring about West Germany's withdrawal from NATO, thus wrecking the alliance and preparing the way for Soviet domination over the whole of Europe.

If Germany represents to the Soviets the principal problem of the Cold War, Berlin stands symbolically even though not geographically at the centre of that problem. In fact, in many respects Berlin can be said to constitute the over-all German problem in microcosm. Hans Morgenthau has observed: ". . . The German issue finds symbolic manifestation in the issue of Berlin, and by raising the latter, Khrushchev raised the former. . . ."[26] One may assume that the Soviets have been concerned for some time over the accident-prone situation in central-east Europe, the only area on the globe where substantial Soviet and US forces confront each other directly. Khrushchev has commented as follows on the United States and Soviet confrontation in Germany: "The armed forces of the confronting military groupings meet in German territory, especially in Berlin, and the slightest carelessness on any side may produce the spark that starts a blaze over it and explodes the powder keg. We want to separate the contacts so as not to cause the spark and so as not to confront the world with the danger of the greatest disaster: a third world war."[27]

The dangers inherent in that confrontation were brought home to the Soviets when successive revolts in Poland and Hungary flared in October, 1956. They displayed their concern at the time of the Hungarian rising when they hastily

[26] "Beleagured Bastion," VII, *The Washington Post*, 2 July, 1961.
[27] Broadcast over the East German radio on 9 March, 1959, as quoted in Mager and Katel, *Conquest without War: An Analytical Anthology of the Speeches, Interviews, and Remarks of N. S. Khrushchev, With Commentary by Lenin, Stalin, and others*. Simon and Schuster (New York, 1961), p. 103.

reinforced their forces in East Germany and alerted the East German security police. They had not forgotten that the East German people had already challenged communist rule in Berlin in June, 1953. They knew that the West Germans, their emotions fired by the Hungarian rising, might not have reacted to a Soviet repression of another East German revolt as passively as they had in 1953. They feared also that any West German embroilment might easily provide the catalyst for a local engagement between Soviet and US forces that could flare into a major conflagration.

Although the Soviets have eased their problem to some extent in eastern Europe since 1956 by strengthening their position in some of the satellites, they have by no means resolved it. The Soviets made it clear in Hungary in 1956 that they were prepared to use force to keep the satellites in line; they may well be concerned lest they be forced to a similar and even more painful decision in East Germany. Moreover, the Soviets probably sense that the US military presence in Berlin encourages some of the Eastern European peoples beyond Germany to cling to the hope of eventual freedom. And while the Soviet military presence is a deterrent to rebellion in the satellites, it also acts at the same time as a potential goad to revolt by these same peoples.[28]

What makes the danger of an embroilment in Europe even more ominous in Soviet eyes is its nuclear implications, imposed by the fact that the US presence in West Germany is to a large extent a nuclear one. The Soviets have consistently challenged the various theories of limited nuclear war, advanced in official and unofficial US circles. For

[28] Shortly after the Polish and Hungarian insurrections, the Soviets made far-reaching concessions to Poland, concessions that included the requirement to consult the Polish government on the movement and stationing of Soviet troops there. They concluded a similar agreement on 12 March, 1957, with the government of their East German satellite. Cf. Cottrell, Alvin J., and Hahn, Walter F., "A New Strategy for Europe," *The Yale Review* (Autumn, 1959), pp. 36-55.

example, Marshal Malinovski, on 15 January, 1960, stated: "In determining the course of the further development of our armed forces in the context of a reduction of numbers, we assume that a future war, if it is unleashed by the aggressors, will be waged with the mass employment of nuclear weapons. We emphasise this because in the West much is now said and written about 'limited nuclear war', about the 'tactical employment of nuclear weapons', about the 'strategy of doses' (graduated deterrence), and about 'strategy of terror', etc."[29] Since, as we have suggested, the Soviet objective of immediate priority is a change in the status of West Berlin, we may assume the dangers inherent in that situation heavily colour their statements on the infeasibility of fighting limited nuclear war. For it is over West Berlin that the Soviet strategy of maintaining pressure on the West is fraught with the greatest risks of triggering a nuclear conflict.

Since the beginning of the Berlin crisis in April, 1958, the Soviets have sought to absolve themselves from legal responsibility for a future crisis over West Berlin by attempting to transfer control of the Western routes of egress and ingress to their East German satellite. Any effort on the part of NATO to break an East German blockade of the routes to West Berlin by military force would confront the Soviets with a difficult decision. If the Soviets were to stand idly by, the East German forces would probably be defeated. The Soviets could permit this to happen only at the risk of endangering their position throughout Eastern Europe. The effect on the other Soviet satellites would be incalculable. It can be assumed, therefore, that the Soviets wish to avoid any action which would amount to leaving the German Democratic Republic to fight NATO forces alone.

No matter what legalistic devices the Soviets resort to in their campaign to sever West Berlin from the West, they

[29] Cited in Dinerstein, H. S., *Soviet Strategic Ideas:* The Rand Corporation, Research Memorandum RM-2532 (January, 1960), pp. 27-8.

cannot easily evade the risk of a US-Soviet military conflict. Nevertheless, the Soviets undoubtedly continue to hope—and with considerable justification—that if they could bring about the West's withdrawal from West Berlin, the impact of this defeat on West German opinion would be such that withdrawal of US troops from the Federal Republic would be only a question of time. In other words, they probably envisage a backdown by the West in Berlin as a major step towards their goal of excising West Germany's participation in NATO, which in turn would constitute a giant stride towards the goal of destroying NATO as an effective alliance. The evidence of recent years would seem to suggest that the Soviets are more interested in bringing about the one-sided dismantling of NATO than in effecting a symmetrical reduction in the level of East-West armaments tension in Europe.

The Soviet penchant for "nuclear-free zones" is also related to their effort to force the West out of Berlin. An agreement on a nuclear-free zone in central Europe would mean a withdrawal of nuclear weapons from the US forces now deployed in West Germany. Should these forces then be utilised in breaking an East German blockade of the routes to Berlin, they at least would not have resort to nuclear weapons at the outset. If the United States should rush nuclear weapons to the scene at a time of crisis, it would have to pay whatever penalties might be attached to breaking such an agreement in the eyes of world opinion. The Soviets seem to have considerable faith in the efficacy of a simple renunciation of the use of nuclear weapons for ultimately inhibiting their employment or their "diplomatic use" by the West. In any event, the Soviets may think that an American agreement to denuclearise US forces in West Germany would give them an enhanced flexibility in exerting pressure on the West's position in Berlin.

The exigencies of Soviet internal politics may be another factor in Moscow's Berlin policy. If the solution of the German problem is the highest priority objective of the

Soviet Union's foreign policy, it would seem to follow logically that the Soviet leadership, particularly Mr Khrushchev, is being judged against the record of his progress in achieving this goal. There is some evidence that the present Soviet political leadership is now deeply and irretrievably committed to changing the status of West Berlin.[30] If this is true, Mr Khrushchev may no longer be in a position to defer indefinitely a showdown on the West Berlin-East German question.

Perhaps the Soviets' confidence in the inevitability of communism's world triumph offers a further clue to the source of their concern over West Germany's alliance with the United States. If the Soviets are as confident of final world victory as some of their statements suggest,[31] then they undoubtedly view the US military presence in and rearmament of West Germany as a formidable obstacle which, however, can do no more than delay their inevitable progress towards this goal.[32] West Germany may drag the United States into a conflict which would make the Soviet victory much less meaningful. Hence, it is not inconceivable that, weighing their prospects conservatively, they see in the US-West German alliance the possibility that the victory of world communism can be won only at an exorbitant price. Indeed, given the unpredictability of the outcome of war in the age of nuclear missiles, they must at moments of honest reflection wonder whether all might not ultimately be lost if they push their

[30] Cf. Lippman, Walter, *Herald Tribune,* 19 April, 1961.
[31] Cf. the text of a statement issued by the Conference of Representatives of Communist Parties held in Moscow in November, 1960. *New York Times,* 7 December, 1960.
[32] It is significant that the Communist Manifesto for 1960 (the statement issued in December, 1960, by the Conference of Communist Parties) places the blame for the Cold War on the West's trying to block the inevitable "March of History." The West is charged with refusing to bow to the inevitable and with endeavouring to stave off the inevitable by military means.

luck too far in Berlin. In any event, the US military presence in West Germany forces the Soviets to tread warily in their efforts to solve the German question on satisfactory terms. Perhaps after five years of gamesmanship in Berlin, they may occasionally suspect that the old capital of Germany constitutes one of these Gordian knots which one can try for years to untie but dare not cut.

SOVIET VIEWS ON DISENGAGEMENT AND DENUCLEARISATION IN CENTRAL EUROPE

A recent study of Soviet policy shows quite compellingly that, whatever local security concerns may have motivated Soviet conduct in Europe after the Second World War, the withdrawal of the American presence has been the consistent goal of Soviet policy in Europe and Asia since the end of that conflict. "Stalin's ambitions in the final phases of the war ran, of course, well beyond the objectives explicitly stated to the Allies as the war came to an end, and beyond those that were implicit in the military advances of the Soviet armies at that time. What Stalin was really after was the expulsion of American influence from the Eurasian land mass generally, and its replacement by that of his own regime. In Western Europe, these ambitions were frustrated by the Marshall Plan and other measures taken to stiffen the independence of Western peoples in the post-hostilities period."[33]

The NATO alliance has military resources greater than those possessed by the Soviet bloc, excluding communist Chinese manpower, and the Soviets seek to prevent this potential strength from being developed into a major obstacle to communist world goals.[34] They obviously believe they can take a great step towards their goal by liquidating

[33] Kennan, George F., *Russia and the West Under Lenin and Stalin*, op. cit., p. 386.
[34] See Chapter 3, pp. 93-4.

the American overseas military deployment which now exists in Europe in the form of bases and troops. The Soviets are aware that, so long as US bases and forces remain stationed in the NATO area, the prospects of significant political or military changes in the orientation of Western European foreign policy are dim. Hence, the Soviets view all proposed modifications of the US forward military posture in West Germany as political issues of the first magnitude. This would seem to be the primary motivation behind Soviet advocacy of proposals for disengagement, nuclear test bans, thinning out of forces, and, to a lesser extent, "denuclearised" zones of the Rapacki type.

At the time the US overseas base system was established, the Soviets probably viewed the US basing arrangements largely in terms of the military advantage which they gave the West in the strategic balance of power. But, as the Soviets have developed their own nuclear delivery systems as a counter-weight to US strategic power, they have come to consider the US overseas military presence more in terms of its political and psychological significance as the major bond uniting the destinies of the United States and Western Europe. This insight is hardly unique. It now appears that the United States, for its part, has begun to recognise that its bases and general military presence in Western Europe are as important politically as they are militarily.

Once they had failed to prevent West German rearmament and membership in WEU and NATO, the Soviets changed their tactics and sought to "neutralise" Germany through various plans for disengaging Western and Soviet forces from their contiguous forward positions in the nation.[35] All these

---

[35] Neutralisation is a favourite technique of the Soviets in their efforts to prevent the growth of collective security arrangements. See Welch, William, "Soviet Commitments to Collective Action," in *Alliance Policy and the Cold War*, Arnold Wolfers (ed.), Johns Hopkins University Press (Baltimore, 1959), pp. 286-7.

Soviet disengagement proposals appear on close scrutiny to have had as their immediate objective the full withdrawal of US forces from Central Europe (i.e., Germany), the termination of West Germany's membership in NATO, and ultimately the emasculation of NATO as an effective mutual security organisation binding Western Europe to North America. That the severance of the tie between North America and Western Europe is the ultimate Soviet objective in Europe may be inferred from a statement by Mr Khrushchev: "When we speak of reducing these troops, we have in mind that this should be the beginning—only the first stage, since ultimately the matter should end in a complete withdrawal of all foreign troops from the territory of other states."[36]

Since the Soviets appear to see the US overseas military deployment as the political "cement" of the alliance, they undoubtedly feel—correctly or not—that the withdrawal of US military power from Europe would dissolve any effective military, economic and political bonds between North America and Western Europe. Apparently they doubt that cultural or political ties could by themselves sustain the alliance once the US military presence had been removed.[37] Apparently also they believe that, once the physical and static deployment of US forces in West Germany has been eliminated, the United States could no longer effectively

[36] "On Questions of the International Situation"—Speech by N. S. Khrushchev, *Current Digest of the Soviet Press* (New York, 22 January, 1958), p. 22.

[37] In June, 1957, Khrushchev stated: "We are not afraid of withdrawing our troops from all countries where they are stationed. Britain, the United States, and France fear this. The governments of Italy and West Germany are also afraid of foreign troops being evacuated. . . . Adenauer, for instance, asks foreign troops to remain in West Germany. Why? Simply because the governments of these countries do not know what will happen to them when the American forces leave. They do not know how French, Italians, Germans, Greeks and others will behave. . . ."—TASS, 29 June, 1957.

bring its power to bear in Europe for political-military purposes—that, in brief, modern means of deployment and communication could not compensate for loss of physical emplacement of US military power at the very border of the East-West confrontation.

The Soviets probably believe that a comprehensive disengagement of US and Soviet forces from Europe would alter radically the *status quo* in Western Europe, while exerting no commensurate effect upon the situation in Eastern Europe. In the light of Mr Khrushchev's assertion that the *status quo* in Eastern Europe must be preserved,[38] the Soviets apparently assume, with considerable justification, that the political impact of a military *quid quo pro* would not be equal.[39] They apparently realise that the strength of the "counter-revolutionary" trends in Eastern Europe is predicated largely on the proximity of potential Western, i.e., US military support. In short, the Soviets would expect the satellite peoples to keep a wary eye on the USSR as they reorganise their governments following a Soviet military evacuation; they probably believe it unlikely that, under these conditions, any non-communist, let alone anti-communist, regime could come to power.[40]

That the Soviets would expect the *status quo* in Eastern Europe to remain relatively intact following a US-Soviet disengagement is evident from a statement by Mr Khrushchev. Castigating the Eisenhower-Dulles policy of seeking to place the question of Eastern Europe on the agenda of a Big Four summit conference, Mr Khrushchev said: "What

[38] Cf. Hilsman, Roger, "On NATO Strategy," in *Alliance Policy and the Cold War,* op. cit., pp. 156-7.
[39] Cf. Finletter, Thomas K.,: "It needs the withdrawal of both political and military power to make a country free." The Russians have not the slightest intention of withdrawing their political power from the occupied satellites. *Foreign Policy: The Next Phase,* op. cit., pp. 113-4.
[40] Cf. Acheson, Dean G., "The Illusion of Disengagement," *Foreign Affairs* (April, 1958).

do Messrs Eisenhower and Dulles want? Evidently they wish to meet us and have a talk about the liquidation of the people's democratic regimes in the people's democracies. They evidently wish that we should give up socialist building and that we should restore the capitalist order . . . the *status quo* should be recognised . . . there are two systems of states in the world . . . if the *status quo* in the communist bloc is not recognised . . . then it is, of course, absolutely impossible to come to terms."[41] The Soviets would be most unlikely to accept blithely a non-communist status for any state which had been a member of the "Socialist Commonwealth." This would represent a blow to the image which the Soviets project of a dynamic communist bloc advancing steadily towards world domination. It helps explain their brutal suppression of the Hungarian uprising when the Imre Nagy government announced it was leaving the Warsaw Pact. It explains, moreover, their acceptance of neutralism in those newly emergent nations of the underdeveloped world which are located beyond the reach of effective Soviet military power. It would be a blow to the image of "dynamic" communism if communist regimes were established in countries where Soviet military power could not effectively be employed to prevent their overthrow. This is probably why the Soviets exercised extreme caution in formally accepting the Castro regime in Cuba into the communist camp and tried so hard to exact a no-invasion-of-Cuba pledge from the United States in return for their decision to withdraw missiles from Cuba.

Mr Khrushchev declared to the 21st Party Congress in January, 1959: "We are for creating a zone of disengagement of armed forces. The Soviet Union is ready to withdraw its troops not only from Germany, but also from Poland and Hungary, where they are situated in conformity with the

[41] Quoted in Hilsman, Roger, "On NATO Strategy," op. cit., pp. 156-7.

Warsaw treaty, if all the other countries who are members
of the North Atlantic Alliance withdraw their troops back
to within their own frontiers and liquidate the military bases
in other countries."[42]

Nuclear-free Zones

Their more comprehensive disengagement schemes having
thus far fallen on barren soil, the Soviets have shortened their
sights to the "denuclearisation" of West Germany. In their
efforts to achieve this objective, they have argued that the
stationing of nuclear weapons on West German territory
and the equipping of the West German Army with nuclear
weapons would practically doom all hope of eventual
reunification. An early sign of their fear that West Germany
would some day get nuclear weapons was their allegation
that Euratom was merely a device for the nuclear arming of
the *Bundeswehr*. They asserted that the treaty did not pro-
hibit the signatories from using fissionable materials for
military purposes.[43] This is not to suggest that the fear of
West Germany receiving nuclear weapons is the only reason
for such Soviet comments on Euratom; they are opposed to
any projects for Western unity whether it be Euratom, the
Common Market or NATO because they desperately fear
Western unity, and particularly, ". . . the consolidation of
German power with the NATO structure."[44]

[42] Khrushchev, Report to 21st Party Congress, *New York
Times*, 28 January, 1959.
[43] Cited in Yeager, F. J., *The USSR and NATO: A Study
in the Implementation of Soviet Foreign Policy* (unpublished dissertation, Princeton University, 1959), p. 232.
[44] James Reston, *New York Times*, 2 July, 1961. As
Reston argues: "They (the communists) are concentrating
on two things: on forming 'a more perfect union' of their
own states and opposing every effort to form 'a more perfect
union' of the free nations. . . . They are opposing the movement toward European unity through the Common Market

The proposals for a nuclear-free zone in Central Europe vary somewhat, but the Soviets have enthusiastically supported the plan advanced by Adam Rapacki, foreign minister of Poland. In its final form, the provisions of the Rapacki plan relating to nuclear weapons called for a ban on the stationing, production and use of nuclear weapons and missiles in East and West Germany, Poland and Czecho-Slovakia.

It seems apparent that the Soviets, whatever other motivation they may harbour for such proposals, consider the "nuclear-free zones" as preliminary steps looking towards general disengagement of the type described above by Mr Khrushchev. As the chairman of the East German Communist Party, Walter Ulbricht has stated: "The working out of such a peace (i.e., German confederation) is in direct connection with the proposals on setting up a nuclear-free zone in Europe, a zone of reduced armaments, with the gradual withdrawal of foreign forces from Germany and the liquidation of foreign military bases in both Germanys and other European countries."[45] While the very location of West Germany is enough to make that country a key Soviet concern, the Soviets so respect German potential that they deem neutralisation of West Germany as almost synonymous with the disintegration of NATO and, with it, the separation of Western Europe from North America—the prime intermediate objective of Soviet policy and global strategy. The banning of nuclear weapons in the geographic limits prescribed by the Rapacki plan is probably intended as a pilot

---

and the Treaty of Rome. They are opposing British association with the treaty. . . . What Khrushchev did manage to do, however, was to divert attention from the political consolidation of Europe, which is really what worries him. A month ago the British were deeply engaged in a debate about joining the Common Market. Today they are talking about Berlin."

[45] Quoted in Yeager, F. J., op, cit., p. 232.

arrangement which would establish a precedent for a wider ban on deployment and use of nuclear weapons in the rest of Europe and elsewhere. This was clearly implied by the Soviet references, as early as March, 1959, to a "trial" zone in Germany.[46]

As one Soviet specialist has observed: "The Soviet Union seeks to convince the nations of Western Europe that as they reduce their involvement in NATO they simultaneously reduce the danger of war in Europe, and minimise the danger they would suffer if there were a war. The main theme in this propaganda campaign is that a nuclear war would mean total destruction for nations of the Western Alliance in Europe which might possess nuclear weapons, and that each country should take immediate political action to prevent admission of nuclear weapons to its territory, or to eject them if they are already there."[47] This is especially true of Soviet propaganda beamed at the smaller NATO nations. In such propaganda the Soviets remind these nations that countries with small territories are particularly vulnerable to nuclear attack. Thus, they exploit the widespread fear of nuclear war in an effort to bring about the withdrawal of the US military presence. Soviet nuclear blackmail against America's smaller NATO allies has been a conspicuous feature of Soviet diplomacy in Europe. By putting pressure on America's weaker NATO allies, the Soviets are able to bring pressure to bear on the United States. Such Soviet threats are designed to make the weaker NATO allies more amenable to Soviet disarmament proposals in addition to discouraging them from allowing the United States to station nuclear weapons on their soil.

In this chapter it has been the authors' purpose frankly to speculate widely on Soviet motivations *vis-à-vis* NATO

---

[46] *New York Times,* 29 March, 1956, p. 1. Cf. also "Main Trends in Soviet Capabilities and Policies, 1959-64."

[47] Dinerstein, H. S., *Military Force and Soviet Goals,* The Rand Corporation, RM-2771 (2 June, 1961).

and Germany. In doing so the authors have tried to view NATO and Germany as the Soviets conceivably might do. Whatever the motivations behind Soviet behaviour towards the Alliance may actually be, one thing is certain: Soviet postwar behaviour is responsible for the creation of NATO and the rearmament of West Germany and its membership in the Alliance. Even if for the sake of argument we concede, as has been suggested before in this chapter, that some Soviet aggressive moves in Eastern Europe immediately following the Second World War may have been motivated to some extent by traditional military security concerns, they cannot blame Western observers who, having read Marxist-Leninist manifestoes and pronouncements proclaiming eventual communist world domination, viewed Soviet policy as a prelude to even further Soviet expansionist efforts on the continent of Europe and elsewhere. It is almost certainly true that the Soviets have managed to bring about a configuration of power the very opposite of which they hoped to see develop in Western Europe, namely, the formation of NATO, which aligned North America with Western Europe, as well as the rearmament of West Germany and its integration into the Western Alliance. Thus, in Europe, as well as in other parts of the world, Soviet conduct has followed a pattern once aptly described by George F. Kennan: "Their own aggressive intransigence with respect to the outside world began to find its own reaction; and they were soon forced, to use . . . [a] Gibbonesque phrase, 'to chastise the contumacy' which they themselves had provoked. It is an undeniable privilege of every man to prove himself right in the thesis that the world is his enemy; for if he reiterates it frequently enough and makes it the background of his conduct he is bound eventually to be right."[48]

[48] "The Sources of Soviet Conduct," Appendix I, *American Diplomacy 1900-50*, University of Chicago Press (Chicago, 1951), p. 111.

Chapter 3

THE POLITICS OF NATO'S MILITARY STRATEGY

Within recent years it has become increasingly evident that NATO's political and military problems are intimately related. Indeed, NATO's political difficulties stem largely from the inadequacy of NATO's military policy, strategy and posture, and these difficulties invite the Soviets to pursue a strategy of pressure and harassment. This Soviet strategy is actually aimed more at NATO's political solidarity than at NATO's military forces.

Throughout most of NATO's history, the major concern of NATO's military planners has been to formulate a viable strategy for the local defence of Europe. Given the conditions of constantly changing military technology under which modern man lives, this will be a continuing challenge as long as NATO remains in existence. But within recent years, the problems of planning for the effective military defence of Europe have been complicated by the emergence of a new issue—one that is primarily political rather than purely military or technical in nature. This is the issue of the control of nuclear weapons. Should a virtual monopoly of nuclear decision-making power continue to be vested in the United States as heretofore, or should there be some form of "nuclear sharing"—some means of admitting the Europeans to the planning of nuclear strategy, the making of nuclear decisions, and the political and physical control of nuclear weapons? It is important that the reader should understand clearly the distinction between these two issues—military defence and political control. They have often been confused. The major part of this chapter will be devoted to the basic problems of NATO's strategy for the local defence of Europe; the subtle political problems associated with the so-called "European deterrent" will be examined elsewhere in the book, but the military implications of a European deterrent will be dealt with towards the end of this chapter.

The Sword and the Shield Strategy

NATO strategy thus far has rested on the concept of the "sword" (SAC and, more recently, the growing missile capabilities of the United States) and the "shield" (NATO's ground forces) stationed in the centre of Europe. Throughout the entire period of NATO's existence, however, this shield has been deemed inadequate to cope with a large-scale Soviet ground attack. Rather, the forces making up the shield appear to have served in fact, though not officially, as a "tripwire" to activate the SAC sword, which is outside the command of NATO. But, as the Soviets began to develop their own nuclear stockpiles and strategic delivery systems and thus to whittle down US nuclear superiority, America's Western allies have been increasingly apprehensive of a possible failure of its strategy of deterrence. Denis Healey, military specialist of the British Labour Party, gave this view of the emerging situation in 1957: "Now, however, new uncertainties are clouding the European response to NATO's demands. The instrument of America's atomic striking power, the Strategic Air Command, has always been held outside NATO under the exclusive control of the United States. So long as Russia lacked a comparable power, the

presence of a few GIs along the Iron Curtain seemed sufficient guarantee that America would commit the Strategic
Air Command to action if Western Europe were attacked.
Now that Russia may have the power to retaliate in kind on
the United States itself, can the peoples of Western Europe
take it for granted that America will invite her destruction by committing the Strategic Air Command to their
support?"[1]

What Mr Healey says about the future utility of SAC
applies with equal validity to all the strategic missile delivery
systems which the United States is now in the process of
developing. It was concern for the continued reliability of
the American strategic retaliatory force for deterring an
attack on individual NATO countries which prompted
Alastair Buchan, Director of the Institute of Strategic
Studies in London, to propose the creation forthwith of "the
least vulnerable" NATO strategic nuclear force. Buchan
proposed the creation of an Intermediate Range Ballistic
Missile system deployed along the entire periphery of the
NATO area from "North Cape to Alexandretta" under
the direct control of the Supreme Commander Allied Powers
in Europe (SACEUR) or some other suitable command.[2]

The strategy to which NATO is committed was formulated
during the period when the United States enjoyed a clear-
cut superiority over the Soviet Union in nuclear weapons
and the means of delivery. Yet, as has been noted, this
superiority is waning. The West's ability to deter a communist attack on Western Europe or to deter more provocative Soviet efforts to harass the Allies in the area (e.g.,
Berlin) may in future depend largely on the strength of the
NATO ground forces deployed in Central and Western
Europe. These ground forces have never been adequate to

[1] Healey, Denis, "NATO and the Cold War," *Confluence*,
Vol. 6 (Autumn, 1957), p. 222.
[2] Buchan, Alastair, *NATO in the 1960s*, Frederick A.
Praeger (New York, 1960), p. 71.

repel a ground attack of the magnitude the Soviets are capable of launching. Throughout most of the period of the Alliance's existence—i.e., up until the Berlin crisis of 1961 —scarcely more than half of the thirty divisions called for by SACEUR have been in position and ready to fight. These forces have confronted approximately twenty-two Soviet divisions in East Germany and over 100 more stationed elsewhere in East Europe and European Russia. The Soviet forces are equipped to wage both nuclear and non-nuclear warfare. By contrast, the NATO forces, by dint of their size and armament, have been committed almost entirely to a nuclear defence.

In the early days of NATO, the West apparently believed it possible to erect a conventional force barrier against a potential Soviet thrust across the River Elbe. At Lisbon in 1952, the NATO Council adopted a force goal of ninety-six divisions. Of these, the forward force was to consist of approximately thirty-five to forty divisions. However, only twenty-five of these divisions representing the forward screen were to be positioned on the vital central front—a line extending from the Baltic Sea in the north to the border of Switzerland in the south;[3] the others were to be distributed largely in the Trieste-Brenner Pass area and along the Scandinavian front. The remainder of the ninety-six divisions were to be manned by reservists and to be ready to fight in from D+15 to D+30 days. However, it became quite obvious shortly after the Lisbon goals were set that the European members of NATO could not or would not take the necessary political and economic measures to raise the forces agreed upon at the 1952 Council meetings. Thus these over-all force goals were eventually scaled down and the United States increasingly urged West German rearmament

[3] Hilsman, Roger, "NATO: The Developing Strategic Concept," in *NATO and American Security*, Klaus Knorr, ed., Princeton University Press (Princeton, 1959), pp. 29-34.

in order to fill the gap in NATO's conventional defences.

The revised NATO force goals called for the equivalent of thirty ready divisions on the central front—five more than under the Lisbon plan—and a considerable number of reserve divisions, but not so many as had been envisaged at Lisbon. It has been estimated that, counting reserve divisions, the total number of divisions called for in the new plan is in the neighbourhood of seventy-five.[4] Thus the disparity between the Lisbon force goals and the force now deemed desirable is not so great as it would seem at first glance. The principal difference between the Lisbon plan and the Norstad goals seems to be the latter's emphasis on the ready force to be deployed at all times along the central front and its de-emphasis of reserve forces. If advances in firepower and mobility are calculated along with the increase in the number of divisions, the ready force is substantially stronger than that provided for at Lisbon.

An important reason behind this shift in emphasis away from reserve towards ready forces is the doubt in the minds of many NATO planners that a war in Europe would remain limited very long.[5] Some European members of the Alliance were unwilling to make the necessary economic and political sacrifices involved in raising and maintaining forces which they believed would be of little or no value, since a war in Europe was likely to be nothing more than a prelude to general war. In fact, many Europeans seemed to fear that too large a NATO ground force might serve to make sure that a war between the United States and the Soviet Union would be confined largely or solely to Western Europe,

[4] Ibid.

[5] For a discussion of the reasons why it seemed harder to limit wars in Europe than in other regions of the world, see the authors' article, "Nuclear Weapons, Policy and Strategy," *Orbis,* Vol. I (Summer, 1957).

leaving the homelands of the two superpowers "out of bounds".

Estimates on how long a Soviet attack can be contained without flaring into general war vary from several days to one month. It is just such estimates which led to a British proposal to NATO that the mobilisation base of the Alliance be reduced from ninety days to a maximum of one month. It has been the view of some British leaders, for example, that either general nuclear war or a return to negotiations would limit a local conflict in Europe to no more than one month.[6]

NATO spokesmen have frequently reiterated that the thirty-division force goal is not a "magic number". A part of the rationale behind the size of the force to be in a position on the central front can be partially explained by the fact that the shield has always been related to the size of the Soviet force poised in East Germany, a force which has for several years approximated twenty-two divisions. The idea has been to have in position along the central front line, i.e., from the Baltic Sea to the Swiss border, a force adequate to cope with the Soviet forward force deployed in East Germany. In short, the NATO force goal has envisaged a ready force which would make it impossible for the Soviet forces in East Germany to carry out a successful surprise attack on Western Europe without heavy reinforcement. In the view of NATO planners, the Soviets could not increase substantially their forces in East Germany without thereby giving the West valuable warning time and enabling NATO to bring up its own reinforcements. As W. W. Rostow has written: "Europe's ground forces might not be able alone to meet a fully mobilised ground attack by the Soviet Union; but, on the other hand, NATO was clearly a force which could obstruct a march from East Germany to the Channel. Its

6 *New York Times,* 30 March, 1960.

capabilities would evidently demand a major further mobilisation of forces in East Germany by the Soviet Union before an attack could be contemplated, thus giving important warning to the United States and the West. . . ."[7]

A Soviet attack of the force necessary to overwhelm thirty NATO divisions would have to be so large as to make Soviet intentions unmistakably clear. A shield of thirty divisions would be adequate to force upon the Soviets what SACEUR has termed "the pause". In other words, it has been hoped that a communist ground probe could be contained long enough to give the Kremlin time to weigh the question as to whether it is willing to proceed further along a course that could grow into general war to achieve its objectives or whether it might be more prudent to halt military operations and seek to return to the conference table.

Moreover, the Soviets would have to accept the risk that a large-scale ground probe into NATO territory might provoke the United States into striking the first nuclear blow, an advantage which is now generally conceded to the Soviet Union. If a nuclear holocaust is likely to be the logical result of a ground probe, then the Soviets might consider such an operation merely as a foolish and costly prelude to general war.

An important and controversial change took place in NATO strategy in 1954. Soon after it took office in 1953, the Eisenhower Administration announced the "New Look" in American defence policy, indicating a shift towards primary reliance on nuclear weapons to meet the full range of communist conflict challenges. The new policy, whose effect among other things was to reduce sharply the level of conventional forces, was often characterised by the phrase, "a bigger bang for a buck". In the words of General Maxwell D. Taylor, the immediate consequence of the New Look

[7] Rostow, W. W., *The United States in the World Arena*, Harper (New York, 1960), pp. 332-3.

was ". . . the reduction of personnel strengths for the armed services for the fiscal years 1955 and 1956 and a sharp increase of the size and level of nuclear air forces at the expense of conventional forces."[8] The "Radford Plan", as the reorientation was frequently called, did not altogether dismiss the need for conventional forces, but these were to be supplied largely by America's allies under the US Military Assistance Programme.

In December, 1954, the NATO Council incorporated the American New Look military policy into NATO strategy when it scaled down the over-all Lisbon force goals and integrated nuclear weapons into NATO strategy in order to compensate for the projected loss of conventional man- and fire-power. This post-1954 strategy has caused a great deal of concern within the Alliance, for many observers have questioned whether a strategy that envisages limited nuclear war is feasible in some areas. For example, in an area as densely populated as Western and Central Europe, can atomic weapons be used without endangering civilian populations? The proponents of a strategy which calls for semi-automatic resort to tactical atomic weapons in the event of a Soviet attack argue that a distinction must be made between large and small nuclear arms. They contend that the side-effects of clean weapons in the low kiloton range can be kept to a minimum, so far as harm to local population goes. But on both sides of the Atlantic many ask: "How high is minimum?" Military and civilian targets in Western Europe are virtually inseparable; even if megaton weapons were not used, the level of destruction is likely to be quite extensive. It is the opinion of Alastair Buchan, that "the indefinite maintenance of our present nuclear posture in NATO will demoralise the Alliance, and in particular the officers and commanders within it who have to live under the shadow of

[8] Taylor, Maxwell D., *The Uncertain Trumpet*, Harper (New York, 1959).

this policy."[9] In support of his view Buchan quotes a distinguished European officer who stated at the Oxford Conference of the Institute of Strategic Studies: "There is a not inconsiderable danger that European opinion might choose that the United States did not honour her commitments to NATO, if it involved the use of tactical nuclear weapons in Europe."[10]

European opinion is first and foremost a political factor. It imposes certain constraints upon the actions and policy choices of European statesmen as they seek to maintain a credible defensive position during a period of protracted international conflict. But it is not likely that the attitude of the European public, or a segment of it, would control strategic decisions in a time of crisis. Nevertheless, it must be recognised that if NATO is to enjoy popular support in the years ahead, it will require a military posture and strategy which will inspire confidence in its strength without giving rise to undue fears among Europeans.

Irrespective of public opinion, it is possible to question excessive reliance upon a nuclear strategy in purely military terms. The predominant military doctrine which emerges in the open literature emphasises the importance of dispersal and mobility. But dispersal and mobility of forces is by no means easy to achieve and to maintain on a nuclear battlefield. The greater the dispersal, the harder it would be to preserve the communications network needed for effective command and control under the chaotic conditions sure to prevail on a nuclear battlefield. After being under tactical nuclear fire for two or three days, and confronted with serious shortages of uncontaminated food and water, the willingness of men to continue the struggle in radioactive areas will indeed be impaired.[11]

[9] *NATO in the 1960s,* Frederick A. Praeger (New York, 1960), p. 38.   [10] Ibid.
[11] See Dupuy, T. N., "Can America Fight a Limited Nuclear War?" *Orbis,* Vol. V (Spring, 1961).

Apart from the obvious physical dangers to populations on both sides of the Iron Curtain inherent in a nuclear strategy, and apart from the difficulties of command and control in a nuclear battlefield environment, there is the question also of the psychological implications of the new weapons. Considerable doubt prevails in many quarters that nuclear weapons provide a credible deterrent to the full range of Soviet options. This problem has been summed up by Captain Carl H. Amme, USN: "Deterrence is in effect a psychological posture. We attempt to create in the Soviet mind a fear or a belief in our willingness to act. Certainly no rational enemy would deny that we would have the will to employ nuclear weapons if the stakes were right. On the other hand, he would hardly conceive that we would be irrational enough to use these weapons when the stakes were minute."[12] Deterrence, then, involves a kind of strategic mind-reading, and the Soviets may calculate wrongly what is in the "mind of the United States".

One of the principal military arguments adduced in support of a strategy which would rely primarily on nuclear weapons is that, for fear of excessive casualties, troop concentration in an atomic war must be held to a minimum and that there is, therefore, an inherent upper limit to the size of forces which can be effectively deployed on a nuclear battlefield. While this argument has much validity, there is no evidence that even in a conflict in which tactical nuclear weapons are employed, the size of forces used would cease to be a meaningful factor in the determination of victory or defeat. A good big atomic army is likely to remain superior to a good small atomic army, despite the fact that the defending side in such a conflict would appear to hold some inherent

[12] Amme, Capt. Carl H., Psychological Effects of Nuclear Weapons," *US Naval Institute Proceedings*, Vol. 86 (April, 1960), p. 33.

advantages.[13] That nuclear weapons necessarily favour the defensive side has been disputed by Dr Malcolm W. Hoag of the Rand Corporation: "If valid at all, the defensive advantage accrues only after nuclear hostilities are under way. . . . And when we are on the defensive at the outset, as we expect to be, the one clear advantage that nuclear weapons would appear to confer is upon the side that initiates their employment, especially if it does so suddenly and in considerable numbers. And if we have made clear our intent to use nuclear weapons, an aggressor has an obvious interest in being the one to initiate their use in overwhelming power."[14] Also, while it is true that the aggressor may be unable to gamble on massing its forces for fear of nuclear attack, it is equally true that the defensive side will be similarly inhibited. Glenn H. Snyder has noted that ". . . effective defence must always include an ability to counter-attack since the aggressor will almost automatically make an initial gain by virtue of the advantage of surprise and momentum. A further point is that if neither side can risk concentrating for a breakthrough, the war is likely to be one of small unit action, infiltration, and the like, verging on guerrilla tactics. If the enemy has an advantage in manpower, he is likely to be able to make gains in this type of warfare."[15]

But even if tactical nuclear weapons could be used in such a way as drastically to scale down civilian casualties, there still remains the danger that their use will spiral inexorably into all-out nuclear war. The proponents of a tactical atomic strategy have argued that the level of the conflict, not the weapons used, will govern its scale and intensity. This

[13] Hilsman, Roger, "On NATO Strategy," in *Alliance Policy and the Cold War*, Arnold Wolfers, ed., Johns Hopkins University Press (Baltimore, 1959), p. 174.

[14] Hoag, Malcolm W., "NATO's Strategy and Limited War," in *NATO and American Security*, Klaus Knorr, ed., Princeton University Press (Princeton, 1959), p. 119.

[15] Snyder, Glenn H., *Deterrence and Defense*, Princeton University Press (Princeton, 1961), pp. 138-9.

argument presupposes that the enemy will tacitly agree to adhere to certain nuclear ground rules. Since he presumes that the NATO powers do not want to start a thermo-nuclear war and since he himself is reluctant to start one, he will surmise that the introduction of lower yield nuclear weapons by the West is not intended to signal the start of all-out war. Moreover, the advocates of a tactical nuclear strategy insist that, even though the commanders of an attacking Soviet army may be confused over NATO's inten-tions in invoking tactical nuclear weapons for tactical pur-poses, Soviet military planners in Moscow will be in a much better position to gauge the real situation and to act with restraint.

The opponents of this line of reasoning on both sides of the Atlantic believe that such a strategy is, to say the least, fraught with considerable risk. It is their view that, in the heat of battle, an enemy may very well mistake the opponent's intentions and refuse to abide by such vaguely adumbrated rules of nuclear war. This might be especially true if medium-range American missiles deployed in rela-tively forward positions should be fired for purposes which NATO considers tactical but which Soviet decision-makers regard as approaching the strategic.

Inadequate Non-nuclear Shield

Despite the change wrought in the balance of power by the growing Soviet nuclear missile arsenal, NATO apparently has continued to base its NATO military policy largely on the assumption that the Soviet Union is aware that Western Europe is so vital to American foreign policy that any attack on the NATO countries would automatically lead to general war.[16] Since, as this line of reasoning goes, the

[16] This premise may soon no longer be valid on grounds of military strategy alone. Roger Hilsman points out that the loss of Europe prior to the missile age would have been

Russians have as little desire as the West to detonate a nuclear holocaust, the latter needs very little in the way of limited war capabilities for the defence of the area. Thus, for strategic reasons which happen to fit in conveniently with budgetary predilections, only half-hearted efforts have been made to develop adequate conventional capabilities. The policy of primary reliance on nuclear weapons has had considerable bearing on the unwillingness of the European Allies to make a substantial contribution to the shield. In the words of Denis Healey: "It is not surprising that the European peoples have made so inadequate an effort to provide the troops demanded by SHAPE. If major aggression in Europe is going to lead to all-out thermo-nuclear war, why bother about holding a line in a radioactive desert? Moreover, if the Russians are convinced that a major aggression in Europe will lead to nuclear retaliation by strategic delivery forces, they will either refrain from such aggression altogether or start with an all-out attack on US strategic delivery bases all over the world. In other words, by basing Western defence on the idea of massive retaliation, NATO appeared to deny America's Allies any real role in their own defence, except in circumstances so catastrophic that defence hardly seemed worthwhile."[17]

This is not to say that America's European Allies are blameless. They have seized upon the inconsistencies in American strategic doctrine as a convenient pretext for their

---

tantamount to a final defeat for the United States. "The Soviets must recognise this, and it would seem unlikely that they would launch such an attack without forestalling United States reprisal by a strike on SAC bases and the continental United States. But the coming of missiles will sharply reduce the strategic significance of Europe for the defence of the continental United States, and the Soviets may not regard the high psychological stake the United States has in Europe as sufficient motive for transforming a purely European war into the ultimate one."—Op. cit., p. 32.

[17] Healey, Denis, op. cit. (see note on p. 78), pp. 221-2.

own failure to make the difficult but necessary economic and political decisions. As Henry A. Kissinger has pointed out: "Our continental Allies have been torn between a strategy of limited risk and the desire for economy, between the wish for protection against Soviet occupation and the reluctance to face harsh realities. Each economy measure has been justified, much as in the United States, by the argument that the new weapons permit a reduction of forces. Yet the more fearful the resulting strategy, the more it has emphasised the sense of impotence among our Allies."[18]

The supposedly high cost of conventional armaments is a reason that is frequently advanced in NATO policy circles for NATO's failure to maintain an adequate non-nuclear shield. But Dr Malcolm W. Hoag, of the Rand Corporation, has written: ". . . one can only argue that strategically acceptable alternatives [to a conventional capability] are unlikely to be any cheaper." Dr Hoag contends that if the United States and its Western Allies were to design an adequate nuclear strategy for NATO, one which would enable NATO to engage in a limited nuclear war with the Russians in Europe, such a strategy would be "tremendously expensive", especially if it were based on a second-strike capability. He proposes that nuclear weapons be relegated to a secondary position for meeting challenges in the NATO area and that NATO forego weapons such as surface-to-surface missiles which are so inaccurate as to be useless in non-nuclear conflict.[19]

The opponents of increased conventional capabilities at times have argued that if the NATO powers undertake to build up a fair-sized conventional force, they might one day discover that the Russians had completely abandoned the capability to wage non-nuclear war, leaving us with an

[18] Kissinger, Henry A., *Nuclear Weapons and Foreign Policy*, Harper and Brothers (New York, 1958), p. 173.
[19] "Interdependence for NATO," *World Politics*, Vol. 12 (April, 1960), p. 386.

expensive and practically useless conventional establishment. Indeed, Mr Khrushchev's announcement on
14 January, 1960, that the Soviets were reducing their ground
forces was offered as evidence that the USSR was following
the American lead and adopting its own version of the "New
Look" in Soviet defence policy. (The counterpart of "a bigger
bang for a buck" seemed to be "more rubble for a rouble".)
It is undoubtedly true that the Russians are modernising their
armed forces and that this modernisation will continue and
entail a reduction in their conventional force levels. The
fact that the Russians are accelerating the integration of
atomic weapons into their strategy, however, is by no means
certain proof that they are preparing to abandon the
capability to wage conventional war. On the contrary, as
F. O. Miksche points out: "Naturally, the Soviet General
Staff is also occupying itself with the problem of atomic
reorganisation. So far, however, the reformed units have
been so organised that they can operate independently of
atomic weapons. Further, atomic weapons come under the
control of the army commands and not that of the divisions.
. . . Unlike the Americans, the Soviet General Staff has taken
care not to incorporate atomic armaments into all its army
units."[20] Even if the Soviet Union were to withdraw thirty
divisions, the total NATO ground force called for by
SACEUR, and transform them into a nuclear striking
force, it would still be able to maintain approximately
seventy conventionally armed divisions. This is a fact of
considerable diplomatic significance.[21] Raymond L. Garthoff
argues in the same vein in his study on Soviet military
thought, *The Soviet Image of Future War*: "The Soviets
have been guided not by a replacement of the capacities for
conventional warfare, but by the addition to them of capacities for either general or limited nuclear war."[22]

---

[20] *The Failure of Atomic Strategy,* Frederick A. Praeger
(New York, 1958), p. 164.   [21] Ibid.
[22] Public Affairs Press (Washington, D.C., 1959), p. 16.

Conventional Russian Forces

Indeed, Soviet conventional capabilities have been an integral element in the crisis confronting the West in Europe. A few Western advocates of greater reliance on non-nuclear forces have argued that the forces which have the greatest manoeuvrability along the Iron Curtain, and which vest Kremlin diplomacy with flexibility, are the Soviet Union's non-nuclear forces. Should the Soviets, in the face of a NATO build-up of non-nuclear forces, decide to shift to an exclusive nuclear strategy, they would forfeit to the West the very advantages of diplomatic manoeuvrability which they now derive from conventional manpower. There is reason to believe that the American conventional build-up as a result of the Berlin crisis of 1961 prompted Soviet strategists to entertain second thoughts about the reduction of conventional forces.

Strategically, the most profound objection to re-emphasising a local defence capability in Europe has been the argument that efforts to build such a defence would weaken the over-all deterrent. It is contended that the deployment of more than tripwire forces might serve only to convey to the communist bloc NATO's reluctance to respond to an attack with nuclear weapons. Thus, the argument runs, reputed statements to the effect that NATO intends to limit its response may have the affect of restoring war to its historical position as an instrument of national policy. Some proponents of this view even contend that the more NATO appears to reduce its reliance on conventional forces, the more credible becomes our willingness to resort to all-out nuclear war. The argument in favouring a semi-automatic nuclear NATO response posture has been summed up succinctly by Glenn H. Snyder: "If the Soviets were to attack conventionally a nuclearised shield, this would show a willingness to take risks which might justify a massive response.

Thus, tactical nuclear weapons help to link up the deterrence of minor aggressions, which can be accomplished with relatively small conventional forces, with the deterrence of major aggression exercised by the strategic retaliatory forces. They do so by increasing, or at least increasing the chances, that any determined aggression would be interpreted, at its outset or soon after, as having a major objective, since only far-reaching aims would justify the enemy in risking the high costs of tactical nuclear warfare.

"This linking up of tactical nuclear weapons, and their deterrent value in general, would be strengthened if it could be made to seem that a tactical nuclear response would automatically follow any aggression, or at least any attack sufficiently powerful to break through the shield at the conventional level. . . . The NATO shield can still fight conventionally, but with the increasing equipment of the forces with atomic arms and the miniaturisation and sophistication of tactical atomic weapons, the conventional response is likely to seem less feasible in practice. . . . These trends will not be lost on the Soviets. . . . As NATO becomes more and more committed to a tactical nuclear response the burden of the initiative in starting a nuclear war shifts more heavily to the Soviets."[23]

The contention that an increase in the local conventional deterrent will detract from the over-all strategic deterrent is superficially convincing. Yet, as pointed out above, Soviet nuclear progress has already put in doubt the willingness of the United States to resort to massive nuclear retaliation in response to limited communist challenges. The great danger of total war in the next decade may not be a pre-emptive strike on the part of either side, but rather the "degeneration" of a local engagement into all-out war. The Soviets may at some future time calculate that they can effect a "smash-and-grab" of weakly defended areas in Western Europe or

[23] Snyder, Glenn H., *Deterrence and Defense*, op. cit., pp. 140-1.

elsewhere and thus confront the United States with a *fait accompli* which the latter will be reluctant to reverse at the cost of initiating nuclear war. The same estimate of US intentions, however, would not necessarily apply to a large-scale and intensively contested local conflict. In Soviet calculations, an American nuclear riposte may be much more likely in the excitement of a large-scale conventional ground engagement like those of the Second World War. Hence, the ability of NATO to meet a Soviet ground probe at a very high conventional level of violence may enhance, rather than diminish, the deterrent to general war, provided that the conventional pause does not become too protracted, in which case the willingness of the Western governments to shift to a nuclear defence may begin to decline.

The decision to place primary reliance on nuclear weapons appears to have been born of despair that NATO could ever achieve adequate conventional force levels to deal with a Soviet ground attack. In opting for a nuclear strategy, however, the NATO powers chose to ignore their inherent material and demographic superiority over the Soviet Union and its satellites. The disparity between communist and Western forces in the European theatre is due not to a disparity of resources, but rather to a lack of will on the part of the NATO countries and apparently, as we have said before, to American strategic precepts. A few statistics will make this fact clear. At present, the United States has approximately 31 million fit males of military age; the Soviet Union has 41 million. By 1965, it has been estimated that the available manpower figure for the United States will have risen to 35·2 million as compared with the slight increase to 41·5 million for the Soviets. If NATO is included, the West's relative position is even better. The Soviet bloc (excluding China) has 58·4 million fit males; NATO has 85·4 million. By 1965, this ratio will be 59 million versus 95·4 million.

It may be wishful thinking to expect the members of the

Atlantic Alliance to draw on their superior reserves of manpower in order to match the Soviet ground strength man-for-man. But so extensive an effort may not be necessary. It is possible that a thirty-division NATO shield will be adequate to deter a Soviet ground probe in terms of forcing the Soviets to go all out or attempt nothing at all. It is important to bear in mind, however, that even the goal of thirty NATO ready divisions was agreed upon when the United States held a clear strategic nuclear advantage. Thirty divisions would not be an adequate shield to cope with the entire force which the Soviets now presumably have mobilised in a protracted military engagement. In short, the thirty-division shield will probably be adequate only if the invulnerability of American striking capabilities is maintained and the Soviets are convinced that they will ultimately be employed, and if NATO prevents the Soviets from massing its quantitatively superior manpower by leaving open its option to employ tactical nuclear weapons.

Still, it seems likely that the West may have exaggerated the actual Soviet ground-force capabilities in Europe. One close observer of NATO strategy has stated: "Recently the Pentagon has begun to look seriously at the question of what the actual Soviet conventional capability is and what would be required to deal with it effectively. Press reports indicate that we may have underestimated NATO capability and overestimated Soviet strength in Europe. There remains a real possibility that if the European NATO countries became convinced of the importance of a conventional capability, capable of holding even a large-scale attack, they could develop one."[24] In an address before the graduating class of the University of Michigan on 16 June, 1962, the Secretary of Defense, Robert McNamara, stated: "The Soviets have superiority in non-nuclear forces in Europe today. But that

[24] Halperin, Morton H., "The Dilemma of the Western Alliance," *The New Republic* (7 May, 1962).

superiority is by no means overwhelming. Collectively the alliance has the potential for a successful defence against such a force. In manpower alone, NATO has more men under arms than the Soviet Union and its European satellites." Mr McNamara went on to urge America's European allies "to strengthen further their non-nuclear forces". "These achievements," he said, "will complement our deterrent strength. With improvements in alliance ground-force strength and staying power, improved non-nuclear air capabilities, and better equipped and trained reserve forces, we can be assured that no deficiency exists in the NATO defence of this region, and that no aggression, small or large, can succeed." On the other hand, few knowledgeable Western commentators and analysts have suggested that it would be feasible for NATO to adopt a strategy of complete reliance on conventional weapons both for deterrence and defence in Europe. Unfortunately, however, except for their response to the Berlin crisis, the European members of NATO have given no indication that they are prepared to make any sustained effort to meet NATO conventional force goals, despite the fact that the rapidly changing technological-military environment would appear to be making the need for such forces even more pressing.

The role of nuclear weapons in NATO strategy thus far has been psychological. They are indispensable as a deterrent against general war, but they are already inadequate to deter Soviet gambits which fall below the threshold of a clear issue of Western survival (e.g., they are not now deterring Soviet harassment in the Berlin area even though they undoubtedly are responsible for some Soviet circumspection in that area). With the approach of a mutual strategic invulnerability in nuclear delivery systems, an American threat of all-out nuclear war may remain a credible counter to a rapidly diminishing range of communist diplomatic-psychological-military pressures and probes. Under such conditions, it will tax the energies of the United States and its allies to convince the communists of NATO's willingness to implement an all-out nuclear response to Soviet gambits. The increasing Soviet acquisition of reliable long-range delivery systems may tend to make direct communist military action more plausible in the future. And in any event, no matter what Soviet intentions really are, it is possible that the Soviets and the West may become involved in a military engagement in the European area regardless of their precise respective intentions, in which case the same NATO capabilities would be required as those which would be necessary to meet a deliberate Soviet attack in the area.

With the impetus provided by the Berlin crisis and the attitude of the Kennedy Administration towards placing more reliance on the local deterrent, NATO in 1962 edged closer to the thirty-division shield-force goal established in 1954. Some press reports indicated that the thirty-division goal might be realised in the following year. At the time of writing, there is a reported equivalent of twenty-five divisions committed to the NATO central front. During the peak of the 1962 crisis in Berlin, NATO force strength was increased by approximately 25 per cent, largely due to the fact that the United States increased its contribution to the Alliance by 50,000 troops and sent equipment to Western Europe adequate to equip an additional two divisions. Also, the European members apparently honoured their share of the build-up. It was hoped optimistically in some quarters that the gap between the equivalent of twenty-five divisions available in the summer of 1962 and the anticipated equivalent of thirty divisions expected to be available during 1964, might be bridged by a French commitment of two more divisions and perhaps as many as three more divisions from West Germany. These developments led SACEUR (General Norstad) to state: "We have reached a point in the development of our forces and equipment where we can now definitely think in terms of a true forward strategy", i.e., a strategy of confronting the Soviets with more than a mere holding action east of the Rhine. Whether the goal of thirty divisions will actually be met is, however, still open to doubt.

The difficulty all along in meeting the NATO force goal of thirty divisions has, to a large extent, been due to what many have believed to be the inadequacy of the strategic rationale justifying such a force. Morton Halperin, of Harvard University, has presented the issue succinctly:

"The [US] Administration has proposed a substantial increase in NATO's conventional capability. It has built up American forces and is pressing our European allies to increase substantially their conventional capability in ground forces and tactical air forces. However, the Administration has not been able to state a doctrine which satisfactorily explains the urgency of the build-up. The notion of the 'pause' has been re-emphasised to explain the requirement for conventional forces. According to this concept, the purpose of conventional forces in Europe is to hold long enough for the Russians to recognise that they are engaged in a 'serious' military operation which might have unfortunate consequences, and to give the Russians an opportunity to stop before the West is forced to resort to nuclear weapons. The ground forces are no longer seen as a tripwire but as a rather more impressive force, designed not to hold indefinitely but to buy time in which to convince the opponent of our determination.

"But so far as I can discover no Administration official has ever attempted to explain why the proposed thirty-division defence against Soviet attack would be a more convincing demonstration of our resolve than the present twenty-two division defence. Both, according to the Administration, are doomed to failure in a relatively short time, although, of course, the larger force could hold out somewhat longer. If the present twenty-two divisions are in fact sufficient to achieve the proclaimed purpose of thirty divisions, it is only fair to ask why the United States and its European allies should make major (albeit clearly acceptable) sacrifices to move from twenty-two to thirty.

"Unless the United States is prepared to propose to its European allies the goal of the development of a NATO conventional defence, there may not be a sufficiently clear rationale in the long run run for a major build-up in conventional forces."[25]

Henry A. Kissinger has also criticised the strategic rationale of NATO as it relates to the thirty-division force goal in a similar vein. He writes: "The thirty-division goal of 1957 did not make much sense when first advanced, except as an estimate of what our allies might reasonably be expected to contribute. However, that goal furnished a convenient target for the Kennedy Administration when it decided that conventional forces should be increased. As a result, goals which originally were not met because, in terms of traditional NATO doctrine, they were too high may now not be met because they are too low for sustained local defence.

"Actually, and fortunately, the size of the military establishment on the Continent—some twenty-two divisions when the Administration took office—has always been largely inconsistent with NATO strategic theory. Had NATO carried out the implications of the prevalent strategic doctrine, the sole function of the shield forces, the forces deployed on the Continent, would have been to determine that a general Soviet advance had in fact begun. At that point, SAC would have launched its counterforce strike.

"It was no accident that the thirty divisions called for in 1957 were never provided. For it did not require thirty divisions to establish that something more than a border incursion was taking place. To be sure, in order to rationalise NATO force goals various other functions were conceived, expressed in such terms as 'forward strategy' and

[25] *The New Republic* (8 October, 1962), p. 17.

'broken-back warfare', but they were equally inconsistent with basic NATO strategy. In case of war, the crucial factor would not be the units on the ground in Europe, but the effectiveness of SAC. Only if SAC were successful could the Soviet advance be stopped, and then the precise number of divisions would not make much difference."[26]

Thus a completely acceptable doctrine for the local defence of Europe has never been fully agreed on within the Alliance. The issue between the United States and its major allies is over the relative role to be allotted to conventional and tactical nuclear weapons in the local defence of Europe.[27]

Ever since the Suez crisis of 1956 and the launching of the first Soviet *sputniks* in the autumn of 1957, there has been increasing support in Europe for the creation of nuclear deterrent capabilities which would not depend entirely upon the decision of American policy-makers. The diplomatic position adopted by the Suez states at the time of the invasion of Egypt, when Washington sided with Moscow against London and Paris, placed a heavy strain upon the Atlantic Alliance and caused among many Europeans an erosion of confidence in the willingness of the United States to back up the policy objective of European governments outside the immediate area defined in the NATO Treaty. A year later, Soviet space successes served to demonstrate in a most dramatic way that the USSR was in the process of acquiring an intercontinental ballistic missile capability which might, in the not too distant future, neutralise the effect of the American nuclear deterrent in Western Europe. Herman Kahn stated the problem very clearly in the following hypothesis: "Imagine, for example, that the Soviets had done some very provocative thing, such as invading Western Europe with conventional armies, on such a large scale that

---

[26] *Foreign Affairs* (July, 1962), pp. 518-9.
[27] Buchan, Alastair, *The Washington Post* (Outlook), "Refashioning NATO: A Partnership Puzzle" (12 August, 1962).

we felt that we could not stop the invasion by any limited actions, and that we would not be able to rescue Europe at a later date. We might still not be willing to strike the Soviets with SAC, in view of the terrible price we would have to pay in their retaliatory blow."[28]

It is important to note that Kahn was speculating about a remote possibility, not an imminent probability. The model which he described was obviously oversimplified. Even the contingency of a Soviet conventional attack is treated in a political and strategic vacuum. (This should be clear from what has been said above about the subtleties and complexities of deterrence in Europe.) It is no easy task to forecast just how the United States would respond to a Soviet attack in Europe. But the point is that *some* Europeans have been concerned in recent years over the possibility, however remote, that the leading partner in the Alliance might be expected to hedge at the idea of pulling the nuclear trigger if Europe alone were subjected to a conventional invasion, and that this very assumption might some day tempt the Soviets to gamble. One of the motives, therefore, which has impelled the Europeans to seek a share in the control of nuclear weapons is to make it perfectly clear to the Soviets that the Europeans themselves will have the option to launch nuclear warfare if a Soviet conventional thrust cannot be contained by conventional means. A second motive has been to obtain a larger voice in the formulation of Western nuclear strategy and in the making of nuclear decisions at times of crisis. A third motive has been to acquire at least a modest power to extend a European deterrent to non-European regions of the world (such as the Middle East and Africa) where Britain, France and other allies still hold important interests. A fourth motive has been to enhance national prestige by gaining possession of the

[28] Kahn, Herman, "The Arms Race and Some of Its Hazards," *Daedalus,* Vol. 89 (Autumn, 1960), p. 757.

indispensable symbol of strategic power in the atomic age.

Great Britain was the first of the European states to build her own nuclear deterrent force. The British, whose scientists had co-operated closely on atomic development with those of the United States during the Second World War, were in a favourable position to obtain nuclear weapons information from their long-time ally. It has generally been recognised that the acquisition of thermo-nuclear weapons by the British in 1957 (less than a year after the Suez débâcle) has helped to consolidate the privileged position which Britain has held within the Atlantic Alliance since its inception. Perhaps it does not appear entirely coincidental to France that a Britain in command of nuclear weapons has experienced somewhat less difficulty in protecting her interests in Malaya and Kuwait than a non-nuclearised France has encountered in Indo-China and North Africa. The British do not claim to own an "independent national deterrent". Rather they prefer to say that they are making an "independent contribution to the deterrent". Mr Macmillan, in explaining his government's defence policies to the House of Commons, pointed out that the government deems itself "constitutionally free" to order the use of nuclear weapons if a critical occasion warranting such action should arise, but that "as a matter of practice" the plans to use the V-bombers of the Royal Air Force have always been closely co-ordinated with the plans of the United States Strategic Air Command.[29]

The French, determined to restore their nation to a status comparable to that enjoyed by Britain, have embarked upon the quest for a national deterrent. Even before General de Gaulle's advent to power, the government of Guy Mollet had initiated the French nuclear weapons programme. De Gaulle has been deeply chagrined at the refusal of the United States to make available to France the same kind of technological secrets as it has given to the British. As Raymond

[29] *The Times,* London, (27 June, 1962).

Aron has written: "The privileged position of Britain in the atomic field is something which will never be accepted in Paris, no matter who may happen to be in power. . . . I must repeat that the policy presently pursued by Washington, which consists of pressing the six Common Market countries into admitting Britain while it maintains an atomic co-opera- tion with Britain, would irritate a man less prone to irritation than de Gaulle. . . . To de Gaulle's way of thinking a *défense nationale* is as much an end as a means. Even if it afforded less protection than America's atomic might, he would go on demanding it, since it is the symbol and con- secration of France's political self-affirmation."[30] The French have argued that it is illogical to withhold from a trusted ally military secrets which are well known to the chief adversary of the alliance, viz., the USSR, and that such a policy on the part of the United States may really mean that, when it comes to certain nuclear questions (such as the avoidance of pro- liferation), the United States is more closely allied with the Soviet Union than with France. Partially for the purpose of showing his pique at the American policy towards France, the French President refused to integrate French fighter planes into the NATO air defence system, withdrew French units from CINCSOUTH (NATO's naval command in the Mediterranean) and prohibited the establishment of Ameri- can missile bases and atomic weapons stockpiles on French territory.[31] These actions did not seem to mean at the time that de Gaulle was entirely opposed to the concept of NATO; on more than one occasion he declared explicitly that the Alliance is indispensable to the defence of the West. But

[30] *The Atlantic Monthly* (August, 1962), p. 36.
[31] Stebbins, Richard P., *The United States in World Affairs, 1959,* for the Council on Foreign Relations, New York: Harper (1960), pp. 196-201. *Cf.* also Furniss, Edgar S., Jr., "De Gaulle's France and NATO: An Inter- pretation," *International Organization,* Vol. XV (Summer, 1961), pp. 349-365.

there can be little doubt that de Gaulle was resentful of certain aspects of U.S. NATO policy, and that his resentment at times coloured his attitude towards NATO military policy.

The United States has been extremely reluctant to co-operate in the multiplication of national deterrent forces. Whether such forces could effectively perform the function of deterrence by themselves, independently of the United States, has been questioned by many strategic analysts on both sides of the Atlantic. It is true that a national nuclear force would place in the hands of its owner a "triggering deterrent", as A. L. Burns called it,[32] one which might enable an ally of the United States to act as a catalytic agent of general nuclear war. But there is good reason to doubt that a country such as France, acting alone, could wield a significant nuclear-diplomatic leverage against the Soviet Union. Nearly everyone recognises that a single European state cannot rationally opt for nuclear war. It would not in all probability launch a first strike, and it could hardly deal a very potent blow in retaliation, after absorbing a Soviet first strike.[33] Henry Kissinger sums up the strategic arguments against national deterrents in the following passage: "None of our European allies is capable of creating from its own resources a retaliatory force capable of defeating the USSR, *even* by striking first. For all practical purposes, then, the strategic striking power of the Soviet Union is invulnerable in relation to the retaliatory force of any single European nation. Thus it is extremely unlikely that any European country would retaliate by initiating nuclear war, even in the face of considerable provocation. . . . Europe is more densely populated than the USSR. The distance to targets in

[32] Burns, A. L., "NATO and Nuclear Sharing," in Klaus Knorr, op. cit., p. 153.
[33] See Raymond Aron's article in the symposium, "The Future of Western Deterrent Power," *Bulletin of the Atomic Scientists,* Vol. XVI (September, 1960), pp. 266-8.

Western Europe from Soviet missile bases is relatively short. Compared with an attack on the United States, a retaliatory blow by the Soviet Union would therefore be more accurate and, because each missile would be able to carry a heavier payload, more destructive."[34]

Other arguments can be adduced against the proliferation of national nuclear deterrents within the West. If European governments concentrate upon nuclear programmes, they will be less likely to budget military expenditures needed to maintain conventional forces at levels sufficiently high to provide SACEUR with military flexibility in Europe. From a purely economic point of view, national deterrents in Europe represent a wasteful duplication of productive effort. Furthermore, as Albert Wohlstetter has pointed out, it is difficult enough for the United States to bear the burden of economic and technological resources required to maintain an up-to-date "invulnerable strike" capability; it is questionable to say the least, that a single West European country can afford to engage effectively in deterrence competition for an indefinitely long period of time.[35] Perhaps the most compelling technical arguments of all against national deterrents were made by the US Secretary of Defense, Robert McNamara. After calling such independent capabilities potentially "dangerous, expensive, prone to obsolescence and lacking in credibility", he said: "We are convinced that a general nuclear war target system is indivisible, and if, despite all our efforts, nuclear war should occur, our best hope lies in conducting a centrally controlled campaign against all of the enemy's vital nuclear capabilities, while retaining reserve forces, all centrally controlled."[36]

The United States appeared to have the better of the

---

[34] Kissinger, Henry A., *The Necessity for Choice*, Harper (New York, 1961), pp. 112-3.

[35] Wohlstetter, Albert, "NATO and the N+1 Country," *Foreign Affairs*, Vol. XXXIX (April, 1961), pp. 361-2.

[36] *New York Times*, 17 June, 1962.

military-technical argument, but the mere recitation of technical reasons why the control of the West's nuclear weapons should not be shared has not satisfied the advocates of a European deterrent. Nor have the American efforts to create a so-called "NATO deterrent" proved to be any more satisfactory thus far. Official efforts in this direction began when General Norstad proposed in 1960 that NATO itself be made the "fourth nuclear power". Since the members of the alliance have never been able to reach agreement on a set of credible political controls for a NATO deterrent, controls which would circumvent the problem implicit in the phrase "fifteen fingers on the trigger and on the safety lock", the United States has acted unilaterally to bolster European confidence and sense of security by establishing something that looks superficially like a NATO deterrent but which is not such in fact. At the Athens meeting of the North Atlantic Council in May, 1962, Mr Dean Rusk announced that the United States would assign five Polaris submarines to American Admiral Robert Dennison in his capacity as NATO's Supreme Allied Commander, Atlantic (SACLANT). The European allies, however, were well aware that such a transfer would not really affect the ultimate political control of these five vessels, which would continue to be manned by American crews and which could fire their nuclear missiles only upon receipt of an order from the President of the United States. The Europeans, in sum, did not think that the problem of "nuclear sharing" within the Alliance had yet been resolved in any genuine way. Hence the discussion on both sides of the Atlantic concerning the possible establishment of a European nuclear force under multilateral control waxed and waned throughout 1963. The major problems involved were: to develop workable political controls; to make certain that it would not facilitate the creation, at some future date, of additional national deterrents, including a German one; to decide whether a European deterrent organisation should extend to both conventional and nuclear forces, or only nuclear; to determine whether a European nuclear deterrent should consist primarily of strategic nuclear weapons or be a balanced combination of both; to work out feasible arrangements for the planning of viable European nuclear strategies and for properly co-ordinating a European nuclear deterrent with the American deterrent in a NATO framework.

In early 1963, in another effort to meet European desires for a more active role in the management of the Alliance's nuclear forces, the United States dispatched career diplomatist Livingston Merchant to Western European capitals to discuss the creation of a NATO multilateral force. The Merchant mission appeared to be a follow-up of the Nassau Agreement of December, 1962 (see Chapter 5), under which a NATO submarine missile force was to come into existence in the late 1960s. But Ambassador Merchant, once in Europe, modified the original concept and tried to enlist support for a fleet of twenty-five surface vessels, equipped with Polaris and manned by international NATO crews. There was a good deal of discussion over the feasibility of creating such a "mix-master" force. Not a few military authorities on both sides of the Atlantic found the idea impractical on organisational grounds and feared that it might lead to too heavy a reliance by NATO on a single weapons system. In Western Europe, only the West Germans seemed favourable to the plan. This fact caused some disturbance among those in the West who thought that the creation of a multilateral NATO force at that particular time might spoil the chances of reaching a nuclear test ban agreement with Moscow. Following President Kennedy's trip to Europe in June, 1963,[37] it was reported that the American

[37] President Kennedy, during his tour of the Federal Republic, attempted to allay European misgivings, stirred by General de Gaulle, that the United States would not invoke nuclear weapons against a Soviet attack on Western Europe because such action would place American cities in danger of

proposal for a NATO multilateral deterrent had, at least for the time being, been shelved. Meanwhile, it appeared that Chancellor Adenauer, who was scheduled to step down from the leadership of West Germany before the end of the year, was playing the role of broker between the United States and France, encouraging President de Gaulle to shift his policy in the direction of closer military co-operation with NATO in return for American assurances (announced at the Ottawa Council meeting in May) that French air squadrons assigned to SACEUR would be equipped with US nuclear weapons.

In conclusion, it can be said that the problem of sharing the control of nuclear weapons is an extremely complex one, and raises political and military issues of the most subtle nature. For the most part, political considerations rather than purely military ones will determine whether or not a European deterrent force will come into being and what its character will be if it does. But if such a force should be created, military factors will come to play an increasingly important role in the shaping of year-to-year policy. A European deterrent will inevitably have to be tailored, as it were, to the shape of the European defence programme. Some form of nuclear sharing will probably be necessary to resolve certain political tensions which have arisen within the Atlantic Alliance. Nuclear sharing, however, will not solve the fundamental problems of European defence. These exigencies will remain, changing as military technology changes, but lasting so long as the ideological-political conflict between the Soviet bloc and the West poses a threat to the security and the vital interests of Europe.

---

immediate Soviet missile attack. Speaking at the Paulskirche in Frankfurt, he said: "The United States will risk its cities to defend yours because we need your freedom to defend ours." *New York Times*, 26 June, 1963.

Chapter 4

THE POLITICS OF EUROPEAN AND ATLANTIC ECONOMIC INTEGRATION

One of the most remarkable developments of the era since the Second World War has been the rapid economic expansion and technological progress of Western Europe. Indeed, since the mid-1950s, the average rate of economic growth among the free countries of Europe has been running higher than that of the United States. Within little more than a decade, a striking change has occurred in the economics of the Atlantic Community. The late 1940s had witnessed conditions of severe privation and stagnation in Europe as a result of wartime losses and dislocations. But by the early 1960s, the Europeans were enjoying what seemed to many economic observers to be the fastest-rising standard of living in the world. The economic successes of Western Europe contain several interesting implications—for the Atlantic Community as a whole (and particularly for the two English-speaking partners); for the Sino-Soviet bloc (both its ideological outlook and its global strategy); and for the under-developed countries of Latin America, Asia and Africa, whose peoples are experiencing a "revolution of rising expectations". But before examining these implications, it is useful to look at how these significant economic changes have come about.

The end of the Second World War found the economies of Western Europe bordering on chaos. But it was not merely the destruction and dislocations of the war which caused the distress. Ever since the beginning of the First World War, profound changes had been operating in the international economic order. Britain had been slipping from her position of world dominance, while the United States, Japan, Canada and other non-European countries had been improving their position relative to the Old World. As the United States had shifted from a debtor to a creditor position, espousing policies of economic nationalism and protectionism more ardently than some of the European countries, the latter saw themselves shut out from the American market and confronted with chronic dollar shortages. The world-wide depression completed the breakdown of the prewar international economy based upon the gold standard and the assumption of free movement of capital and goods. The nations of the world had become preoccupied with the goal of economic self-sufficiency and tried to insulate their domestic recovery programmes against interference from forces outside their control. World trade languished and business stagnated in the worst cyclic crisis the capitalist system had ever experienced. Economic conditions played no small part in the rise of undemocratic "isms", and these in turn helped to catalyse a war which aggravated Europe's economic woes not only because it brought about the physical destruction of productive wealth, but also because it set the stage for the liquidation of Europe's colonial empires overseas.

THE MARSHALL PLAN

The first important step in the building of the economic structure of the Atlantic Community was the Marshall Plan, which antedated NATO by nearly two years. At a time when

Europe was feeling most keenly the effects of factory bombings, transport breakdown, fuel shortages, grain crop failures and dollar deficits, the United States Secretary of State declared that his country's policy should aim at "the revival of a working economy in the world so as to permit the emergence of political and social conditions in which free institutions can exist." Between 1948 and 1952, the European Recovery Programme (ERP) resulted in grants totaling about 12·3 billion dollars. The bulk of the aid took the form of shipments of coal, petroleum, machinery, grain, fertiliser, fibres and other raw materials. Long before the American appropriations were terminated, there were impressive signs that the Europeans were getting back on their feet, economically speaking. By 1951, European industrial production had risen to 40 per cent above the levels achieved in 1938.[1]

Needless to say, the Marshall Plan alone could not have ensured Europe's economic resuscitation. Indeed, a massive aid programme could not have produced comparable results in any other region of the world, for Europe alone could boast the technological skills, managerial experience and economic incentives required for the sustenance of rapid economic restoration and growth. In the last analysis, it must be reckoned that the indigenous resourcefulness and energies of the Europeans were the prime factor in Europe's postwar economic miracle. Undoubtedy, however, United States assistance greatly speeded up the process, not only by facilitating the flow of imports which the Europeans lacked the necessary dollars to purchase, but even more importantly by inducing intra-European co-operation on recovery planning.

Continuing aid grants under the Marshall Plan were made

---

[1] For a thorough discussion of the European Recovery Programme, and the work of the OEEC, see Price, Harry Bayard, *The Marshall Plan and Its Meaning*, Cornell University Press (Ithaca, 1955).

contingent upon the Europeans' getting together and working out a co-ordinated approach to their problems. The result was the establishment in April, 1948, of the Organisation for European Economic Co-operation (OEEC), which eventually came to include: Austria, Belgium, Denmark, France, West Germany, Greece, Iceland, Ireland, Italy, Luxemburg, the Netherlands, Norway, Portugal, Spain, Sweden, Switzerland, Turkey, the United Kingdom and Yugoslavia.[2] The OEEC, at the insistence of the British, was set up as a purely intergovernmental body, whose Council was bound by the rule of unanimity. The OEEC embraced a few neutral states as well as those which later elected to ally militarily with the United States in NATO. Although OEEC could not authoritatively direct the member governments to undertake any adaptations of national economic policy which they were unwilling to accept, it could facilitate discussion and planning, and exhort them to harmonise their policies. Even though each nation wielded a veto power in theory, it was usually possible to prevent one or two states from causing a stalemate through the application of informal diplomatic pressure. As a matter of fact, the Organisation enjoyed considerable success in its primary function of making joint recommendations for the most efficient allocation of ERP aid. Moreover, it took important initiatives beyond that primary function. It encouraged the maximum possible interchange of goods through the relaxation of restrictions on trade and payments. Content to see the problem of tariff reduction dealt with mainly under the General Agreement on Tariffs and Trade (GATT), OEEC focused its efforts upon what was then the more crucial prerequisite of trade liberalisation—eliminating the quota system which

---

[2] Spain and Yugoslavia never became fully-fledged members, but took part in the work of certain OEEC committees. The United States and Canada were subsequently affiliated in an associated status.

most of the European countries had imposed against a wide variety of imports.[3]

The Europeans quickly realised that genuine trade liberalisation would not be possible without fundamental changes in the intra-European payments network. If, let us assume, the Netherlands had a payment surplus with Britain while running a deficit with France, a Dutch businessman would find it more difficult to order French than British goods irrespective of his own preferences. The desire for something approaching greater currency convertability led to the creation of the European Payments Union (EPU) in 1950, which embraced the eighteen OEEC countries and provided for the multilateral rather than merely bilateral settlement of international accounts. In other words, EPU served as a sort of international financial clearing house which permitted member nations, within limits, to use their payments surpluses with certain countries to cancel out payments deficits with others. Although the EPU was occasionally criticised by economists on the grounds that, by making it easier for nations to strike payments balances, it reduced the effectiveness of one of the major restraints upon inflationary tendencies, on the whole the payments union produced beneficial effects and facilitated an increased flow of trade within Western Europe.

Throughout the period of economic recovery, United States policy-makers encouraged the Europeans to move towards closer integration at the economic level, as a prelude to political unification. This was clearly stated in the Economic Co-operation Act of 1949. The Congress, however, was extremely vague about the objective it had in mind, and gave no hint of what it meant by "European unification", either geographically, politically or economically. It is true that the Organisation for European Economic Co-operation

[3] Cf. Gordon, Lincoln, "The Organisation for European Economic Co-operation," *International Organisation*, Vol. X (1956).

was the most significant regional organisation that had ever
been formed in that part of the world. But the membership
of the OEEC was so broad (stretching from Iceland to
Turkey) that it could furnish no definitive answer to the
question: What constitutes Europe for purposes of
economic and political unification? Mr Paul G. Hoffman,
the ECA (Economic Co-operation Administration—now
MSA) Administrator to OEEC, was unable to clarify United
States policy aims to the satisfaction of the Europeans. When
he called upon the latter to show some progress towards
integration, his specific demands were quite limited; they
included nothing beyond measures towards free intra-
European trade. On 28 February, 1950, Mr Hoffman told
the Congress: "So the reason that we are driving hard for
unification is, first, that it is a goal; that is, a progress goal;
and it does not cost any dollars directly to bring about unification and the integration of the European economy. . . .
That is the goal they (the Congress) gave us and it is a goal
we are seeking because, in our opinion, unless we make real
progress towards breaking down trade barriers in Europe,
freeing trade, it will be impossible for Europe to realise its
potentialities either for prosperity or security."[4]

Nevertheless, because it lacked a consistent and unified
theory of the geographic, political, strategic or cultural basis
on which a united Europe might be founded, the United
States continued its promotional work in a rather pragmatic
if not haphazard way, sometimes lending its support to
different approaches which were not entirely reconcilable.
During this period there were some Europeans, including
M. Paul Reynaud who charged the United States with applying not too much but too little pressure towards unification.[5]

[4] *Foreign Aid Appropriations for 1951,* Hearings before
the Subcommittee of the House Committee on Appropriations, 81st Congress, 2nd Session, p. 2.
[5] See Reynaud, Paul, "The Unifying Force for Europe,"
Foreign Affairs (January, 1950), especially pp. 262-3.

The Americans were indeed cautious, and sometimes not a little confused. But it must be remembered that there were very few people, if any, during that period who had a vision of European unity that was at once precise and realistic. Even Sir Winston Churchill, the most eloquent of the early spokesmen for unity, a man who could afford to be eloquent in 1946 because he was the Leader of His Majesty's Loyal Opposition rather than His Majesty's Prime Minister, seemed deliberately obscure when, at the University of Zurich, he called for a "United States of Europe". Before it had ever become clear as to whether he favoured a European federation, he shifted his attention to the need for the development of a broader Atlantic defence community. The Council of Europe which finally came into being in May, 1949 could make no grander claim than to call itself "the first permanent European institution". But the Council, though it fell far short of the hopes of many of its original architects, provided a convenient framework within which the first practical scheme for European economic integration came to life.

THE EUROPEAN COAL AND STEEL COMMUNITY

A few days after the Consultative Assembly of the Council of Europe held its initial meeting in August, 1949, one of the French delegates, M. Bonnefous, said of the unity problem: "There is only one solution—the pooling of wealth. In spite of their natural dislike for so doing, countries must agree to hold and administer their natural resources in common. A basic industry should be chosen in order to break down national frontiers and to invade state sovereignty on a substantial scale. Everything points to the choice of the coal industry."[6]

Next day, a British Labour Party representative indicated

---

[6] Quoted in *The Council of Europe and the Schuman Plan*, published by the Council of Europe, Directorate of Information (Strasburg, 1952), p. 3.

that he favoured the integration of the coal, iron and steel industries of the Ruhr, Britain, Belgium, Luxemburg and Lorraine under the direction of a supranational authority. Four months later, a commitee of the Assembly drafted a convention for the establishment, under the auspices of the Council of Europe, of companies which would have a European instead of a purely national registration. A few weeks after Germany and the Saar were admitted to the Council of Europe in March, 1950, M. Robert Schuman, the French Foreign Minister, showed a considerable interest in the proposal for European companies. On 9 May of the same year, he presented to the Assembly the essential elements of his plan for a European Coal and Steel Community. Under the "Schuman Plan", the entire production of French and German coal and steel would be pooled under a joint High Authority in which other European countries would be eligible for membership. This Authority would create a single market for coal and steel, without subsidies, tariffs, and any discriminatory or restrictive practices. The members would not be subject to the definite instructions of their governments. Rather, the Authority, which would not be simply an industrial association comparable to the prewar cartels, would be the first example of an independent supranational institution in which the participating countries would abandon some degree of sovereignty. Schuman was convinced that the general aims of increased production and trade, lower prices and a higher standard of living for Western Europe could be achieved without creating a bureaucratically controlled economy. M. Schuman noted that his proposal contained "potentialities that cannot yet be fully measured, but which will rapidly lead us on towards the complete economic and political unification of Europe".[7]

[7] Quoted in Robertson, A. H., *European Institutions,* Stevens and Sons (London, 1958); Frederick A. Praeger (New York, 1958); for the London Institute of World Affairs; p. 18.

It came as no great surprise that France should officially put forth such a plan. The Third Force in France, recognising the inferior efficiency of the nation's steel industry and its weaker currency structure compared with Germany's, foresaw the Coal and Steel Community as a spur to "economic rationalisation".[8] Looming even more ominously in the background was the spectre of an economically recuperating Germany which would soon be expected by the United States to rearm itself and make a substantial contribution to the system of NATO defence which was then being constructed against the threat of Soviet military attack. The Community would furnish an apt instrument by which France could bind the western part of Germany into Western Europe and keep the bases of its future industrial power under some kind of joint planning control. Thus it was for reasons of long-range security that France was willing to face the competition posed by Germany in a single market to France's own steel mills, less favourably situated as they were with respect to coal deposits. The Germans, for their part, looked upon the ECSC with hopes and misgivings, for it meant not only expanded industrial production but also prolonged international control over the Ruhr. Italy and the Benelux countries, too, similarly analysed the projected community in terms of gains and losses, hoping that the former would outweigh the latter.

Among the Western Europeans, there were some who branded the plan as a clever effort to create a super-cartel. The industrial cartelists claimed that it would lead to *superdirigisme*, that it was, in brief, a socialist plot. The socialists criticised it as a step to forestall nationalisation and

---

[8] "Without some binding Franco-German agreements, the vertical combines in the Ruhr which control their own coal supply . . . were expected to revive the old cartel tactics of dual pricing and restriction of production." Sethur, Frederick, "The Schuman Plan and Ruhr Coal," *Political Science Quarterly* (December, 1952), p. 511.

economic planning by individual governments.[9] Oddly enough, there was a grain of truth in each of these charges, for the Schuman Plan embodied a mixture of liberal economics, quasi-cartel practices, and centralised planning. One favourable circumstance which helped to reduce misgivings among the six governments adhering to the Coal and Steel Community Treaty (France, West Germany, Italy, Belgium, the Netherlands and Luxemburg) was the common philosophy of international co-operation and the *via media* between individualism and collectivism shared by the Christian Democratic statesmen who made policy in the signatory countries. This circumstance, among others, prompted many European socialists to manoeuvre themselves into awkward and apparently nationalistic positions against the European integration movement.[10]

The British government was invited to participate in the ECSC but decided to remain aloof. The Labour Party was unwilling to submit to any supranational authority which might be controlled indefinitely by a non-socialist majority. Labour supporters had noticed serious tensions in the Benelux Union, especially over the wage-price issue, growing out of differences between the planned economy of the Netherlands and the capitalist system of Belgium. The Attlee government feared that if Britain should join the Coal and Steel Community, its full employment policy could be jeopardised. The Conservatives were cool towards any kind of supranational planning, socialist or not. But their hostility could not be reduced to mere economics. In their view, the Schuman Plan represented a major step towards a European

[9] Cf. McKesson, John A., "The Schuman Plan," *Political Science Quarterly* (March, 1952), pp. 30-2.

[10] Erich Ollenhauer, then leader of the German Democratic Party, threatened to boycott the Special ECSC Assembly after it had voted to draft plans for Western European political federation. *New York Times,* 14 September, 1952.

federal structure to which Britain was not prepared to commit herself. A federation requires a written constitution, something which the British have regarded with suspicion since the days of Cromwell. Furthermore, most Conservatives and many members of the Labour Party were convinced that Commonwealth obligations were incompatible with too intimate an association with Europe. Both parties preferred to carry on co-operation through such intergovernmental agencies as the OEEC, the EPU and the Council of Europe, rather than become involved in the movement towards the federal union of Europe. Towards supranational institutions, most Britons were inclined to adopt the attitude tersely formulated by Sir Winston Churchill: "We are *with* them, not *of* them." But, although Britain did not wish to become a member of the ECSC, she was interested in maintaining close associative contact. Within three weeks of the assumption of powers by the High Authority, London appointed a permanent delegation to the Community, headed by Sir Cecil Weir.

The Scandinavian countries—Norway, Sweden and Denmark—took sides with the British on the question of the Coal and Steel Community. All three were ruled by Labour governments, and all three viewed the issue in terms of public national planning for full employment versus free-market economics and continental cartels. Another reason for the lack of enthuiasm among the Scandinavian states was the fact that the Schuman Plan provided for integration only in the realm of coal and steel production, whereas Norway and Denmark would have been more interested in a project for creating a single agricultural market, or "green pool". Sweden, of course, in contrast to the other two states (which were both members of NATO), was committed to a neutral policy and hence was reluctant to enter an economic community that had as an avowed objective the eventual political unification of Europe. The membership of the other

European members of NATO—Greece, Turkey and Portugal—was hardly relevant, since those countries were not major producers of coal and steel.

In the United States, official reaction to the Schuman Plan was most cordial. The Department of State tendered "warm approval and support. . . . It will represent an experiment in new concepts of sovereignty and of international organisation which will help to knit the free nations of the world with stronger and more enduring ties."[11] President Truman endorsed it publicly. The United States took a keen interest in the negotiations of the Treaty and looked upon the ECSC as an important new channel through which aid might be given more efficiently. Congress, in the Mutual Security Act of 1951, provided for a transfer of funds directly to the Community without passing through the hands of the participating governments.[12] American benevolence towards ECSC can best be explained as a desire to see Franco-German co-operation fostered. To be sure, American industries were not entirely happy over the idea of the United States government encouraging the growth of Europe's heavy industry through the establishment of a pool which was likely to restrict international competition. The government, anxious to support the experiment in integration because it would contribute to the achievement of political and security objectives, placated the domestic opposition by giving assurances that it would try to dissuade M. Jean Monnet and the High Authority from courses of action detrimental to the interests of American producers. After the High Authority headquarters was established in Luxemburg, the United States accredited an ambassador to it, granted a $100-million loan in 1954, helped the Community to obtain

[11] *Department of State Bulletin*, 2 April, 1951.
[12] Brown, W. A., Jr., and Opie, R., *American Foreign Assistance*, Brookings Institution (Washington, D.C., 1953), p. 270.

a set of concessions from GATT and concluded a reciprocal trade agreement with it in 1956.[13]

The Community which grew out of the Schuman Plan warrants close examination for even to this day it represents the high point in the "sector approach" to European integration, an approach whereby quasi-federal bodies are given regulatory authority over designated areas of international functional activity. No detailed description of the Community's structure and powers can be attempted here.[14] But in order that the full significance of this experiment may be grasped, at least a brief sketch of its political institutions must be made. The instrument establishing the Community reads more like a constitution than a treaty. The Community itself was vested with certain delegated powers hitherto exercised only by national governments, as well as some powers which appear to override even the traditional sovereign prerogatives of nation-states. Indeed, it is this "supranational" feature which has made the ECSC such an object of attention on the part of political scientists. Title Two of the Treaty establishes the four institutions responsible for accomplishing the Community's purposes:

(1) *The High Authority*   This body, which might aptly be thought of as an international ministry for coal and steel,

[13] See "The Economy of Western Europe," Section VI of *United States Policy: Western Europe,* a report prepared at the request of the US Senate Foreign Relations Committee by the Foreign Policy Research Institute, University of Pennsylvania (October, 1959). Study No. 3 in *United States Foreign Policy: Compilation of Studies* (Washington: GPO, September, 1960), Vol. I, p. 259.

[14] The reader is referred to Diebold, William, Jr., *The Schuman Plan,* Harper, for the Council on Foreign Relations (New York, 1959); Haas, Ernest B., *The Uniting of Europe: Political, Social and Economic Forces 1950-7,* Library of World Affairs, Stevens and Sons, Ltd. (London, 1958); and Ball, M. Margaret, *NATO and the European Union Movement,* Frederick A. Praeger, for the London Institute for World Affairs (New York, 1959), chapter 9.

consists of nine members selected for six-year terms from among citizens of the member states. Eight of the nine members were originally appointed by agreement among the six governments; the ninth was co-opted by the other eight. A third of the membership is renewed every two years by two methods which are employed alternately as terms expire: (a) five-sixths vote of the member governments and (b) co-option by majority vote of the remaining members of the High Authority. No more than two members may be of the same nationality at a given time. Each country is assured of having at least one of its nationals on the High Authority, and it is understood that France and Germany, the biggest producers, will always have two each. The ninth place is rotated among the other four countries. The Treaty declares: "The members of the High Authority shall exercise their functions in complete independence, in the general interest of the Community. In the fulfilment of their duties, they shall neither solicit nor accept instructions from any government or from any organisation. They will abstain from all conduct incompatible with the supranational character of their functions. Each member State agrees to respect this supranational character and to make no effort to influence the members of the High Authority in the execution of their duties."[15]

What made the High Authority unique among existing international institutions was its ability to do the following four things: (a) to act directly upon coal and steel enterprises without going through the national governments; (b) to issue not only opinions and recommendations, but also legally binding decisions and to punish violations by imposing fines

---

[15] *Treaty Constituting the European Coal and Steel Community*, Title Two, Article 9. See also Merry, Henry J., "The European Coal and Steel Community: Operations of the High Authority," *Western Political Quarterly*, Vol. VIII (June, 1955).

and other economic sanctions; (c) to finance its own operations, at least partially, by placing direct levies on the production of the commodities over which it has jurisdiction; and (d) to arrive at binding decisions by majority procedures. Certain measures of a more administrative nature the High Authority can decree simply by majority vote of its own members; other measures which involve more delicate political questions may require the additional concurrence of an absolute majority, a qualified or weighted majority or the unanimous membership of the Council of Ministers, which in a sense shares the executive powers of the Community.

Either alone or with the approval of the Council, the High Authority promotes economic research; issues trade forecasts; raises revenues; polices those treaty provisions which forbid illegal trade practices (e.g., price-fixing, limitation of output and division of the market); plays a key role in the industrial investment process by granting loans, guaranteeing loans, co-ordinating investment plans for modernisation and expansion, and actually financing projects which facilitate production and marketing; and acts as a relief agency for workers displaced by Community decisions, paying indemnities, granting allowances for re-adaptation and financing technical retraining. Should the Community be faced with a serious decline in demand, the Authority can, with Council approval, impose production quotas to forestall a market crisis; conversely, in the event of a major shortage, the Authority can install a system of resource allocation. In stipulated cases, the Authority may set maximum or minimum prices for coal and steel products within the single market, make recommendations on wage levels and propose tariff modifications. The High Authority is advised by a Consultative Committee comprising an equal number of producers, workers and consumers drawn from a list of organisations compiled by the Council of Ministers. Finally, the High Authority must report annually to the

Community Assembly to which it is, in limited respects, responsible.

(2) *The Council of Ministers* The Council, which may consist of either the Foreign, Finance or other relevant ministers of the six countries, was assigned the task of "harmonising the action of the High Authority and that of the governments, which are responsible for the general economic policies of their countries". The Council must, therefore, work very closely with the High Authority. Whereas the Authority embodies most clearly the supranational principle at work within the Community, the Council, established at the insistence of the smaller powers which were apprehensive of Franco-German domination, is designed to operate more along the lines of the traditional intergovernmental diplomatic grouping in which the delegates frankly represent the national interest of their states. The Council was really intended to serve as a check upon the High Authority, but it is not true to say that in this forum the Six necessarily always bargain as sovereign equals. Council decisions in support of High Authority actions can be taken by absolute majority (i.e., four votes), provided that either France *or* Germany is in this number, or even by three votes if they include both France *and* Germany. In other situations where unanimity is required, the national veto can operate through the Council. With the accumulation of Community experience, and especially since the advent to power of General Charles de Gaulle in France in 1958, there has been a noticeable tendency to strengthen the role of the Council in the ECSC decision-making process.[16] Perhaps it is not wide of the mark to conclude that the High Authority and the Council of Ministers have become more or less equal partners in the formulation of

---

[16] On the relations between the High Authority and the Council of Ministers, see Diebold, William, Jr., op. cit., pp. 594-601.

coal and steel policy, and that the supranational character
of the ECSC as originally conceived by the first High
Authority President, M. Jean Monnet, has been modified by
a moderate shift towards the co-operative methods of an
intergovernmental organisation.

(3) *The Common Assembly*   The architects of the Coal
and Steel Community, as Sir Cecil Weir has pointed out,
were "anxious that all the interests of the member states
should be represented in one way or another", and they
were equally concerned that "the method of operation of
the Community should as nearly as possible reflect that of
a modern democratic State".[17] Hence they created a Common
Assembly to represent the people or, more accurately, the
parliaments of the six member states, since it was the national
parliaments which were to select from among their own delegates the seventy-eight delegates to the Assembly. The member states were given the option of electing their delegates
by direct universal suffrage but none took advantage of this
privilege prior to the change which occurred in the Assembly
structure in 1958. West Germany, France and Italy were
entitled to send eighteen representatives each; Belgium and
the Netherlands ten; and Luxemburg four. From the beginning there has been a wide overlapping between the membership of the ECSC Assembly and that of the Assembly of
the Council of Europe. But the ECSC Assembly, unlike the
Assembly of the Council of Europe, is more than a merely
consultative body and can exercise supervision, even if not
control, over the executive organs of the Community. It
meets annually to review the work of the High Authority
and it can also meet in extraordinary session at the request
of the Council of Ministers. Although the Assembly lacks
legislative powers and is unable to initiate policy, it wields

[17] Weir, Sir Cecil, *The First Step in European Integration,*
The Federal Educational and Research Trust (London,
1957), p. 7.

one important weapon: by adopting a motion of censure on the High Authority's annual report by a two-thirds vote, the Assembly can force the collective resignation of the High Authority's nine members.[18] This has never happened. Since 1958, the ECSC Assembly has been integrated with the Assemblies of the European Economic Community and the European Atomic Energy Community; the combined body has been renamed the European Parliamentary Assembly.[19] The rights and duties of the former Coal and Steel Assembly remain unaltered.

(4) *The Community Court of Justice*   The Court, which acts as an instrument of judicial review for the Community, is made up of seven judges appointed by unanimous agreement of the member governments. It is empowered to annul the acts of the High Authorty "on the grounds of lack of legal competence, substantial procedural violations, violations of the Treaty or of any rule of law relating to its applications, or abuse of power".[20] Appeals may be carried to the Court by the Council, by any member state, or by any effective enterprise or non-governmental association. If the Court finds the Community liable for damages, the High Authority is obliged to make redress. The High Authority, however, is not the only institution whose actions are subject to review. On petition of a member state or of the High Authority, the Court may annul the acts of the Assembly or the Council. But most of the appeals made so far have been against the most active initiator of policy—the High Authority. Sir Cecil Weir has summed up the record as follows: "The Court of Justice has shown itself to be an impartial arbiter. . . . Its judgments, which have sometimes gone against the High Authority, or a member government,

---

[18] *Treaty,* Title Two, Chapter II, Article 24.
[19] Cf. Lindsay, Kenneth, *European Assemblies: The Experimental Period 1949-59,* Stevens and Sons (London, 1959), Frederick A. Praeger (New York, 1959).
[20] *Treaty,* Title Two, Article IV, Chapter 33.

or an industry, have without exception been accepted and respected. No problem has been created by the fact that there can be no appeal against this Court."[21]

When the European Economic Community and Euratom came into existence, it was decided that a single Court should serve all three Communities. The new Court of integrated jurisdiction is the very same in structure as the former ECSC Court and exercises the same powers with respect to the ECSC.

On the whole, the ECSC has proved to be a successful experiment in European economic integration. The common market for coal and steel was established in February, 1953, with provision for a five-year transition period to facilitate gradual adjustment without serious economic dislocation. A number of special cushioning arrangements had to be devised, e.g., to help marginal coal producers in Belgium and Italy to remain competitive during the five-year period, and the French government was allowed to continue certain subsidy programmes temporarily. But the general movement was in the direction of removing tariffs and quantitative restrictions and thus increasing the flow of trade; eliminating discriminatory practices (such as dual pricing and charging higher transport rates for trans-boundary trade); making prices more uniform throughout the six-nation area; controlling cartels and breaking up some of the more notorious concentrations of industry; and facilitating labour mobility.[22] In 1952, despite charges of trade discrimination from the

---

[21] Weir, Sir Cecil, op. cit., p. 14.

[22] ECSC re-adaptation provisions have not been applied on a grand scale. There have been some moderate accomplishments and a few failures. The latter must be attributed not to defective treaty provisions but rather to the existence of national cultural differences. European workers in stricken areas have often been reluctant to uproot themselves and begin life anew in an unfamiliar environment, and sometimes even to move from their own native province to another part of their country.

Scandinavian countries, the ECSC obtained a waiver from the GATT (General Agreement on Tariffs and Trade) obligation to extend any trade privileges granted to one country to all GATT members.

EURATOM

No doubt the greatest disappointment of the architects of ECSC was that it did not lead more quickly to other experiments in European integration. The movement towards a European Defence Community and a European Political Community, for which the ECSC was intended to serve as a model, suffered a reversal at the hands of the French Parliament in August, 1954.[23] For a time, the European federalists feared that functional supranational institutions as vehicles of European unity had a bleak future. But the experiment in coal and steel integration taught several interesting lessons: (1) At the mid-1950s stage of evolution towards European unification, economic integration seemed easier to achieve than military or political integration. (2) Supranational institutions can be made to work in a way that takes into account the problems and policies of member national governments. (3) Integration in one economic sector sooner or later usually creates a desire to expand the scope of integration. Certainly some of the problems encountered by the ECSC had to be attributed to the fact that its control did not extend beyond the realm of the coal and steel industries.[24]

[23] See below pp. 178-80.
[24] "Distortions in costs arising from differences in social security systems, taxation and transportation charges are difficult to tackle in two industries alone. The ECSC has no responsibility for harmonising national policies generally in trade, credit or investment. Trade among the Six in coal and steel is important and growing but it still represents only a fraction of their trade with each other in all commodities. Freeing it has so far had little impact in the balance of payments among the member countries. If, however, the sector-by-sector approach to integration were to be extended

It was not surprising, therefore, that the European federalists, stunned by the defeat of EDC, should decide to press forward with their unity offensive along the economic front. The result was the formation of two other organisations of a somewhat modified supranational character—the European Economic Community (popularly known as the Common Market) and the European Atomic Energy Community (or Euratom). The concepts of the two Communities were formulated at a meeting of the Foreign Ministers of the Six in June, 1955. Both were based upon a report drafted under the chairmanship of Paul-Henri Spaak of Belgium. The treaties for Euratom and the EEC were negotiated in parallel. Both were signed together at Rome in March, 1957 and were put into operation on 1 January, 1958. Since Euratom poses less complex issues than the Common Market, it may conveniently be taken up first.

Euratom, like the ECSC, seeks to integrate a single, narrowly defined industrial sector—the field of nuclear energy. Moreover, it bears resemblance to the Coal and Steel Community in so far as it mixes the principles of supranationalism and intergovernmental co-operation. Management is vested in a Commission of five, which serves as the administrative organ of Euratom and decides by majority vote, and in a Council of Ministers of the Six, which co-ordinates Euratom policies with those of the member states. As indicated previously, Euratom shares the Assembly[25] and the Court of Justice with the other two supranational Communities of the Six.

---

gradually to enough industries to account for a significant portion of the total trade of the ECSC area, the inability to harmonise the general economic policies of its members would soon loom up as a serious handicap."—Moore, Ben T., *NATO and the Future of Europe,* Harper, for the Council on Foreign Relations (New York, 1958), pp. 142-3.

[25] The new integrated Assembly consists of 142 instead of 78 parliamentary delegates.

One of the principal factors underlying the creation of Euratom was the growing realisation on the part of the Six that they were lagging far behind the two super powers and Britain in the one technological field which had become the primary symbol of power in the modern world. Unless they pooled their national resources for the purpose of creating nuclear capabilities which no one of the Six could efficiently achieve by itself, they would remain permanently dependent upon the atomic technology of the United States. One should not draw the conclusion, however, that the Six were originally motivated by the desire to achieve an independent nuclear *military* capability. Economic considerations were, it appears, more immediately compelling. Of all the regions of the world, Europe is one of those most urgently in need of expanding energy production. The steady postwar growth of the European economy has placed a great strain on conventional sources of power, as the Europeans became acutely aware when the Suez crisis interrupted the politically vulnerable flow of oil from the Middle East. Yet apart from coal, which has gradually been losing its competitive position in the European pattern of solid-fuel consumption, Europe is not richly endowed with natural energy resources. A few countries, such as Switzerland, Sweden, Norway, Italy and Austria, are in a good position to produce hydro-electric power cheaply, but France, Germany, and the Low Countries are not. As for oil, all the free countries of Europe combined can produce from indigenous fields less than ten per cent of their needs. The discovery of oil deposits in Algeria and Libya and the coal production surpluses of recent years have brightened the European energy picture somewhat, reducing the motif of urgency in Euratom's mission of developing industrial nuclear power. But in the long run, the growth of Western Europe's gross national product will necessitate an even more rapid rate of expansion in energy capabilities, and it seems likely that nuclear reactors as sources of electric power will become competitive in costs with conventional fuels earlier in Europe than in most other regions of the world.[26]

Euratom is designed to promote research in the peaceful uses of atomic energy by training scientists and technicians in a Joint Nuclear Research Centre which receives two-thirds of its financial support from France and Germany and the remainder from the other four countries. The Centre has also been assigned the function of co-ordinating all peaceful atomic programmes among the Six governments, Western European universities, industrial firms and private institutes. It is hoped that wasteful duplication of effort can thereby be avoided and a consistent European programme of nuclear technology developed. The Commission is to make the results of nuclear research available to any government, organisation, enterprise or individual within the Community provided that the ability to use them effectively and for authorised purposes can be demonstrated. As from 1 January, 1959, a common market without any tariff barriers or quantitative restrictions was established for all nuclear materials and equipment among the Six, and the unfettered mobility of nuclear scientists and technicians throughout the Euratom area was guaranteed.

The field of nuclear energy seemed like a natural one for an experiment in integration because the Six are for the most part (except for Luxemburg) at comparable levels of development in this sector. Each stands to gain something from the combination of effort; each can contribute something which will help to satisfy relatively similar needs in the future. Furthermore, in Western Europe nuclear energy is a totally new industrial frontier, one which raises unique

[26] *United States Foreign Policy: Western Europe,* A Study Prepared at the Request of the US Senate Committee on Foreign Relations by the Foreign Policy Research Institute, University of Pennsylvania (see note, p. 120). Cf. especially Appendix "C," "Europe's Energy Problem," pp. 79-81.

problems of finance, technical application and political control. There are no vested interests which demand escape clauses and other devices to cushion them against the effects of the merger. "Euratom, of all the European supranational institutions, probably poses fewest problems under the heading of pure 'integration'. There was little difficulty in abolishing all tariffs on items deemed clearly essential to the growth of industrial nuclear power. More complicated are the questions of raising the needed investment capital for an industry that is not yet competitive; fixing the relations between Euratom and private enterprise; negotiating outside agreements for purposes of development, on which Euratom's promising research programme depends; and determining the connection between Euratom's peaceful purposes and the military objectives of member nations, especially France."[27]

This last point leads logically to the thought that there can hardly be any such thing as "purely economic" integration—totally divorced from politics—on a significant scale. When nations embark upon a Euratom project, their decisions inevitably have political implications, if not immediate then proximate or remote. If, for example, the Europeans go in for nuclear specialisation, with each nation contributing its part to the over-all effort, it may well prove difficult for any single country to disengage itself at some future date and attempt to embark upon its own fully-fledged national programme. Perhaps this was one of the major reasons why the British were not attracted to the idea of Euratom at its inception. Compared with the Continent, Britain already possessed a relatively self-sufficient nuclear industry. The player who holds the most chips does not stand to gain when everyone throws his chips into the kitty for the purpose of equal redistribution. Furthermore, the British in the late 1950s were still extremely wary of the

[27] *United States Foreign Policy: Western Europe*, p. 59.

ultimate political implications of the various economic communities of the Six. They were most unwilling to submerge into a general European atomic pool their own nuclear industry, the possession of which had helped to assure them of a privileged relationship with the United States within the NATO alliance. It would have been awkward indeed for British scientists to try to participate with European scientists in Euratom research projects while at the same time maintaining complete secrecy concerning the military applications of the atom. Until the British were willing to commit themselves fully to the European unification movement, membership in Euratom seemed to be out of the question.

It is highly doubtful whether a sharp and lasting distinction can be drawn between peaceful and military uses of the atom. To begin with, many strategic analysts would argue that if the acquisition of nuclear weapons is intended to strengthen the deterrent against the outbreak of war, then military nuclear programmes can be brought under the rubrics of peaceful uses. But even apart from this argument, which is essentially political, no unscalable wall can be built between nuclear programmes for power production and those for weapons production. True, nuclear reactors which are designed for purposes of power production will not be *efficient* for the accumulation of fissionable materials suitable for the manufacture of weapons, but they will permit the *inefficient* pursuit of this latter goal, since every reactor is capable of yielding some fissionable materials.[28] Thus, as Ben T. Moore has pointed out, "the creation of an independent European nuclear industry to produce power and other outputs for peaceful uses will certainly carry with it the capability of turning out nuclear weapons".[29]

[28] Cf. Murray, Thomas E., *Nuclear Energy for War and Peace,* World Publishing Co. (New York, 1960).
[29] Moore, Ben T., op cit., p. 189.

Under an agreement signed at Brussels on 8 November, 1958, the government of the United States agreed to co-operate with Euratom to bring into operation within the Community before the end of 1965 nuclear reactors which have been developed to advanced stages in the United States, and having a total capacity of one million kilowatts. The United States, determined not to facilitate the process of nuclear weapons proliferation, insisted upon the inclusion of Article XI in the Agreement:

> 1. No material, including equipment and devices, transferred pursuant to this Agreement to the Community or to persons within the Community, will be used for atomic weapons, or for research on or development of atomic weapons, or for any other military purpose. . . .[30]

At the insistence of the Europeans, however, Euratom itself undertook the exclusive responsibility for establishing and maintaining the control system. The United States had no choice but to withdraw its original request for the right of inspection of Community installations.

Actually, there is little fear that Euratom itself might ever depart from its announced intention of concentrating upon peaceful applications without formally revising the Treaty. But, as Ben T. Moore has observed, although Euratom itself will not produce nuclear weapons, "it has no authority to prevent any member country from going ahead with a nuclear military programme."[31] France has had its own nuclear weapons programme since 1957. Other countries are free to develop nuclear military technology except West Germany, which is prohibited from manufacturing nuclear

[30] *Agreement between the United States of America and the European Atomic Energy Community,* Signed at Brussels 8 November, 1958, Treaties and Other International Acts Series 4173, US Department of State, p. 8.
[31] Moore, Ben T., op. cit.

weapons by the Protocol of 1954 to the Brussels Treaty. It cannot be denied that Euratom, by training atomic scientists and by facilitating the production of fissionable materials in Europe, has made an important contribution to the French military effort, and may prove to be significant if at some future time a decision should be made to establish a genuine European nuclear deterrent.

THE COMMON MARKET
(EUROPEAN ECONOMIC COMMUNITY)

The European Economic Community went far beyond the single-sector approach and sought to establish a common market on a scale roughly equivalent to that which had historically developed under the aegis of the "interstate commerce" clause of the US Constitution. The total population of the Six in 1958, when the construction of EEC began, was 165 millions, while that of the United States was 174 millions. In the same year, the combined gross national products of the Six amounted to about £56 billion; the gross national product of the United States was £157 billion. The advocates of integration argued that, by creating a single market economy, Western Europe could sustain longer than otherwise the high rate of economic growth which it had achieved as a result of recovery thrust. Moreover, they declared, the economies of scale to be expected from integration of the region would strengthen the Atlantic Community for the protracted struggle against a growing Soviet economic system. Even before launching the experiment, the Six could boast a total output in the production of basic commodities which compared favourably with the Soviet performance, and the total external trade of the Six was much greater than that of the Soviet Union.[32] The United States, discerning

[32] In 1957, the Six produced 219 billion k.w.h. of electric power; the USSR 209 billion k.w.h. The corresponding

a greater potential on the far side of the Atlantic for sharing the economic burdens of NATO defence and the process of international development, staunchly supported the movement towards comprehensive integration.

The latter 1950s, however, witnessed serious disagreements among the Europeans over precisely how economic integration could best be achieved. Even within the ranks of the Six there were misgivings. Many influential groups wondered what effects the projected Common Market would have upon their own interests. High-cost producers feared that they would be wiped out of existence if national tariff barriers should be abolished. Concern ran especially high among the French, who were apprehensive that their wage-price-social security structure would render them uncompetitive in comparison with the Germans and other neighbouring peoples. The French government, therefore, felt compelled to insist upon several cushioning devices (such as special import taxes and export subsidies), the eventual "harmonising" of national economic policies to bring social security and other welfare programme costs into line, and a prolonged period, twelve to fifteen years, for carrying out the transition to conditions of a completely homogeneous market. Then, just when it appeared that the Six were close to reaching agreement on the internal mechanics of market-building, the French raised another issue of far-reaching implications. Anxious to modernise the administration of the overseas territories in Africa, they demanded that these must be included as an integral part of the EEC. This demand was not received enthusiastically by Germany, Italy and the Netherlands. But the French remained adamant and the other members of the Community finally acquiesced.

---

figures for crude steel were 60 million metric tons for the former and 51 million for the latter. Data from *The United Nations Statistical Yearbook* (1958).

This was the price that had to be paid to obtain French adherence to the Treaty of Rome.[33]

Despite their internal difficulties, the Six moved with a steady determination towards EEC, encouraging one another as they went. The governments managed to convince most of the interested groups within the various nations that the Common Market was to be founded not on Utopian vision or abstract economic theory but on something much more solid—a sober, business-like assessment of mutual advantage. France stood to benefit the most from the provision creating an Overseas Territories Development Fund,[34] since she held more non-European territories than all the other members combined. By contributing $200 million to this fund, Germany would in effect be underwriting France's effort to convert her African colonies into a cluster of independent states permanently linked to the metropolitan country by economic ties. Germany and the Benelux countries anticipated that their primary gain would derive from the elimination of tariff walls within the Community and the vast expansion of a single "domestic market" for their manufactures. Italy, deeply concerned throughout the postwar period over the effects of population growth and the poverty of the country's southern provinces, hoped to find some relief in those treaty clauses promising labour mobility throughout the Community and the establishment of a European Investment Bank which would, among other things, finance projects for developing underdeveloped regions within the Community. France, besides receiving welcome aid in the task of African development, also expected to reap profits

[33] Article 131 of the Treaty stipulates that all the non-European countries and territories having a special relationship to Belgium, France, Italy and the Netherlands will be brought into association with the Community.

[34] France and Germany each agreed to contribute $200 million; the other four countries were to contribute a total of $181 million.

to her farmers, who would be cast in the role of "grocers of the Common Market", once the proper agricultural adjustments could be made.[35] The Six, in sum, perceived more assets than liabilities in the contemplated merger.

Along the outer edges of the Six, reactions were quite different. The British, from the very beginning, were cool towards the proposal for a European Economic Community. They were no more willing in 1958 than they had been in 1950 (when the Schuman Plan was unveiled) to subordinate their national independence to European institutions. The British trade unions were not at all friendly to a plan which might some day involve the immigration of cheaper Continental labour. Labour intellectuals could not exorcise the suspicion that an EEC Commision vested with supranational powers would take decisions certain to interfere with Britain's public policy objective of full employment. Several economic analysts, inside and outside of Britain, were of the opinion that the less efficient segments of British industry which would find themselves hard-pressed by the competition of Germany's modernised producers might be embarrassingly large. The British were further dismayed at the prospect of seeing the new states of French West Africa incorporated into EEC whereas it was taken for granted that, even if Britain should join, she could not bring her Commonwealth partners in with her, not those in Africa or anywhere else. Finally, most Britons deemed intolerable the thought that, by entering EEC, they would be obliged to subscribe to a common external tariff against imports from Commonwealth countries while admitting goods from across the Channel duty free. Few Englishmen were prepared to buy Danish dairy products (at higher prices!) and

[35] The authors of this book called attention to the mutual self-interest aspects of the Treaty of Rome in an article on the European Economic Community in the *Encyclopedia Britannica Yearbook* for 1958.

to tell the New Zealanders that they would have to find other markets for their butter.

FREE TRADE AREA

Great Britain was, nevertheless, interested in liberalising intra-European trade. But she wished to accomplish this objective by continuing to work through the existing inter-governmental mechanisms of OEEC without resorting to any new supranational institutions. This had been the gist of the Eden government's proposal at a meeting of OEEC Ministers in July, 1956 for a Free Trade Area (FTA). FTA was similar in concept to the Common Market in that it called for the removal of all tariffs and quotas among the seventeen OEEC countries. FTA differed from EEC in so far as it would not require the setting of a common protective tariff against outsiders. Each member of FTA was to be left free to fix his own tariffs on goods coming from non-signatory countries. Hence the Six could erect a common barrier as high as they pleased against non-FTA countries, while Britain would be permitted to maintain her system of Imperial Preferences, under which agricultural products from Canada, New Zealand, Australia and other Commonwealth countries found their way into the United Kingdom through the non-tariff gate. Under the British plan, food and agricultural products were to be excluded from the coverage. FTA was to encompass manufactures only. The scheme did not extend beyond mere free trade measures. It carried no intention of trying to harmonise the economic and social policies of the member nations.[36]

[36] See Worswick, G. D. N., "Britain, the Common Market, and a Free Trade Area," *Year Book of World Affairs 1958*, Stevens and Sons, Ltd., for the London Institute of World Affairs (London, 1958): Frederick A. Praeger (New York, 1958), pp. 181-198; and the article "The Negotiations for a Free Trade Area," *The World Today*, Vol. 14 (June, 1958), pp. 236-247.

The British did not underestimate the difficulties of trying to superimpose a Free Trade Area upon the Common Market. They recognised, for example, the nettlesome problem of determining the "origin of goods", which would arise out of the disparity of FTA and EEC external tariff policies. Sweden, for instance, might maintain a very low tariff or none at all on certain manufacturers on which the Six wished to preserve a protected market. If these items were imported into Sweden from the United States, they might be re-exported to France under free trade arrangements, thereby undercutting the common tariff of the Six, perhaps to the detriment of a German producer. An OEEC working committee concluded that, in order to cope with the problem of re-shipment, FTA would probably have to introduce a rather cumbersome system of "certificates of origin". Even this type of safeguard could be evaded in the case of goods imported in one form and re-exported in another after processing.

Most of the European countries which shunned the political goals of the Six were very much attracted to the British free trade idea. In fact, although Britain was generally looked upon as the leader of the free trade movement, she had less reason then to be concerned at the possibility of trade discrimination by the Six than had the smaller peripheral countries. "In 1956, only fourteen per cent of British exports went to Community countries. The comparable percentages for some of the other OEEC countries were: Austria 49, Denmark 31, Norway 25, Sweden 34, Switzerland 39. Thus, for the smaller countries, the stake in the Community market was equal to from one-fourth to one-half of their total exports."[37]

Hence it was not fair to charge, as some critics did, that

[37] Frank, Isaiah, *The European Common Market: An Analysis of Commercial Policy*, Frederick A. Praeger (New York, 1961), p. 204.

the British were trying to form a bloc of the so-called "Outer Seven" (including those states just named, plus Portugal) against the "Inner Six". A more accurate judgment would be to say that Britain was acting as spokesman for those OEEC members who needed no one to persuade them that the erection of a Common Market unaccompanied by broader European trade agreements could pose a serious issue to their national economic interests.

The reaction to the FTA proposal among the Six was not homogeneous. Germany and Belgium were interested in obtaining the widest possible market for their industrial products and hence they were willing to negotiate for a free trade area, but not at the cost of weakening the Common Market. The Netherlands and Italy, on the other hand, were unwilling to open up their markets to British manufactures without extracting from Britain some reciprocal concessions for Dutch dairy products and Italian fruits and vegetables. Undoubtedly, the most strident opposition to the FTA proposal came from the French, who charged that the British and others were seeking to cash in on the benefits of the enlarged West European market without paying the price that the Six were preparing to pay—in concessions on domestic, social and economic policies, mobility of labour, and the creation of common investment, development and readjustment institutions. Isaiah Frank concludes that the Six were basically suspicious of FTA for two reasons. The first was a political concern that incorporation of the Six in a larger free trade area would dilute the supranationality of the EEC's institutions and militate against its ultimate political objective of political union. "The other concern was economic and was at the core of almost every specific issue that arose. It was the belief that any arrangement consisting simply in a commitment for the total dismantlement of trade barriers would be either unworkable or grossly inequitable in the absence of comprehensive understandings for the co-ordination of other aspects of economic policy such as were included or implied in the Treaty of Rome."[38]

The British government, upon realising that the Six were pressing forward rapidly toward the establishment of EEC while apparently losing interest in FTA, proceeded at a meeting in Stockholm in late June, 1959 to encourage the consolidation of trade policies among the "Outer Seven". At a subsequent meeting in Stockholm on 20 November, 1959, the Seven initiated a convention establishing a European Free Trade Association for manufactured goods.[39] The EFTA convention entered into force on 3 May, 1960. Since the EEC countries had gained a head start in tariff reduction and were putting their second ten per cent cut into effect on 1 July, 1960, the EFTA members agreed to reduce their mutual tariffs by twenty per cent on the same date. In an effort to keep the gap between the two trade groupings from growing wider than absolutely necessary, each side extended its initial tariff reductions to the other. Thus during the first year or so, the EEC caused no "felt discrimination". But it was generally recognised that the real problem would arise when the low tariff countries among the Six (especially Germany and the Benelux states) would reach the point where they would have to start raising their external tariffs to conform to an EEC average. Towards the later part of 1959, the United States as leader of the Western alliance began to worry about two things: (1) the possibility that the EEC external tariff would some day adversely affect American trade with Europe; and (2) the danger that the European Allies would become divided into two hostile economic blocs.

[38] Frank, Isaiah, op. cit., p. 297.
[39] Finland adhered to EFTA as an associated state on 1 March, 1962.

ORGANISATION OF EEC

The EEC which came into existence on 1 January, 1958 differed perceptibly in structure and operation from the Coal and Steel Community. Instead of being headed by a High Authority wielding a substantial executive power in defined areas, the EEC is managed by a nine-member Commission which is armed, for the most part, only with administrative and planning powers. The Commission's main function is to propose measures, while it is up to the Council of Ministers, representing the six national governments, to make the authoritative decisions. This feature should not be construed to mean that the designers of the Common Market had abandoned the principle of supranationalism. Supranational institutions need not always be patterned according to the same rigid formula. In the case of ECSC, the Six knew that they were delegating powers over no more than two industries, coal and steel, and hence they could afford to make those powers specific and plenary. The same was true in the case of Euratom. But when they set up the Common Market, the Six could not forsee precisely what steps would have to be taken to carry out comprehensive integration, or how these steps might affect the various national economies. A greater role, therefore, was assigned to the Council of Ministers. But the Council is not intended to operate as a purely intergovernmental diplomatic conference, bound always by the rule of unanimity. It was decided that during the first of the three four-year transitional stages, most of the important questions could be decided only by unanimous agreement, but with the passage of time the principle of regular or weighted majority decision would come increasingly to the fore.[40] At the end of the first

[40] Article 148 of the Treaty declares: "Except where otherwise provided for in this Treaty, the conclusions of the Council shall be reached by a majority vote of its members. Where the conclusions of the Council require a qualified

four years, for example, the Council was to decide by unanimous vote whether the objectives of the first stage had been achieved so that the second stage might be entered. (This actually occurred early in 1962.) Failing unanimity, the first stage has to be extended for another year. At the end of the fifth year, the same procedure has to be followed. But at the end of the sixth year, the Council could decide by qualified majority to enter the second stage. If at that time any single member refused to be bound by the Council's decision, its only recourse would be to withdraw from the EEC, either destroying it completely or forcing a re-negotiation of the treaty. But now the momentum of the Common Market, with its cumulative mutual benefits, appears to be irreversible.

Almost as soon as the EEC undertook the gradual abolition of internal trade restrictions, European business-men quickened to the significance of a single market in which all goods, services, labour and capital could eventually circulate in perfect freedom. They were already riding the crest of a prosperity wave. Between 1950 and 1958, the gross national product of the six Community countries (calculated at 1954 prices) had increased by fifty-two per cent.[41] Now they were confronted with the prospect of an enlarged and expanding market, one which cried out for new economies of scale as they drafted their production plans for the future. "The climate of business opinion is changing even more rapidly than the architects of the EEC had predicted. Everywhere producers appear eager to capitalise on the opportunities of a greatly enlarged market.

---

majority, the votes of its members shall be weighted as follows: Belgium 2; Germany 4; France 4; Italy 4; Luxemburg 1; Netherlands 2." A qualified majority of the Council consists of 12 out of 17 votes, and in some cases may require the votes of 4 of the 6 members.

[41] *The European Community: The Facts*, European Community Information Service (2nd edition, April, 1960), p. 3.

Dozens of major companies are making merger agreements on either a national or an international basis. Some companies are joining to build bigger power supply sources . . . more efficient than anyone could afford singly. Other companies are working out agreements to specialise their products and market each other's output, thus saving the cost of setting up new sales organisations."[42]

During 1959, intra-Community trade grew almost twice as fast as trade with outside countries. In the first quarter of 1960, trade among the Six was forty per cent higher than it had been in the same period in 1959.[43] By the spring of 1960, the EEC members were seeking to accelerate the process of tariff modification. In August, 1960, the EEC Commission in Brussels issued an official estimate that the growth rate among the Six for that year would be about eleven per cent.[44]

AMERICAN ECONOMIC POLICIES

The remarkable success of the Common Market experiment provoked animated discussion, beginning in the 1959-1960 period, of a whole set of profound economic-political problems within the Atlantic Alliance. Although the establishment of EEC was not the actual cause of all these problems, it certainly helped to impart to all of them a note of urgency. The United States, either for reasons of its own national interest or because of its obligations as leader of the Alliance, had no choice but to concern itself deeply with these problems, most of which are likely to endure in one form or another for several years to come: (1) eliminating the possibility of harmful trade discrimination by the Common Market against the United States and other Free World

[42] *United States Foreign Policy: Western Europe,* op. cit. (see p. 120, note), p. 57.
[43] *New York Times,* 23 June, 1960.
[44] Ibid, 22 August, 1960.

countries; (2) healing the rift between the two European trade groups which, if allowed to go unchecked, could have serious political implications for the solidarity of the Alliance; (3) reversing the deterioration which has occurred in recent years in the international competitive position of the United States; (4) bringing about a more equitable sharing of defence and foreign-aid burdens among the leading industrial members of the Atlantic Alliance; (5) ensuring a more efficient co-ordination of the West's efforts to assist in the process of international economic development; (6) developing methods of parrying Soviet bloc economic penetration into the underdeveloped countries as well as Soviet bloc economic intervention into Western economies; and (7) constructing as between Europe and the United States a genuine Atlantic economic partnership which will enable the Alliance to maintain a rate of economic-scientific technological growth higher than that of the Soviet bloc for an indefinitely long period of time.

The issue of discrimination can be phrased in the form of a different question : Will the Common Market grow more by trade creation than by mere trade dislocation, i.e., more by an expansion of total economic activity, including buying from abroad, than by shifting the factors of production within Europe from smaller and less efficient to larger and more efficient producers? The experience of EEC's early years indicates that the Common Market was, on balance, trade-creating and not just trade-diverting. Although intra-Community trade in 1960 showed at least a thirty per cent increase over 1959, imports from the outside world also ran considerably higher. Hence non-EEC nations profited from the initial impetus of integration. Indeed, the figures for the American trade increase were little short of phenomenal: "That year [1960] Italians increased their buying of American woollen materials and clothes by 467 per cent. . . . That year Frenchmen and Frenchwomen bought 301 per cent more

American textiles; 286 per cent more American kitchen gadgets; 246 per cent more American cosmetics; 169 per cent more American automobiles. That year the United States sold to the Common Market as a whole 412 per cent more aircraft (in value); 164 per cent more metals; 86 per cent more machinery. The total value of all United States exports to the Common Market, already worth $2,500,000,000, rose 44 per cent."[45]

But there was a fear that this upsurge was only temporary, owing to the unusually rapid expansion of Western Europe's industrial capacity and to the policy of extending the original EEC tariff cuts to all GATT participants and the quota reductions to all OEEC members. It was expected that Western Europe's imports from outside industrial suppliers would decline after the period of expansion came to an end and the common external tariff barrier of EEC began to take shape. There was reason to believe that, the higher the common tariff, the greater would be the temptation of American business firms, instead of trying to compete across the hurdle, to leap over the tariff wall and invest in European plants. Naturally, American labour did not find such a prospect very pleasing in view of the nation's chronic unemployment problem, nor did the United States government, which had to cope not only with unemployment but also with a continuing balance of payments deficit in recent years.

Many Americans had become worried of late about an apparent worsening of the international competitive position of the United States. Their concern frequently took the form of the complaint that American producers were being "priced out of the world market". There could be no doubt that a few sectors of American industry had become high-cost producers in comparison with their more modernised com-

[45] May, John Allen, "Common Market Bars Loom," *Christian Science Monitor,* 11 January, 1962.

petitors in Germany, Japan and other countries and were as a consequence losing ground in some foreign markets which they had entered almost by default in the years following the Second World War. But beyond this, not a few economists wondered whether a number of economic factors, including labour productivity, corporation marketing practices, high overhead costs (e.g., for advertising), and national policies regarding interest rates, taxation, social welfare programmes, and strategic spending (for security and foreign aid), had not combined to place the United States in a position where it had to become more careful about the efficiency of its total economic performance.

Throughout the 1950s up to the end of 1957, the United States had normally incurred in its payments balance an average annual deficit of about one billion dollars. Put differently, the United States had been spending about a billion dollars a year more for imports, tourism, foreign aid, overseas investment and the support of military forces and bases in allied countries than it had been receiving from abroad in payment for American goods and services. But in the three-year period 1958-1960, the total deficit exceeded ten billion dollars, and this caused serious concern. One consequence of the imbalance was an outward flow of gold of $2·3 billions in 1959—the largest in US history.[46] There were two general ways in which the drain on American reserves could be reduced: first, by expanding the total volume of American exports; second, by cutting US spending abroad. The government sought to correct the imbalance by taking action along many fronts: (1) adopting a "Buy American" policy by which most monies disbursed through the Development Loan Fund would have to be spent on purchases in the United States; (2) undertaking a campaign to promote US exports by supplying information on foreign marketing opportunities and improving credit facilities for

[46] *New York Times*, 1 May, 1960.

exporters; (3) intensifying diplomatic efforts to convince allied governments that they should continue to liquidate the barriers to dollar imports, now that the international dollar shortage was becoming a dollar surplus, and that they should increase their contribution to financing military defence and foreign aid. Finally, on 16 November, 1960, President Eisenhower ordered the number of US military dependents overseas to be reduced from 484,000 to 200,000.[47] The task of maintaining the "soundness of the dollar" had begun, albeit slowly, to come into apparent conflict with the international strategic commitments of the United States. For many years a debate had raged among Americans over the question whether national security issues should be subordinated to the exigencies of a balanced budget at home. Now, for the first time, large numbers of Americans began to realise that the achievement of economic balance is more than a domestic problem, that security objectives cannot be pursued in patent disregard of economic considerations, and that henceforth it would be necessary for the United States and its Atlantic Allies to think of striking a balance between economic limitations and international strategic goals on a wider regional basis than heretofore.

Although the Allies, under Article 2 of the North Atlantic Treaty, promised to eliminate economic conflict in their international economic policies and to encourage mutual economic co-operation, they have not been prone to look upon NATO itself as an appropriate instrument for the direct co-ordination of their economic activities. NATO, of course, has had to be concerned with the financial implications of the military preparedness programmes of the various member nations. National requirements have usually been measured against national capabilities through a device known as the Annual Review, in which the objectives desired by the military authorities are reconciled with the available

[47] *New York Times,* 17 November, 1960.

resources and defence plans of the member countries. The Annual Review, according to an official estimate, has the merit "of making it possible to find out whether a comparable defence effort is being made by all countries . . . taking into consideration the economic position of each country, its general structure, its gross national product, the trend, good or bad, of its balance of payments, the weight of taxation it bears, and the national living standards; whether, in brief, it can be inferred from certain 'economic pointers' that a country's share of the defence burden is adequate or inadequate, not in absolute terms . . . but in relation to the contributions called for by the military authorities."[48]

Despite the fact, however, that the allied governments have voluntarily submitted their defence budgets to multilateral examination and criticism in the Annual Review, nevertheless NATO as such can do no more than express opinions and recommendations, leaving the final power of decision to the national governments. The cost of modern weapons technology, the shortage of manpower in certain NATO countries, the threat of inflation, national tax policies—all these factors and more have complicated NATO's task of balancing military requirements with available economic resources.

Beyond the realm of military defence matters, NATO has found it even more difficult to discuss alliance economic policies. The United States and Britain, among other allies, had long been reluctant to employ the North Atlantic Council as a channel for co-ordinating foreign aid policies. They feared that if anything resembling a NATO aid policy should be developed, nationalist *élites* in the underdeveloped regions would be sure to brand it with the label of "neo-imperialism". The problem was compounded by the fact

[48] *Economic Problems and NATO,* in the Aspects of NATO Series, NATO Information Service (Paris, October, 1961), p. 7.

that for many years the European colonial powers did not wish to have delicate questions of empire raised within the framework of NATO, largely because they resented the well-known anti-colonial attitude of American policy-makers. In the absence of a co-ordinating mechanism, the various international economic assistance programmes sponsored by the Atlantic nations mushroomed in a dozen different directions—Point Four, the World Bank, the Colombo Plan, the Overseas Countries and Territories Development Fund of the EEC and many others.

It became increasingly obvious that the Atlantic Alliance was in need of some means whereby full and efficient use of the member countries' economic potential could be assured. In December following the Suez crisis of 1956, a Committee of Three submitted to the Council meeting a report on non-military co-operation among the Allies. The Committee observed that NATO was not an appropriate agency for administering programmes of aid for the under-developed areas, or even for trying to concert the aid policies of the Allies. But it called upon the members to keep each other and NATO fully informed of what they were doing in this field, and suggested that NATO might occasionally review the adequacy of existing aid policies in relation to the interests of the Alliance. The Committee then proceeded to focus attention upon a serious problem of economic strategy confronting NATO: "71. The economic interests of the Atlantic Community cannot be considered in isolation from the activities and policies of the Soviet bloc. The Soviets are resorting all too often to the use of economic measures designed to weaken the Western Alliance, or to create in other areas a high degree of dependence on the Soviet world. In this situation it is more than ever important that NATO countries actively develop their own constructive commercial and financial policies."[49]

[49] *Report of the Committee of Three on Non-Military*

The report carried a recommendation that a Committee of Economic Advisers be established under the NATO Council, and this was done in February, 1957. The general attitude, however, continued to be that the job of co-ordinating national economic policies should be left to the specialised international organisations (such as OEEC, GATT and the International Monetary Fund) within which the NATO countries exercised a preponderating influence. The presence of non-NATO states, including some official neutrals, within these organisations militated against any effort to use them as vehicles for the development of "NATO economic policies".

ORGANISATION FOR ECONOMIC CO-OPERATION AND DEVELOPMENT
(OECD)

The pressing nature of the United States balance of payments deficit, the threat of a trade war between the Six and the Seven, and the fear that American exporters would be hurt by tariff adjustments across the Atlantic, combined with a desire to enlarge the role of European states, especially Germany, in the process of international development, led to the formulation in 1959 of the so-called "Dillon Plan", named after the US Undersecretary of State, and designed to promote the strengthening and cohesion of the Western democracies. A special conference of eighteen OEEC members was held at Paris in January, 1960 to discuss the relationship between the Common Market and EFTA, the problems of aid to the underdeveloped countries, and the possibility of re-organising the OEEC to enable the United States and Canada, then associated members, to become full

---

Co-operation in NATO, reprinted from the *Department of State Bulletin,* 7 January, 1957, Department of State Publication 6449, p. 8.

participants. This meant that henceforth the discussion of common economic problems would be elevated from a European to a transatlantic level. After nearly a year of negotiations, twenty nations signed the Convention creating the Organisation for Economic Co-operation and Development (OECD) on 14 December, 1960. Its stated objectives were to assure the highest rate of sustainable growth consistent with financial stability, to contribute to sound economic expansion in the underdeveloped countries, and to work for the growth of international trade on a non-discriminatory multilateral basis.[50]

The debate which occurred in the US Senate Foreign Relations Committee over ratifying the OECD Convention indicated how fraught with political difficulty the task of integrating the Atlantic economies could be. The Convention provides that the OECD Council can take decisions only by unanimous agreement, and that if a member should choose to abstain from voting on any specific question, it would not be bound by the decision taken.[51] Despite these precautions, which were established largely to allay misgivings on the part of the US Congress, the Senate nevertheless raised the "constitutional question", and some Senators expressed concern over the fact that the new international organisation was supposed to be able to take any decisions at all, whether by unanimous agreement or not.[52] The Foreign Relations Committee finally recommended ratification, but appended to its report a statement of understanding of the US position to the effect that nothing in the treaty authorised the Executive to exceed its existing powers, or

[50] Article I of the OECD Convention. Full text in *NATO Letter*, Vol. IX (January, 1961).

[51] Article 6 of the Convention.

[52] *Organisation for Economic Co-operation and Development*, Hearings before the Committee on Foreign Relations, US Senate, EX. E., 87th Congress, 1st Session 14, 15 February, 1, 6 March, 1961, pp. 196-232.

to bind the United States without complying with constitutional requirements and domestic law, or limited any powers of Congress. In March, 1961, the Senate ratified the Convention by a vote of 72 to 18.

The OECD formally came into existence on 30 September, 1961, and by the end of the year all twenty members had deposited their ratifications. Not all the Europeans, however, were sure that OECD represented a significant gain in the field of economic policy co-ordination, or that they were going to like the brand of leadership which the United States was now attempting to furnish. There was little doubt that the speed at which the European countries had been liquidating their colonial empires in Asia and Africa (having brought some thirty-five newly independent states into existence by the end of 1960) would make it easier for the Atlantic countries to discuss economic aid to the underdeveloped countries. But there was still no desire to have the OECD administer aid funds, assume any operational functions, or take up the question of aid to specific countries or projects. Furthermore, several European governments showed themselves cool towards the suggestion advanced by US Undersecretary of State George W. Ball that each industrialised country should aim at an annual aid-figure amounting to one per cent of its gross national product. An English journal was prompted to make the following critical comment: "The view could be taken that America was joining with Europe in the new organisation primarily in order to influence European policies rather than to reorientate her own policies to comply with the demands of economic interdependence. Some such feeling was not uncommon during the negotiating period and contributed to a certain scepticism among British and Continental commentators regarding the potential value of the OECD."[53]

[53] "OEEC into OECD," *The World Today*, Vol. 15 (May, 1961), p. 185.

There was general agreement, however, that the OECD would facilitate systematic long-range economic planning within the Atlantic Community. It would also provide an additional channel through which the EFTA and EEC groupings could intensify their communications and seek ways of resolving their dispute. Moreover, the presence in OECD of the four European neutrals—Austria, Ireland, Sweden and Switzerland—might assist the West in its efforts to build a bridge to at least some of the non-Western neutrals in need of development assistance. At the same time, their membership would render it awkward for the Atlantic Allies to use OECD as a medium for working out economic policies with Cold War implications, such as a strategic embargo on East-West trade. So far as a NATO economic policy is concerned, the OECD operates under the same political limitations as the former OEEC. (In late 1962, NATO itself entered the field of economic warfare for the first time when the North Atlantic Council decided to place a NATO embargo on the sale of Big Inch pipe to the Soviet Union for the construction of oil transport facilities to Eastern Europe. After the Council made the decision, the first half of 1963 saw questions raised as to how long German and British business firms would comply with the ban.)

The one area in which the OECD was willing, under United States prodding, to enter into public competition with the Soviet bloc was the realm of announcing growth goals. At the 22nd Congress of the Soviet Communist Party, held in Moscow in October, 1961, the Premier, Mr Khrushchev, presented a draft programme in which he promised that the USSR would surpass the United States in industrial output by 1970 and bring about such a spectacular increase in the well-being of the Soviet people as to lay the material foundations of communism by 1980. The Western response to this boast was made at a meeting of the OECD Ministers in Paris in November, 1961 when the twenty nations declared their resolution to achieve by 1970 a fifty per cent rise in their combined gross national products, through joint and individual action. The purpose of the declaration was merely to define the goal; the planning required to reach it will require exhaustive consultation within OECD and national policy modifications during the years ahead. Should such a goal be realised, it would mean that the total gross product of the OECD members, which was then about $866 billions per year, would increase within nine years to about $1,300 billions. Mr Ball, who presented the plan, said that the US gross national product, then $520 billions (or about sixty per cent of the total for the Atlantic Community), would amount to $780 billions by 1970. The anticipated nine-year US growth would be equal to what the total Soviet gross national product was estimated to be in 1961, and the combined growth of the twenty nations would be nearly equivalent to the addition of another American economy to the Western side of the economic scale.

To reach their goal within nine years, the OECD nations would have to achieve an average annual growth rate of 4·6 per cent per year; within ten years, 4·2 per cent. A better-than 4 per cent rate would not seem too formidable for West Germany, France and some other European countries, but it might prove extremely difficult for the United States and Britain, whose annual growth rates in recent years had fluctuated around the levels of 3 per cent or lower, to sustain substantially higher rates over the next decade. The incentives for making the effort were great, for success in fulfilling the goal of a fifty per cent production increase would enable the West to stay well ahead of the Soviet bloc, to assure the Western orientation of most developing countries, and to bring about closer Western economic unification all the more easily.[54] But not a few observers wondered whether the

[54] It was expected that economic growth would facilitate the British entry into the Common Market and make it easier to negotiate an agreement between the United States and the EEC on mutual tariff reductions. "Officials note that the

United States and Britain, precisely because they already were among the "richest" nations, much of whose gross national product expansion now occurs in the realm of intangible services, could gird themselves for a race to expand physical output against younger and less complex national economies. On balance, Western policy-makers were moderately optimistic. They reasoned that the OECD goal was considerably more realistic than the 150 per cent increase which Mr Khrushchev forecast for the Soviet Union in the next ten years. Most Western economists seemed confident that by the time 1970 came round, the absolute economic gap between the Atlantic Community and the Soviet bloc would be even wider than it is today.

BRITAIN AND THE COMMON MARKET

Undoubtedly, the most significant development along the economic integration front in 1961 was the announcement on 31 July, by Britain's Prime Minister, Mr Macmillan that the British government would enter negotiations for membership in the European Economic Community. The Prime Minister told the House of Commons that he was not confident of success, but hopeful. He seemed to be acknowledging the fact that Britain, disappointed in her efforts to influence the course of Common Market events from the outside position afforded by EFTA, and seeing that the Six, economically, were moving ahead faster than herself, had no choice except to try to come to terms with the EEC. But his approach did not appear to be too enthusiastic, and for this he was taken to task by a Liberal editor: "Most Europeans . . . will be glad to see Britain as an equal partner

---

Common Market members found that the phenomenal growth in their economies in the last four years made it unexpectedly easy for them to adjust to reduced tariff schedules."—*New York Times,* 12 November, 1961.

in the new Western Europe. But they want us to come in wholeheartedly. . . . Whitehall has never quite believed that the Community would not collapse. It has, however, come into thriving life, although still with many hard and painful adjustments to be made among its existing members. They want us with them, but not at the price of dismantling what they have built. We shall have to accept the measures towards a common tariff already taken before our entry, although scope exists for debate about future tariff reductions. . . . Above all, whatever reservations we feel about methods, we must show that we believe in the ambition of a politically united Europe. This is just what Mr Macmillan has not done."[55]

The British decision was greeted with dismay among the members of the Commonwealth, who feared that Britain's economic and political reorientation towards the Continent would have adverse repercussions upon their trade and would also lead to the disintegration of the world's oldest and in many respects most remarkable association of states. The Macmillan government, reluctant to interpret the issue as a choice between the Commonwealth and Europe, preferred to think that Britain's admission to the EEC would so contribute to a general expansion of world trade as to redound in the long run to the advantage of her Commonwealth partners, especially if arrangements could be devised to cushion the impact of the British entry upon New Zealand, Canada, Australia and the underdeveloped producers of primary products who depended most heavily on exports to the United Kingdom.

The United States enthusiastically supported the British decision to apply for membership in the EEC. Presumably this would bring the British into the Coal and Steel Community and Euratom as well. Washington was pleased at

[55] "Right Decision: Wrong Route," *Manchester Guardian Weekly*, 3 August, 1961.

the prospect that the movement towards European political unification would henceforth be tempered by the presence of prudent and pragmatic English diplomats. The Macmillan government hoped that, as a result of Britain's new initiative, she would be able to achieve a "more dynamic influence in the affairs of Western Europe and the Western world."[56] Throughout the negotiations which got under way in November, 1961, Britain sought to secure her vital Commonwealth interests, to obtain safeguards for British agriculture, and to obtain the most favourable terms possible by which her EFTA partners could join or associate with the Common Market. (Within eight months of the British decision, Denmark, Ireland and Norway had applied for full membership in the Community; Spain and Turkey had applied for an associated status leading towards full membership; Austria, Sweden and Switzerland had requested an associated status. Permission for the association of Greece with the EEC had already been granted.)

The negotiators had to deal with problems that were extremely complex. President de Gaulle complained of Britain's effort to enter in the company of a "massive escort". In the face of Britain's request for "special arrangements" to avoid hurting Commonwealth members whose goods, since 1931, have enjoyed privileged entry into the British market under the Imperial Preference system, the Six at one point displayed sympathetic understanding of London's problem and even seemed willing to grant exceptions for a certain number of years, provided that these exceptions would be no more than temporary and destined eventually to disappear. De Gaulle insisted upon the establishment of a common external tariff in order to preserve the distinctly European character of the EEC. More than once he insinuated that the British were trying to dilute the Common

[56] *New York Times,* 3 April, 1962.

Market by proposing extraordinary concessions to the members of the Commonwealth and of EFTA.

Commonwealth sentiments in Britain, however, were still strong enough to prevent the Macmillan government from agreeing to any terms that would seem to spell the liquidation of the Commonwealth within a period of ten or twelve years. Even the Labour Party, which could not be accused of harbouring nostalgic memories of imperial grandeur, professed deep concern over the future of the Commonwealth. The principal reason for this concern was perhaps not so much the fact that Canada, New Zealand and Australia depended heavily upon the British market as the fact that practically all the other Commonwealth countries were in the underdeveloped category. These would suffer immeasurably if their exports should someday be excluded from the British market and be discriminated against by the entire Common Market area. Mr Edward Heath, speaking before the Council of the EEC, pointed out that Mauritius sends eighty-two per cent of its exports to Britain, Sierra Leone seventy per cent, Nigeria fifty-one per cent and India and Ceylon about thirty per cent each.[57] Important as the Commonwealth countries may be for British trade, Britain is more important for theirs. Indeed, in recent years the Commonwealth has been of gradually declining significance in Britain's export picture. Between 1957 and 1960, Commonwealth imports from Britain dropped off by eight per cent, while during the same period Commonwealth imports from other countries rose by sixty-one per cent.[58] To no inconsiderable extent, Britain was being replaced as a supplier in several Commonwealth countries by the Common Market area, at the same time that the latter was beckoning

[57] May, John Allen, "Mirror on Commonwealth," *Christian Science Monitor*, (11 January, 1962). Cf. also "Commonwealth Ministers Are Apprehensive," *EFTA Reporter* (9 October, 1961), p. 3.
[58] Ibid.

English manufacturers as a buyer. It made economic sense, therefore, for the British to shift emphasis from the Commonwealth to the Common Market. But they could not completely abandon the system of Imperial Preferences, for to do so would leave several Commonwealth nations practically no alternative except to expand their trade links with the USSR, the East European satellites and communist China.

The British-EEC negotiations were hampered from the start by the lack of an agreed agricultural policy among the Six themselves. Nearly all the Commonwealth countries and the EFTA members were keenly interested in the kind of arrangements EEC would make to remove restrictions on the flow of farm goods within the market and to erect a common external tariff against farm imports from outside the market. Among the Six, France and the Netherlands, as the countries with farm surpluses, wished to abolish most agricultural trade barriers internally and to protect their enlarged "domestic" market with a high tariff wall around the outside. The Federal Republic of Germany, however, was reluctant to expose its farmers to French and Dutch competition too rapidly and too soon. The government recognised that national protection would eventually have to be eliminated under the terms of the Treaty of Rome, but wished to delay as long as possible to give the German farmers an opportunity to improve their competitive position. Towards the end of 1961, there was some fear that lack of progress in the agricultural sector would delay for another year the decision to pass on to the "second stage" of the EEC.

The first agricultral trade policy ever to be adopted on a European scale was completed on 14 January, 1962, when the Six accepted a plan named after Sicco L. Mansholt of the Netherlands, Vice-President of the EEC Council. The Mansholt Plan as finally modified deals with cereals, pork, eggs, poultry, fruit, vegetables, wine and rice. It aims to balance supply and demand inside and outside the Community, to stabilise agricultural markets by sheltering them from speculative price fluctuations, and to ensure both a fair return to farmers and a fair deal to consumers. The common market for agriculture is to be established gradually over a period of seven and a half years, by the end of which time, prices, marketing, competitive conditions and legislation will have been harmonised throughout the Community. In the meantime, price differences among the Six will be compensated by variable levies at internal frontiers, which will diminish throughout the transition period. Furthermore, any member country which fears disruption of domestic production as a result of imports from other members will be allowed to invoke safeguard clauses. To shelter the Community against world price fluctuations and to ensure some degree of protection for Community farmers, the EEC will also apply a variable levy on imports from outside the Community to bring their prices up to those of home production. The proceeds of these levies will go into price stabilisation funds, the fund for promoting farm modernisation, and a fund for export subsidies to permit EEC farmers to compete on the world market.[59] The adoption of a common agricultural policy meant that the Common Market had managed to overcome the most severe test in its history, and enabled the Six to embark upon the second stage of their experiment in economic unification.

When Britain resumed her negotiations with the EEC in January, 1962, she knew at last where the Six stood with respect to agricultural policy, but in some ways the problem of arranging entry had now become even more complex.

[59] See "Common Market on the Move" and "EEC Ministers Agree at Last," *Manchester Guardian Weekly,* 18 January, 1962; also "EEC Farm Policy" and "Highlights of the Agricultural Agreement," in *Bulletin from the European Community,* No. 52 (March-April, 1962).

If Britain joined the Common Market, she would be expected to abandon or drastically modify Imperial Preferences and subscribe to EEC's common external tariff.[60] This would pose grave enough difficulties in the realm of manufactures, where it would hurt the trade of Canada, Australia, India, Pakistan and Hong Kong, among others. But since the bulk of Britain's imports from Commonwealth countries consists of agricultural products and raw materials, the EEC farm agreement would greatly compound the problem of working out the details of Britain's admission. Australia in recent years has sold about 25 per cent of her wheat to Britain, and New Zealand more than 90 per cent of her butter and cheese. The traditional practice of admitting Commonwealth exports of food and textiles duty free has made the average worker's cost-of-living lower in the United Kingdom than in most countries of Western Europe. Abolition of Imperial Preferences and acceptance of the common external tariff would mean that the British worker would have to pay substantially higher prices for food and clothing. This helps to explain the lack of enthusiasm for the Common Market within the ranks of the Labour Party. More than a year after the Macmillan government announced the decision to negotiate, the subject of Britain's membership in the EEC was still being hotly debated in England. A year after their initial outburst of resentment in Accra, the Commonwealth foreign ministers, meeting in London, were still not hesitant

[60] On 29-30 May, 1962, Britain and the Six agreed on tariff arrangements for Britain's imports of manufactured items from Canada, Australia and New Zealand. Immediately on joining the Community, Britain would adjust her own tariff for these goods 30 per cent of the way towards the common external tariff. She would make a second 30 per cent adjustment at the beginning of 1967. By 1 January, 1970, Britain would place into full effect the Community's common external tariff on imports of manufactures from those three industrialised members of the Commonwealth. *Bulletin from the European Community*, No. 54 (June-July, 1962), p. 11.

to express their misgivings over the direction of Britain's policy. They were finally reconciled, however, to the fact that Britain seemed determined to press the negotiations on towards an acceptable conclusion, but they reserved "final judgment" until the negotiations were completed.

Probably the most important obstacles in the way of Britain's coming to terms with the EEC were really political rather than economic. At the heart of the matter lay the question as to whether the British were willing to undertake the commitment to some form of eventual political unfica-tion to which the Six had pledged themselves when they signed the Treaty of Rome. The old aversion of Englishmen to subordinating national sovereign prerogatives to supra-national institutions could not be expected to abate rapidly. It would be hard enough for the British to submit to any decision-making by majority procedures in the realm of economic policies. But in recent years President de Gaulle had been calling for the development of a common European defence and foreign policy and it was expected that this would be still more difficult for a British government to accept.

USA AND THE COMMON MARKET

Within the United States, the period beginning in the latter half of 1961 witnessed a growing realisation that the success-ful emergence of the Common Market posed an economic challenge of the first magnitude to the leader of the Atlantic Alliance. The further development of the Market was expected not only to contribute significantly to the total strength of the Atlantic Community, but also to spur the American economy to new competitive efforts, in order to preclude any further deterioration in the nation's balance-of-payments position. Speaking of the potentially discrimin-ating character of the Common Market, President Kennedy said: "One-third of our trade generally is with Western Europe. If the United States should be denied that market we will either find a flight of capital from this country to construct factories within that wall, or we will find ourselves in serious economic trouble."[61]

Not a few prominent Americans went so far as to suggest something approaching full American membership in the Common Market. Christian A. Herter, Secretary of State in the Eisenhower Administration, and Will Clayton, Undersecretary of State for Economic Affairs in the Truman Administration, in a report prepared for the Joint Economic Committee of Congress, declared that "the only way this country can hope to hold its export markets is by associating itself with the Common Market."[62] Eric Johnston, former president of the US Chamber of Commerce, pointed out that the United States had to choose among three alternatives: (1) to go it alone by returning to a fully protectionist policy; (2) to form, along with Latin America and Canada, a hemispheric trading bloc that would rival the Common Market; and (3) to join the Common Market. After dismissing the first two alternatives as being undesirable not only on economic grounds but also because they would imperil Atlantic political unity, Johnston advocated joining the Common Market. "Only by joining can we hope to produce here and sell there, hold on to United States capital and salvage our present losses."[63]

The Kennedy Administration did not regard outright membership as a feasible policy choice within the forseeable future. Washington policy-makers were concerned over some nations, such as Japan and the underdeveloped countries, which lacked the power to apply bargaining leverage

[61] Quoted in *New York Times,* 12 November, 1961.
[62] Ibid., 5 November, 1961.
[63] Johnston, Eric, "We Must Join the Common Market," *New York Times Magazine,* 12 November, 1961. For a fuller analysis of the implications of the EEC for American business, see *The European Common Market,* American Management Association (New York, 1958).

against the EEC. Furthermore, protectionist sentiment was still politically strong among those American industries that feared the prospect of increased competition from Europe. Nevertheless, the Administration was convinced that drastic changes would have to be made in American trade policy to cope with the rapidly developing economic situation on the far side of the Atlantic, where, early in 1962, the Six reached the 40 per cent mark in their internal tariff-cutting drive. Consequently, George W. Ball, Under-Secretary of State for Economic Affairs, began to alert Congress and the public to the need for an overhauling of US foreign trade legislation. The Reciprocal Trade Agreements Act, which had been extended eleven times since 1934 and was due to expire in June, 1962, was fundamentally inadequate to the new challenge, for it permitted only item-by-item tariff reduction, whereas the EEC procedure is to cut tariffs "across the board" on broad categories of goods. In January, 1962, a United States delegation headed by Howard Petersen, Special Assistant to the President for Trade Policy, and Charles Murphy, Under-Secretary of Agriculture, went to Brussels and concluded a tariff-cutting bargain with the EEC Ministers which would reduce trade barriers by 20 per cent (the maximum then permitted by US law) on a wide range of items, mostly industrial. The Brussels negotiations demonstrated clearly that the United States had little choice but to sharpen its tariff-bargaining instruments.[64] In late January, President Kennedy sent to Congress his proposed Trade Expansion Act. He requested (a) "a general authority to reduce tariffs by 50 per cent in reciprocal negotiations, including negotiations on broad categories or sub-categories of products" and (b) "special authority to be used in negotiating with the EEC, to reduce or eliminate all tariffs on those groups of products where the United States and the EEC

[64] See Mr Petersen's statement, "The Common Market: Opportunity Knocks," in *The Christian Science Monitor*, 11 January, 1962.

together account for 80 per cent or more of world trade in a representative period."[65] In order to assuage the fears of third parties, the United States promised in dealing with the EEC to adhere to the "most-favoured-nation" principle. To mollify domestic protectionists, the Administration wrote into the law provisions for federal "readjustment allowances" for injured industries and accepted various concessions on behalf of the cotton, oil, coal, watch, glass, bicycle and other industries. The Trade Expansion Act passed the House of Representatives in June, 1962, and the Senate in the following September. By the autumn of 1962, it appeared that the United States had turned its back upon protectionism and economic isolationism and was beginning to awaken to the full implications of Atlantic partnership in the sphere of trade.[66] As President Kennedy made clear to the Conference on Trade Policy in Washington on 17 May, 1962, the United States expected that trade expansion would both contribute to a grand design of Atlantic partnership and also benefit the American economy by speeding growth, increasing exports, providing new jobs, stimulating domestic investment, spurring plant modernisation and raising the national standard of living.[67]

USSR AND THE COMMON MARKET

There can be little doubt that the emergence of the European Common Market, and the prospect of close economic ties

[65] The Trade Expansion Act of 1962, H.R. 9990. See Aschinger F. E., "The United States and the Common Market," *Swiss Review of World Affairs* (March, 1962).

[66] See Gass, Oscar, "Crusade for Trade," Parts I and II, *The New Republic*, 19 and 26 March, 1962; also *Survey of Trade Relations between the United States and Common Market Nations*, compiled by Senator Kenneth B. Keating, of New York, 19 March, 1962, Washington: Government Printing Office (1962).

[67] *Trade and Atlantic Partnership*, remarks by President Kennedy and Secretary of State Rusk, 17 May, 1962, Department of State.

between it and the English-speaking members of NATO, constitute the most important developments on the world scene during the last decade. It was true that in the past several of the younger, underdeveloped nations of Asia and Africa looked with a certain amount of misgiving on what they regard as a Western "rich man's club." Even though Britain had obtained from EEC an agreement permitting African Commonwealth countries to become associate members of the Common Market, Nigeria and Tanganyika showed themselves wary, at the annual Commonwealth Conference in London in September, 1962, of identifying themselves politically with the Atlantic Community. Prominent neutralist leaders, such as Tito, Nehru and Nasser, also issued warnings against the political implications of the Common Market.

The Soviet Union, as was to be expected, did not miss any oppportunity to attack the Common Market once it became clear that the British were engaged in serious entry negotiations and other European countries were interested in applying for membership. The Soviets were particularly incensed at the thought that Europe's three prominent neutrals—Sweden, Switzerland and Austria—were anxious to link up with the EEC. By mid-1962, Soviet propagandists were levelling regular and vehement attacks against the Common Market as a form of "collective colonialism," "the economic arm of the aggressive militaristic NATO bloc," and the "Holy Alliance of the reactionary forces of Western Europe."[68] The intensely hostile tone adopted by Mr Khrushchev himself indicated that the communist leadership watched with dismay the rise of a great new economic power centre on the western flank of the USSR. The success of the movement towards European economic

[68] Cf. Madeleine and Marvin Kalb, "The Communist Dread of the Common Market," *The Reporter*, 19 July, 1962; and Nove, Alec, "Communists and the Common Market," *The New Republic*, 17 September, 1962.

integration was fraught with serious meaning for the communist bloc. It portended an enhanced Western capability to engage in costly programmes of defence and space-technology precisely at the time when the Sino-Soviet world was running into notorious economic difficulties. Moreover, the Soviets must have realised that the expansion of Western economic activity would make the Atlantic Community more important than ever to the underdeveloped nations of the world, which already carried on more than twenty times as much trade each year with the industrialised Atlantic nations as they did with the communist bloc; the dependence of these yet-to-be-developed countries upon the markets and capital resources of the Atlantic Community seemed destined to grow during the decade of the 1960s.

Perhaps most important of all, the vitality of the Western economic system loomed in the early 1960s as a monumental embarrassment to the validity of the Leninist-Stalinist thesis concerning the fatal "contradictions of capitalism." For many years, communist ideologues had been predicting the imminent decline into chaos of the Western economic system. This decline, they said, would result from extreme cyclic fluctuations, chronic malfunctioning of the distributive mechanism, internecine rivalries and mounting resentment on the part of the exploited classes within the West and within the erstwhile colonial societies. But in the latter part of 1962, it looked very much as though something had gone awry in the communist diagnosis, as the Atlantic Community appeared to be moving steadily towards regional economic integration.

The communist bloc appeared almost ready to adopt the maxim, "If you can't lick them, join them." In late summer 1962, Mr Khrushchev displayed some interest in concluding an agreement that would provide for co-operation between the EEC and its communist-bloc equivalent, the Council for Mutual Economic Assistance (COMECON). The Premier's attitude struck Western observers as a paradox in the economic realm comparable to one with which they were more familiar in the political order. Although the Soviet leader had often denounced NATO as an instrument of aggression, nevertheless more than once he had proposed a non-aggression treaty between NATO and the Warsaw Pact countries. Now, similarly, after condemning EEC as a tool of neo-imperialism, he professed a willingness to come to terms with it. Harry Schwartz, economic analyst for the *New York Times*, was of the opinion that the communist bloc found itself in economic trouble and under mounting pressure to widen trade ties with the West if its plans for expanded output were to be realised. Schwartz pointed out that between 1959 and 1961, the exports from communist countries to the EEC rose by 25 per cent and that these gains would probably be jeopardized as Euromart's common external tariff rose higher."[69] During the latter months of 1962, Mr Khrushchev seemed especially anxious to win special tariff concessions from France and Italy. Then something happened early in 1963 which undoubtedly prompted the communist leadership to wonder whether the movement towards Western economic integration had perhaps reached its peak and passed it.

After fourteen months of negotiations for Britain's entry into the EEC, President de Gaulle, speaking at a press conference on 14 January, 1963, adopted a position which was interpreted as tantamount to a veto of the British application at that time. The French leader criticised Britain for not having joined the Common Market when originally formed, for creating a free trade area and for having tried to slow down the growth of the EEC. Among other things, President de Gaulle said: "England is, in effect, insular, maritime, linked through its trade, markets and food supply to very diverse and often very distant countries. Its activities are

[69] Schwartz, Harry, "Soviet is Pressing Hard on Economic and Political Fronts: The Economic Front,"—*New York Times,* 2 September, 1962.

essentially industrial and commercial, and only slightly agricultural. It has . . . very marked and original customs and
traditions. In short, the nature, structure and economic context of England differ profoundly from those of the other
States of the Continent. . . . For example, the means by
which the people of Great Britain nourish themselves is in
fact by importing foodstuffs purchased at low prices in the
two Americas or in the former dominions, while still granting
large subsidies to British farmers. This means is obviously
incompatible with the system the Six have quite naturally
set up for themselves."[70] A few days later, the French delegation at Brussels demanded that negotiations for British entry
be suspended.

France's five Community partners demurred from de
Gaulle's view. The German delegation pointed out that Britain
was prepared to accept the common external tariff, abolish
Commonwealth preferences (with special arrangements
for certain Commonwealth members) and relinquish her
special links with the EFTA countries. The only remaining
difficulties pertained to the transitional arrangements for
agriculture, primarily a question of phasing the adjustments
out over a fairly long period of time. The Five did not agree
with President de Gaulle's insinuation that Britain was not
sufficiently European, was unwilling to accept the Community on its own terms, and was trying to change completely
the series of adjustments already established among the Six.
The delegates of the Five argued that substantial progress
had been made during the course of the negotiations, albeit
slowly, and that everyone had known from the beginning
that the task of working out the arrangements for Britain's
entry would be immensely complex. They did not believe
that a break-off in the negotiations was warranted. They could
not deny, however, that France had the right under the

[70] Text of President de Gaulle's Seventh Press Conference,
Ambassade de France, Service de Presse et d'Information,
Speeches and Press Conferences No. 185, p. 6.

Treaty of Rome to insist that the negotiations be discontinued. Nor were they willing to argue that all the nettlesome economic and political problems of British entry had been close to solution before de Gaulle delivered his rebuff. Indeed, one leading periodical made this comment: "We should not forget, just because of de Gaulle, that a fair agreement was not immediately in sight. Nor should we forget . . . that the British government has never fully faced the political implications of joining."[71]

President de Gaulle's decision was widely regarded as a setback for President Kennedy's policies of encouraging closer British ties with the Continent and of working for a general round of tariff cuts. For some weeks, an atmosphere of gloom hung over the Alliance. The French action perceptibly slowed down the progress of the Community's movement towards further economic integration. Germany, Italy and the Benelux countries seemed reluctant to condone any tighter economic consolidation of Europe along lines mapped out by France and to the prejudice of closer Atlantic-wide ties. In economics no more than in the realm of defence did the Bonn government wish to be confronted with a choice between France and the United States. In the meantime, the British public, after their initial shock, hurt and dismay, decided to make the best of the situation. Some leaders, including Mr Harold Wilson, who succeeded Mr Hugh Gaitskell as head of the Labour Party, went so far as to express satisfaction at the failure of the Brussels negotiations.

For at least half a year after President de Gaulle's veto of the British application, the progress of Common Market development seemed to slow down markedly. Many Europeans wondered whether the United States, which had for many years encouraged economic integration on the Continent, might begin to have second thoughts about the

[71] "Mr Macmillan's Rescue Operation,"—*Manchester Guardian Weekly*, 24 January, 1963.

EEC, both because American interest groups, especially the farmers, feared the effects of rising tariff walls against American products, and because under French prodding the Common Market seemed to be poised for a movement in the direction of separatism rather than toward closer co-operation with the United States and Britain within the framework of Atlantic unity. The Europeans marked time, while seeking an answer to the question: "Where do we go from here?"

The Common Market was confronted with two main tasks —negotiating with the United States in the so-called "Kennedy round" of tariff talks, and working out a new approach to Britain. In early May, 1963, an American delegation headed by a former Secretary of State, Christian A. Herter, went to Geneva under the authority of the US Trade Expansion Act to obtain an across-the-board tariff cut (about fifty per cent) instead of the product-by-product reduction which had previously characterised negotiations under the General Agreement on Tariffs and Trade (GATT). At Geneva, the United States was somewhat surprised to encounter a fully united Six.[72] The "Friendly Five", as France's partners were then called, sided with de Gaulle in the effort to maintain EEC cohesion and to fend off an American agricultural invasion of Europe at least until the Continent's own farmers' house would be in order.[73] France, however, finally concurred in a compromise accord on the procedures by which the EEC and the United States would negotiate the reduction of trade barriers beginning in May, 1964.

As for Britain, the "Friendly Five" hoped after de Gaulle's veto that it would be possible to keep the door open between Euromart and London. President de Gaulle, however,

[72] Forbath, Peter, "Coming to Terms with the Common Market," *The Reporter,* 20 June, 1963, p. 25.
[73] Giniger, Henry, "De Gaulle Still Tough," *New York Times,* 9 June, 1963.

rejected formal communications between the British government and the EEC Council of Ministers. At this point, British Deputy Foreign Minister Edward Heath, the British government's negotiator at Brussels, attempted to establish connections with the Continent through the Western European Union (WEU), which links the Six and Britain in a formal defence alliance. The French were at first opposed. But one of the effects of President Kennedy's trip to Europe in June, 1963, was a renewed effort on the part of West Germany to "open the line" again between the Continent and London. After President de Gaulle's follow-up visit to Bonn, France agreed to permit consultations in WEU once each quarter on matters of common economic interest.

By late summer 1963, there were signs that the Atlantic Community was beginning to recover from the disappointment of January. There were cautious hopes that interim solutions could be devised until a more solid and durable formula for Western economic integration could be discovered. These hopes were, no doubt, contingent upon parallel political and military developments within the Atlantic coalition, such as the creation of either a NATO or a European nuclear deterrent acceptable to all the Allies. The hopes represented more than mere whistling in the dark. They were founded upon a persistent conviction that the spirit of European unity and the spirit of Atlantic Community had to flourish together, reinforcing rather than opposing each other.

Chapter 5

THE POLITICS OF THE ALLIANCE

NATO was founded primarily to ensure the local defence of Europe, but from the beginning it was recognised as more than a mere military coalition. It was a grouping of states which realised that they had more in common than fear of the strategic threat which Soviet power posed to their security. With the exception of Portugal, they all shared democratic institutions and were interested in strengthening them. All of them had inherited the cultural values of Western civilisation, values which were being challenged not so much by the authentic cultural traditions of the non-Western world as by the rise of militant and hostile ideologies, several of which were, in a very real sense, products of the Western mind. The *élites* of all the Atlantic nations were becoming increasingly convinced of the interdependence of their respective national economies and of the mounting dependence of Asia, Africa and Latin America upon the economic prowess of the Atlantic Community for an improved living standard in a context of relative political liberty. Finally, the NATO partners were anxious not only to deter a Soviet attack upon Europe but also to create the conditions on a worldwide scale for the growth of a reasonably stable international order of law in which the uses of violence would be minimised and the process of peaceful change guaranteed. In short, the NATO countries stood opposed to the forces of destructive revolution on the world scene; they stood *for* the forces of constructive evolution, looking towards a genuine international community.

But in spite of its common ideals and objectives, an alliance of democratic states is bound to encounter difficulties in the co-ordination of national policies. As military technology passes from one phase to another, defence strategies must be modified. There is no reason why the policy-makers of the fifteen nations should necessarily discern the changing defence problem in exactly the same way. Moreover, some of the strategic arguments which arise, although they may be couched in terms of a conflict of theories of defence, will really reflect the fact that even the staunchest allies can at times disagree rather seriously over political objectives and approaches; this is to be expected. All the NATO members have behind them long and proud national traditions. All of them are jealous of their national sovereign prerogatives. Several are concerned over what they regard as vital national interests outside the area precisely defined within the Treaty. A few have far-flung strategic responsibilities beyond the NATO region; most of them have not. They entertain divergent attitudes with regard to colonialism, the various manifestations of neo-imperialism, neutralism and other phenomena in the international scene. They do not always see eye-to-eye on the role of the United Nations in dealing with critical problems. Indeed, they do not all have exactly the same conception of the nature of the threat posed by the communist bloc to the free world and of the possibility of arriving at East-West understandings in such crucial sectors, e.g., as that of nuclear armaments.

It is not surprising, then, that political stresses and strains will from time to time arise within the Atlantic Alliance. A democratic alliance such as NATO is in certain respects comparable to the Democratic or Republican party in the United States. Each national party is a coalition of disparate interest groups, and each is beset by two conflicting forces: (1) the desire of the party to co-operate for the purpose of achieving the joint minimum goal, i.e., the capture of public offices; and (2) the desire of the component groups to maintain their separate interests within the framework of the party, if possible, or outside the party, if necessary.[1] The members of NATO usually manage to come closest to a consensus on those clear-cut security issues which touch upon the central purpose for which the Treaty was signed. This is the centripetal force of the Alliance. When the Soviet Union pursues a "hard line" in Europe, the Allies are generally disposed to close ranks, diplomatically speaking, and present a united front. But there are also centrifugal forces at work, which can adversely affect the solidarity of the Alliance. These arise from the fact that each member has its own identity, prestige and interests which it is determined to preserve. Most of the Allies would prefer, if possible, to defend their own particular interests within a climate of NATO political consensus, i.e., each to win the support of its allies for its own position. But in many instances this is patently impossible, and so the individual ally "goes it alone". The present chapter deals with the interplay of common and separate interests within the Atlantic Alliance.

NATO's Early Years (1949-1954)

The first important political decision of the Council, following the establishment of a unified command for NATO forces, was the agreement of September, 1950, on the "forward strategy" by which NATO forces would resist

---

[1] The analogy of alliance and political party is suggested by Liska, George, *Nations in Alliance: The Limits of Interdependence*, The Johns Hopkins University Press (Baltimore, 1962).

aggression as far to the east in Europe as possible.[2] The motives for this were as much political as they were military. The United States realised that the Europeans were not interested in a NATO strategy of deterrence-retreat-liberation. Many Europeans would have refused to place any political confidence in a NATO predicated upon such defence plans. Hence when the "forward strategy" was proposed in the Council, it received unanimous support.

Closely related to the adoption of the "forward strategy" was the decision to allow Germany to rearm and to participate in the defence of Europe. A defence line as far to the east as possible meant a line along the Elbe. Some military strategists were of the opinion that it would be easier for NATO forces to make their stand on the Rhine rather than the Elbe. Others took the position that even though it might be more difficult to bear the full brunt of an attack in the Elbe region, such a forward posture would assure NATO much greater defence-in-depth. Once it was agreed to defend at the Elbe, a West German military contribution seemed perfectly natural. But at the New York meeting of the Council in September, 1950, France, still concerned over the problem of her national security *vis-à-vis* Germany, forced the postponement of a precise solution to the question of German rearmament, which was advocated by the US Secretary of State, Dean Acheson. Mr Acheson's proposal took on added urgency in view of the drain on American military manpower caused by the outbreak of the Korean War in June, 1950. But not even the crushing defeat suffered by Germany in the Second World War had completely dispelled in the minds of Frenchmen the unpleasant memories of 1870, 1914 and 1940. The French, however, recognising Europe's current defence requirements, were willing to seek a solution. French delegates to the Consultative Assembly of the Council of

[2] Lord Ismay, *NATO, The First Five years, 1949-1954*, The North Atlantic Treaty Organisation (Paris, 1955), pp. 101-2.

Europe, giving extension to the concept of supranational integration as embodied in the Schuman Plan for a Coal and Steel Community (cf. Chapter 4), suggested the creation of a European army.[3] The government of René Pleven drafted a proposal for an integrated European army and presented it to the French National Assembly on 24 October, 1950. Robert Schuman gave this description of the Treaty establishing a European Defence Community (EDC), which was signed by the Six in Paris on 27 May, 1952: "This Treaty sets up a defence community and stipulates that the six existing armies are to be replaced by one common army. Only France is to retain additional forces of her own, for the defence of her overseas territories. No element of the common army is at the disposal of any government acting alone; all six must approve its use. The Council of six Foreign Ministers defines the general policy and gives the general directions, which are to be carried out by a nine-man executive commission. Command is integrated on the model of the Atlantic Army of which the European Army will be one of the chief land forces. But in the European Army integration is carried still further. Not only is the high command integrated, but the same is true of all units larger than a division, as well as of the services of supply and other auxiliary services; each will be composed of officers and men of different nationalities. There will be German soldiers but no German Army; German officers at every level but no German general staff; and the same will hold true for continental France and the other signatory nations."[4]

The Council meeting at Lisbon in February, 1952, which stressed the importance of building up NATO ground forces, gave its approval to the idea of the EDC. But almost as soon

[3] See Walton, Clarence C., "Background for the European Defence Community," *Political Science Quarterly,* Vol. LXVIII (March, 1953).

[4] Schuman, Robert, "France and Europe," *Foreign Affairs,* Vol. 31 (April, 1953), p. 355.

as the EDC draft treaty was signed, opposition to its ratification mounted within the country which had originally proposed European military integration. Criticism of the EDC came from many quarters: (a) from nationalists who resented any effort to subordinate French national sovereignty to supranational institutions; (b) from pacifists who disdained policies based upon traditional concepts of military defence; (c) from socialists and others who feared that France alone could not control a rearmed Germany and hence would require the kind of British participation which Britain was reluctant to undertake; (d) from those who thought that German rearmament ought to be carried out within the framework of NATO;[5] and (e) from those who deemed the closing of the humiliating Indochinese war an inappropriate time for abolishing the "glorious traditions" of the French Army on the Continent and merging it with a colourless international force. The prolonged debate over EDC delayed the decision concerning a German contribution to Western defence. In December, 1953, the US Secretary of State, Mr Dulles, warned the European Allies that unless progress were made towards improving Europe's indigenous military capabilities, the United States might have to make an "agonising reappraisal" of its policy. Meanwhile, the Six proceeded to draft a treaty for a European Political Community which would at first encompass the two functional communities, Coal and Steel, and Defence, but which would gradually extend its scope until a European federation would be established.[6] Nevertheless, on 30 August, 1954,

[5] The EDC plan did not specifically provide for German membership in NATO.

[6] See the *Draft Treaty Embodying the Statute of the European Community*. Prepared by the *ad hoc* Assembly Instructed to Work Out a Draft Treaty Setting Up a European Political Community, Secretariat of the Constitutional Committee (Paris, 1953). The purpose of the draft treaty was not to create a third community but to merge the other two into a new European Community which would

after the other five signatories had ratified the EDC Treaty, the French National Assembly cast a vote of 319 to 264 on a technical procedural matter and thereby killed the Treaty.[7] The draft treaty on the Political Community, which was contingent upon the acceptance of EDC, became irrelevant. A high point in the history of the European movement towards political unity *via* sector integration had passed.

After the defeat of EDC, another set of arrangements governing the rearmament of West Germany had to be worked out swiftly. Within a month of the French Assembly's decision, Sir Anthony Eden (now Lord Avon) made a quick tour of the European capitals. The result was a late-September conference in London of the five Brussels Pact powers (Britain, France and the Benelux countries) plus Germany, Italy, the United States and Canada. It was generally recognised that, since the collapse of EDC had been caused in part by the unwillingness of Britain to participate in any joint European defence undertaking which involved a commitment to the federal goal, the new plan would require a somewhat looser structure in which the British would be included. The solution lay in extending and revising the fifty-year Brussels Treaty of 1948, making it the cornerstone of a Western European Union (WEU) which would include the Federal Republic of Germany and Italy. This was done in the Paris Agreements of 23 October, 1954. At the same time, the occupation regime in Western Germany was terminated, and the Federal Republic assumed its place, for all practical purposes, as a sovereign member of the

---

have the powers of the ECSC and the EDC, as well as additional powers in the fields of foreign affairs and economic policy.—Robertson, A. H., "The European Political Community," *British Yearbook of International Law* (1952), pp. 383-401.

[7] The full story is told by Lerner, Daniel, and Aron, Raymond, *France Defeats EDC*, Frederick A. Praeger (New York, 1957).

international community.[8] Furthermore, it was decided that the Federal Republic would accede to the North Atlantic Treaty. (Germany was actually admitted to NATO in May, 1955.)

The collective defence commitment of WEU remained just as it had been stated in the Brussels Treaty of 1948 : "If any of the High Contracting Parties should be the object of an armed attack in Europe, the other High Contracting Parties will, in accordance with the provisions of Article 51 of the Charter of the United Nations, afford the Party so attacked all the military and other aid and assistance in their power."[9] It is to be noted that the wording of this pledge, stronger than that contained in the North Atlantic Treaty, bears a striking resemblance to that often found in alliance documents of the period before 1914.

Under Article 6 of Protocol II on Forces of Western European Union, the British government undertook to maintain on the European Continent the effective strength of the UK forces which were assigned at the time to SACEUR —i.e., four divisions and a tactical air force—or a force acceptable to SACEUR as having equivalent fighting capacity. The British government agreed not to withdraw these forces from Europe so long as a majority of the members of WEU deemed their presence necessary. Britain, however, was not to be bound by this provision in case of a serious overseas emergency. She also reserved the right to request the North Atlantic Council to review the financial

---

[8] The text of the *Protocol Modifying and Completing the Brussels Treaty* is in Robertson, A. H., *European Institutions,* published under the auspices of the London Institute for World Affairs, Stevens and Sons (London, 1958): Frederick A. Praeger (New York, 1958), pp. 294-7. Protocol III and its four Annexes specify that Germany shall not manufacture atomic, biological or chemical weapons, as well as certain other stipulated weapons, such as guided missiles, warships and strategic bombers.

[9] Article 4 of the Brussels Treaty.

aspects of living up to this commitment if the maintenance of UK forces on the Continent should cause undue economic strain.[10] Notwithstanding these reservations, the British commitment to the defence of WEU is of considerable significance, for it stands as the only instance in history of a willingness on the part of Britain to submit formally to the wishes of an international majority on questions that might have a crucial bearing upon her national security policy.

The WEU is worthy of attention on several counts: (1) It stands midway between such purely intergovernmental institutions as OECD and NATO on the one hand and the supranational European Communities on the other. (2) Its executive body, the WEU Council of Ministers, can take certain decisions by simple majority. (3) The WEU Assembly, whose membership overlaps that of the Common Assembly of the supranational Communities, is the only parliamentary body in the Atlantic Community which is authorised to debate defence questions. (4) The Council is empowered under the Brussels Treaty to consult with regard to any situation which may constitute a threat to peace "in whatever area this threat should arise."[11] (5) The WEU is the world's only international organisation which has devised practical procedures for the control of armaments, and the Agency for the Control of Armaments may submit to the Council questions which can be decided by simple majority.[12]

[10] See Ball, M. Margaret, op. cit. (see p. 32, note), pp. 392-3.

[11] Article 7 of the Brussels Treaty.

[12] The duties of the Agency are "to inspect and report on the level of stocks on the mainland of Europe and to ensure that prohibited weapons are not being manufactured. It is also charged with determining the level of the stocks of atomic weapons produced on the mainland of Europe that its members may maintain there. This has not so far been applied, but it will presumably have to be done once French production of nuclear weapons passes the experimental stage."—Mulley, F. W., *The Politics of Western Defence,* Thames and Hudson (London, 1962): Frederick A. Praeger (New York, 1962), p. 26.

(6) Finally, the WEU is closely linked to NATO, to which it has delegated all its defence and military functions. The Vice-President of the Western European Union Assembly has given the following assessment of the work of the WEU: "In general, the WEU Council has been loath to take any decisions in defence matters, or to take any initiatives in this field within the North Atlantic Council, for fear of creating the impression in NATO that the seven members are acting in consort or forming a Western European Union pressure group. However, . . . [the WEU] has been of great value as a framework for political consultation between the Six and the United Kingdom. . . ."[13]

The decision to bring about the controlled rearmament of Germany within the framework of NATO was the most important single development within the Alliance during its first six years. Ever since the failure of the Soviet attempt to drive the Western powers out of Berlin with the blockade of 1948, the Soviet leaders had hoped that once West Germany became sufficiently independent to conduct its own foreign policy, it would be willing to steer clear of the Western Alliance and pursue a course of neutrality in quest of national re-unification. The admission of the Federal Republic to NATO represented a major blow to Soviet policy in Europe. In a final endeavour to entice the Germans towards neutrality, the USSR in the spring of 1955 quickly negotiated the Austrian State Treaty, which entailed the mutual withdrawal of Soviet and Western forces from that country, along with a declaration of abstention from military alliances and foreign military bases.[14] The Soviet gambit, however, failed

[13] Mulley, F. W., *The Politics of Western Defence*, pp. 26-7. For a fuller elaboration of these and related points concerning the possibility of a WEU nuclear force, see Strausz-Hupé, Robert, Dougherty, James E., and Kintner, William R., *Building the Atlantic World*, Harper (New York, 1963), pp. 267-274.

[14] *New York Times*, 16 May, 1955.

to produce the desired effect upon West Germany (cf. Chapter 2).

The early years of NATO's existence witnessed the gradual development of the Alliance's institutions and operating procedures. The NATO Council meeting in Ottawa in September, 1951, established a committee made up of the representatives of Belgium, Canada, Italy, the Netherlands and Norway to explore the possibilities of Article 2 of the Treaty, which provides for joint efforts to strengthen free institutions and to bring about economic collaboration. At the Lisbon meeting in February, 1952, the committee recommended that the Council itself inquire into the possibilities of foreign policy co-ordination, closer political consultation among the members, and economic, cultural and social co-operation.[15] Norman J. Padelford has suggested that in the early 1950s the United States and Britain, anxious as they were to build the basic military structure of the Alliance, were somewhat cool towards proposals that NATO should expand its political, economic and cultural activities.[16] This seemed slightly paradoxical, inasmuch as it was the larger powers in NATO, those with strategic commitments and vital political interests outside Europe, which stood to gain the most from closer political co-operation.

During the early 1950s, each of the leading NATO Allies, the United States, Britain and France, faced a serious communist military threat to its interests in Asia: the United States in Korea, the British in Malaya and the French in Indo-China. At one time or another, each of the Allies had the feeling that its partners were doing little or nothing to lend more than *pro forma* support, despite the fact that the

[15] Communiqué of the Ninth Session of the North Atlantic Council Meeting at Lisbon, *New York Times*, 27 February, 1952.

[16] "Political Co-operation in the North Atlantic Community," *International Organisation*, Vol. XI (Summer, 1955).

North Atlantic Council at its meeting in December, 1952, proclaimed moral support for the resistance of the free nations against communism in Korea and Indo-China, and declared these efforts deserving of continuing support from NATO governments. In the case of Korea, disagreements arose between the United States and Britain, even though the latter did support the Korean War effort by committing forces. The authors elsewhere have described the divergence of basic interests as follows: "The United States had scarcely begun to construct a defence of Europe through the North Atlantic Treaty Organisation when the Korean War broke out. The Europeans, especially the British, were inclined to dissociate the crisis in the Far East from their security interests and feared that an American emphasis on Asia might slow down the development of the Atlantic Alliance. The United States, on the other hand, had historically been oriented more towards Asia than Europe, and emerged from the Second World War as the dominant power in the Pacific. Whereas Great Britain was in the process of reducing her political commitments in Asia, the United States, which had borne the greatest burden among the Western powers in fighting the Axis on both fronts, realised its growing strategic responsibilities in both theatres."[17]

The British, worried over Hong Kong, became even less enthusiastic about the vigorous prosecution of the war after the communist Chinese entered it in November, 1950. When President Truman, at a press conference in that same month, hinted that the use of atomic weapons was under consideration, the British Prime Minister, Clement Attlee, flew hurriedly to Washington to obtain American assurances that the war would not be expanded to the nuclear level.[18] Throughout

[17] Cottrell, Alvin J., and Dougherty, James E., "The Lessons of Korea," *Orbis,* Vol II (Spring, 1958), p. 58.
[18] Ibid., p. 50 Cf. Truman, Harry S., *Memoirs,* Garden City: Doubleday (1956), Vol. II, *Years of Trial and Hope,* pp. 395-6.

the remainder of the war, the British opposed American suggestions that a total economic boycott and blockade be applied against China, that UN pilots be permitted to engage in "hot pursuit" of enemy aircraft into Manchuria, or that any action be taken which might lead to an extension of the war on to the mainland of China. But since the US Secretary of State, Dean Acheson, assigned top priority in the nation's foreign policy to the construction of the Atlantic Alliance, the Anglo-American differences over the conduct of the Korean War never became critical.

In the meantime, Britain and France were tied down in their own wars against communism in south-east Asia. In Malaya, the British were favoured by the fact that the communist guerrilla force was entirely Chinese in composition; the Malayan population supported the British.[19] After two years of difficulties, the British developed an effective counter-guerrilla strategy which, when combined with a programme of social reform, enabled them to break the logistical links between the communist guerrillas and the Chinese population. Although the effort was costly, the British preferred to accomplish it without calling upon their leading NATO ally for any special assistance. The "emergency" in Malaya never became either an issue within NATO or a source of friction among the Atlantic Allies.

The situation with respect to the war in Indochina, however, was quite different. Early in 1950, it appeared that the United States might supply military aid directly to the government of Vietnam to carry on the struggle against Ho Chi Minh. The French regarded such a suggestion as

[19] See Pye, Lucian W., *Guerrilla Communism in Malaya,* Princeton University Press (Princeton, 1957); Purcell, Victor, *Malaya: Communist or Free?* published under the auspices of the Institute of Pacific Relations, Stanford University Press (Stanford, 1954); and Dougherty, James E., "The Guerrilla War in Malaya," in Franklin M. Osanka, ed., *Modern Guerrilla Warfare,* The Free Press of Glencoe (1962).

tantamount to American intervention in a region of French influence, and argued that any direct US aid to the Associated States of Indochina would be wasted.[20] So anxious was the United States to dissociate itself from the colonialist aspects of French operations in south-east Asia that at one point the US government refused "to allow the re-export of American war material from France to Indochina, so that propellers of American manufacture had to be removed from Spitfire aircraft which were being shipped to the Far East."[21] The United States, although anxious to promote the independence of the Indochinese states of Vietnam, Laos and Cambodia within the French Union, finally in May, 1950, agreed with the French view that the successful prosecution of the war against the communists required that aid should be given to the Associated States *and* France. During the years that followed, the United States supplied ammunition, automatic weapons, aircraft, artillery and amphibious vehicles, while intermittently criticising the French for their conduct of the war and for their policy towards the Associated States.

The Indochinese War reached its crucial stage early in 1954, a few months after the Korean War ended. In January, the United States sent a few hundred aircraft technicians to Indochina to aid the beleaguered French. In the same month, the US Secretary of State, John Foster Dulles, by way of warning the Chinese communists not to press their luck too far in south-east Asia, laid down his famous threat of "massive retaliation"[22]—a strategic doctrine which itself became a subject of heated controversy throughout the Atlantic nations. In March, 1954, the French garrison at Dien Bien Phu came under massive assault by Viet Minh

---

[20] Lancaster, Donald, *The Emancipation of French Indo-china*, Oxford University Press (London, 1961), pp. 203-6.
[21] Ibid., pp. 207-8.
[22] *New York Times,* 13 January, 1954.

forces, backed by Chinese "volunteers", technical assistants and advisers. Mr Dulles, speaking to the Overseas Press Club on 29 March, declared that the effort to impose communism on south-east Asia "should be met by united action", even though this might involve serious risks.[23] Admiral Radford, then Chairman of the Joint Chiefs-of-Staff, apparently favoured limited naval-air intervention, and the French government requested the United States to bomb objectives round Dien Bien Phu. Congressional leaders in Washington, however, sensitive to the post-Korean mood of the American public, were reluctant to see the United States become involved in another frustrating military engagement along the periphery of Asia.[24]

Mr Dulles appeared to be in favour of intervention, but other political leaders in Congress and in the Administration advised him that he should sound out America's allies on the extent to which they could be expected to participate. Many of these leaders were willing to support joint Allied intervention, but not unilateral US intervention. When Mr Dulles approached the British, he found them cool towards the idea of undertaking any military measures in Indochina which might jeopardise the outcome of the Geneva Conference, scheduled for the latter part of April.[25] The British

[23] *New York Times,* 30 March, 1954.

[24] Not only the political leaders were opposed. The Army Chief-of-Staff took the position that the jungles and rice-paddies of Indochina would be an inappropriate area for the commitment of US troops. See *Soldier: Memoirs of Matthew B. Ridgway,* Harper (New York, 1956), pp. 275-7.

[25] Sir Winston Churchill, then Prime Minister, told the House of Commons: "The timing of the climax of this assault (i.e., on Dien Bien Phu) with the opening of the Geneva Conference is not without significance, but it should not be allowed to prejudice the sense of world proportion which should inspire the Conference. . . . Her Majesty's Government are not prepared to give any undertaking about United Kingdom military action in advance of results of Geneva." Hansard, Parliamentary Debates, 5th Series, Vol. DXXVI (27 April, 1954), pp. 1455-6.

were also reluctant to form a coalition for the defence of south-east Asia which might alienate the neutralist members of the Commonwealth, especially India. Consequently, the proposal for intervention collapsed, and the war in Indochina was brought to an end at the Geneva Conference. Although the diplomacy surrounding the Indochinese crisis was not, strictly speaking, a NATO affair, since it involved non-NATO allies of the United States (e.g., Australia, New Zealand and the Philippines) and was carried on outside NATO channels, nevertheless the developments in southeast Asia had repercussions within France (including the defeat of EDC)[26] which had an important bearing upon the Atlantic Alliance.

One other issue in the latter part of 1954 disturbed the smoothness of relations between NATO's two English-speaking leaders: the question of Western policy towards China, Formosa and the offshore islands. In the Autumn of 1954, the United States entered into a bilateral defence treaty with the Nationalist Chinese government of Formosa. This action carried with it the implication that the US policy of non-recognition of the communist Chinese government in Peking would become a rather permanent feature of the international scene. Some members of the British Labour Party demanded that for the sake of peace in the Far East, the United States ought to turn Formosa over to mainland China. But the British government, which already maintained diplomatic relations with the People's Republic, did not espouse the Opposition's proposals. It did, however, favour a "two Chinas" policy under which both

[26] Clubb, O. E., Jr., notes that "French critics have accused Mendès-France, never a strong advocate of EDC, of having made a tacit deal with the Soviets." The agreement, presumably, was that the French Premier would ensure the defeat of the EDC project in return for a settlement in Indochina. *The United States and the Sino-Soviet Bloc in South-East Asia*, The Brookings Institution (Washington, 1962), p. 17. Cf. also Lancaster, Donald, op. cit., pp. 336-7.

the communist regime and the nationalist regime on Formosa would be admitted to the United Nations. The Eisenhower administration was unwilling to accept this suggestion. The situation assumed critical proportions when it appeared that the communists might try to seize the offshore islands of Quemoy and Matsu, held by the nationalists. On 28 January, 1955, the US Congress passed a joint resolution authorising the President to take such action as he deemed necessary to secure Formosa, the Pescadores and other "related positions" important to their defence. This commitment on the part of the United States was arranged by Mr Dulles, the US Secretary of State, without prior consultation with the NATO allies, some of whom feared that it might lead to major hostilities in the Far East into which they would eventually be drawn. The dispute over China policy among the NATO allies was to flare up even more acutely in the late summer of 1958, at the time of the communist bombardment of and threatened attack upon the offshore islands. Technically, of course, the United States was under no obligation to consult with its allies with respect to its policy in the Western Pacific, since that region was halfway round the world from the area covered by the Atlantic Treaty, and it was a region where the United States alone felt that it had strategic responsibilities. But the disagreement over the China question and over the proper methods of dealing with its dangers underlined the difficulties of achieving political solidarity within a regional alliance in the face of conflicting allied interests and policies outside the scope of the alliance.

The Middle Years (1955-1960)

After the wars in Korea and Indochina had been brought to an end; after the United States and communist China had settled down for a period of glaring at each other across the Formosa Straits; after it had become obvious that

Soviet efforts to forestall the entry of West Germany into NATO had failed; and after Mr Khrushchev had begun to manifest a different foreign policy style from that which had marked the Stalinist era—to many policy-makers the time seemed ripe for undertaking high level negotiations on some of the outstanding problems of East-West relations. Accordingly, on 10 May, 1955, the United States, Britain and France suggested to the Soviet Union that a "Summit Conference" be held in Geneva during the summer. The Western proposal was discussed fully at the Ministerial meeting of the NATO Council which was then in session. Speaking of that Council meeting, the Canadian Foreign Secretary, Lester Pearson, said that the exchange of views among the members was more complete and more candid than it had ever been up to that time.[27] This was to be expected, since the subjects to be discussed at the Summit would pertain primarily to Europe and hence would bear vitally upon the future of the Alliance.

As finally agreed upon, the agenda for the Geneva Conference contained four items: (1) the re-unification of Germany; (2) European security; (3) disarmament; and (4) the improvement of contacts between East and West. The Soviets had made it clear prior to the meeting that they would not countenance any discussion of the situation in Eastern Europe, but the powers reached an early agreement on the need for linking the questions of Germany's future and European security. The USSR submitted a draft proposal outlining the progress to be made by stages towards European security. "At first the NATO and Warsaw alliances would remain intact, but by means of gradual reductions of troops, improved contacts, and solemn agreements on the renunciation of the use of force in settling international problems,

[27] Padelford, Norman, "Political Co-operation in the North Atlantic Community," *International Organisation*, Vol. XI (Summer, 1955), p. 359.

both security organisations would be replaced by a single European treaty."[28] The rejoinder of the Western powers was that the greatest threat to the peace of Europe was the division of Germany. They argued that before there could be any guarantees such as those suggested by the Soviets, Germany must be reunified on the basis of free elections, after which the Four Powers would sign a general settlement treaty with a single Germany. At this juncture in the conference, Sir Anthony Eden, the British Prime Minister, suggested the creation of a demilitarised zone in Central Europe, involving a system of controlled limitation of armaments on the territory of Germany and her neighbours, and thus he opened the "disengagement" debate which was to run for the next three or four years. The directive of the four heads of government to their foreign ministers declared that "the reunification of Germany by free elections should be carried out in conformity with the national interests of the German people and the interests of European security."[29] During the Summit Conference, President Eisenhower made a dramatic proposal calculated to reduce reciprocal fears of surprise attack; his "open skies" plan called for the exchange of information between the United States and the USSR concerning the location of military installations and the permission to fly aircraft of one country over the territory of the other for purposes of inspection. This was intended to serve as a confidence-building measure.[30] The Soviets, how-

[28] Mackintosh, J. M., *Strategy and Tactics of Soviet Foreign Policy*, Oxford University Press (London, 1962), p. 109. The subject of disengagement proposals is discussed at greater length below, pp. 204-10.

[29] Text of the communiqué in the *New York Times*, 24 July, 1955.

[30] European surveys at the time showed a rising popular disaffection for nuclear weapons, lack of enthusiasm for keeping American bases in Europe, and indifference towards NATO. The United States wanted to "retain its nuclear weapons but still make it clear for all to see that its purpose was peace." The formula hit upon was to revive earlier plans

ever, unwilling to forfeit the strategic advantage which the secrecy of their system afforded them, received the "open skies" proposal with considerable caution. They refused to commit themselves, and merely reiterated the proposals which they had made to the UN Disarmament Sub-committee on the previous 10 May.[31]

Although the Summit Conference ushered in a brief period of relaxation of international tensions, an atmosphere known as the "Spirit of Geneva", it soon became apparent that no fundamental breakthrough had been made towards a resolution of the major East-West problems. The foreign ministers of the Four Powers held a follow-up meeting at Geneva in October, 1955. Prior to this meeting, the three NATO powers co-ordinated their negotiating positions through the medium of the North Atlantic Council. The Western foreign ministers, upon arriving at Geneva, found that the Soviets had decided to oppose both the aerial inspec-tion suggested by President Eisenhower and the reunification of Germany by free elections, which had been tentatively agreed to in principle at the Summit Conference. The West was not surprised at the Soviet *volte face*. Within three days of the ending of the July summit meeting, Khrushchev, speaking in East Berlin, had stressed the fact that he would never consent to any form of free all-German elections which would result in the fall of the East German communist government.[32] Khrushchev's summit policy indicated that he was interested in keeping alive among all Germans the hope of eventual national re-unification. But the performance of the Soviet Foreign Minister, Mr Molotov, at Geneva in the

---

for aerial inspection and exchange of blueprints. Donovan, Robert J., *Eisenhower: The Inside Story,* Harper (New York, 1956), pp. 344-6.

[31] A summary of the Soviet proposals can be found in Noel-Baker, Philip, *The Arms Race*, Stevens and Sons (London, 1959): Oceana Press (New York, 1960), pp. 19-22.

[32] Mackintosh, op. cit., p. 112.

autumn of 1955, and especially his proposal for an all-
German council made up of the representatives of the East
and West German parliaments on an equal footing, left no
doubt that the reunification of Germany within the near
future was out of the question. Thus did events bear out a
judgment made by Lord Strang a few months before the heads
of government had ever met at Geneva : "If the intentions of
the Western powers and the Soviet Union in regard to Germany are to be judged by their acts, then it is clear that their
immediate objective has been and remains to bind their
respective spheres more and more closely to their own
political systems. . . . The two sides seem to be agreed in
this, if in nothing else, that if they cannot bring about the
reunification of Germany on terms which they deem to be
vital to their own security, then they think it better that
Germany should remain divided, and that no thought of
future reunification, which both declare to be their ultimate
objective, should deter them from promoting in their respective areas the political orientation that best suits their
major policies in the contest now engaged for the future of
Europe and the world."[33]

The Middle East Crisis

Within two months of the Geneva Summit Conference,
President Nasser of Egypt announced that he had concluded
an arms-for-cotton agreement with Czecho-Slovakia, i.e.,
with the Soviet bloc, and thereby set in motion a critical
chain of events which placed a severe strain upon the
Atlantic Alliance.

In the Middle East, perhaps more than in any other region
of the non-Western world, United States policy had oscil-
lated back and forth unsteadily between the exigencies of
Alliance solidarity and the attractiveness of an independent

[33] Lord Strang, "Germany Between East and West,"
Foreign Affairs, Vol. 33 (April, 1955), p. 393.

American policy on the world political scene. During the years from 1949 to 1952, while the US Secretary of State, Dean Acheson, was doing his utmost to lay the foundations of NATO, the Department of State had not been manifestly unsympathetic towards British and French efforts to maintain their interests in the Arab world. The Eisenhower administration, which came to power shortly after the Egyptian nationalist revolution of mid-1952, apparently hoped that by reducing economic and diplomatic support for Israel and by disassociating itself from "Anglo-French" imperialism in the Middle East, the United States might win the friendship of emerging nationalist forces within the Arab world, and recruit them to the cause of regional defence against Soviet communism. If this latter objective could not be accomplished, at least Arab nationalism might be kept benevolently neutral towards the West provided that the vestiges of Western colonial control could be liquidated— or so Mr Dulles seems to have thought. Consequently, the United States used its influence to bring about a British military evacuation from the Nile valley; in effect, it supported the Egyptian Arab nationalists in their efforts to realise their two major aspirations, viz., prising the British loose from their positions in the Sudan and in the Suez Canal Zone.[34] "Later," according to John Marlowe, "and almost entirely as a result of President's Nasser's objections, the United States refused to join the Baghdad Pact, although this pact had been regarded by the Americans themselves as an integral part of the American-inspired defence system for the Middle East."[35] But as one of the authors of this book

[34] The Egyptians gave credit to the United States for the assistance rendered in bringing about the accords on the Sudan and the Suez Canal. See *Department of State Bulletin*, Vol. 31, 16 August, 1954, p. 234.

[35] Marlowe, John, *Arab Nationalism and British Imperialism*, Frederick A. Praeger (New York, 1961): The Cresset Press (London, 1961), p. 122.

has observed previously, the United States, despite its amicable overtures, was unable to establish a genuine rapport with Egypt. "American efforts to draw aloof from Britain and France in the Middle East and to achieve quasi-neutrality in the Arab-Israeli dispute failed to reverse the gradual deterioration of relations between Washington and Cairo. The Arabs remained unconvinced that the United States could really detach itself from its friends in the Middle East. The Egyptians were moderately pleased with American diplomatic support on the Sudan and Suez questions but they realised that Britain and France, still holding important interests in the Arab world, were the two major allies of the United States. The use in Algeria of American arms supplied to France through NATO was branded as an affront to the whole Arab nation."[36] Moreover, Nasser had tried at one time or another to acquire arms not only from the United States but also from several of its European allies and had never been able to procure them in the desired quantities. When Nasser agreed to accept the arms from the Soviet bloc, the United States and Britain withdrew their joint offer of aid for the construction of the Aswan High Dam. This action precipitated Egypt's nationalisation of the Suez Canal Company and the crisis which culminated in the Anglo-French-Israeli invasion of Egypt in late October, 1956.

Until shortly before the invasion, Washington was careful to co-ordinate its policy closely with that of London, for the Department of State was deeply concerned about the penetration of Soviet-bloc military equipment and political influence into Egypt during the first half of 1956. But after the Canal Company was nationalised, American policy-makers wished to rely exclusively on diplomatic and legal

[36] Dougherty, James E., "The Aswan Decision in Perspective," *Political Science Quarterly*, Vol. LXXIV (March, 1959), p. 32.

admonitions in order to ensure the future freedom of navigation through the Canal. Mr Dulles, however, would not
agree to lend American support to Anglo-French military
measures in the event of desired objectives not being achieved
through negotiation. At the international conference of
Canal "user" nations held in London in August, 1956,
there was little evidence of NATO's political solidarity.
Greece, embroiled with Britain over Cyprus (see below),
refused to attend. West Germany, anxious not to jeopardise
her own new economic interests in the Arab world, adopted
what to the British and the French appeared to be a neutral
posture in their controversy with Egypt. Even though
Western Europe was heavily dependent upon oil from the
Middle East, much of which had to pass through the Canal,
it would not have been appropriate for any member of
NATO to make official reference at the conference to a
collective interest of the Alliance in the settlement of the
Suez question, and no member did.[37] But it seems from all
accounts that there was a reluctance within the "NATO
household" itself to discuss the Middle Eastern problem
frankly. The result of this failure was a major crisis of confidence within the Alliance. During September and October,
the misunderstanding between the US Secretary, Mr Dulles,
and the British Prime Minister, Sir Anthony Eden, mounted
by the week, until it appears there was almost a complete
breakdown of communication between Washington and
London. In preparing for military action, Britain and France
deployed in the Mediterranean forces which had originally
been assigned to NATO (or withdrawn specifically for service
in Algeria) without consulting the NATO Council. Not until
the day before the outbreak of hostilities did the United

[37] See the verbatim record of the Twenty-two Power
London Conference, August 16-23, 1956, in *The Suez Canal
Problem*, Department of State Publication 6392, United
States Government Printing Office (Washington, October,
1956), pp. 55-293.

States, Britain and France enter into consultation concerning the crisis in the Middle East, and then under the Tripartite Declaration of 1950, ostensibly for the purpose of guaranteeing Egypt's borders against impending Israeli attack. Britain and France informed the United States of their decisions only at the last moment, probably to eliminate the possibility that the Eisenhower administration might press them into abandoning their plans, but it seemed inconceivable to some that the United States had no intelligence of impending developments in the Eastern Mediterranean. Some of the disappointment felt by the British Prime Minister at the lack of US support for his position was evident in his statement to the House of Commons the day after the Suez war began: "The decisions which we and the French Government took were . . . taken on our own account and on our own responsibility. The Government remain convinced that we could have done no other and discharge our national duty. Now it is, of course, an obvious truth that safety of transit through the Canal, though clearly of concern to the United States, is for them not a matter of survival as it is to us and indeed, to all Europe and many other lands. . . . Mr Dulles himself made this clear on 28 August, when he said the United States economy is not dependent upon the Canal. Of course that is true. We must all accept it, and we should not complain about it, but it is equally true that throughout all these months this fact has inevitably influenced the attitude of the United States to these problems, as compared to that of ourselves and France."[38]

The period from mid-October until mid-November, 1956 was one of almost incredible confusion. There was a significant shift in Polish policy towards the Soviet Union and a full-scale anti-Soviet revolution in Hungary. The United

[38] Statement in the British House of Commons by the Prime Minister, Sir Anthony Eden, 31 October, 1956. Text in *United States Policy in the Middle East*, Department of State Publication 6505 (August, 1957), p. 146.

States passed through the final throes of a presidential election campaign. Israel attacked Egypt, and Britain and France occupied key positions along the Suez Canal to separate the belligerents and preserve freedom of navigation. President Eisenhower announced, on 31 October, that the United States would not become involved in the Middle East hostilities, but would strive to localise and end the conflict. On the same day that the Soviet government issued threats of rocket war against Britain and France, it proposed to the United States joint military action "to put an end to the aggression."[39] Although the United States categorically rejected the Soviet proposal, the two leading world powers did align themselves within the United Nations against the Anglo-French-Israeli actions. For a time, it appeared that the political solidarity of NATO had undergone complete disintegration. The leader of the Alliance had sided diplomatically with the major adversary of the Alliance against two members who claimed to be acting in defence of their vital interests. It may be true, as Susan Strange has argued, that Sir Anthony Eden was completely mistaken in thinking that "what ought to have been the Anglo-French reaction to Hitler in 1938 ought also to be their reaction to Nasser in 1956", and that the Mollet government was equally mistaken in attributing all France's troubles in North Africa to the interventionist policies of Egypt.[40] Nevertheless, the United States, as the premier Atlantic ally, cannot be entirely

[39] The texts of these notes will be found ibid., pp. 108-86, and also in *Middle Eastern Affairs*, Vol. VII (January, 1957). For a discussion of the Soviets' use of threats in the Suez crisis, see Strausz-Hupé, R., Kintner, W., Dougherty, J., and Cottrell, A., *Protracted Conflict*, Harper (New York, 1959), pp. 88-9, and Speier, Hans, "Soviet Atomic Blackmail and the North Atlantic Alliance," *World Politics,* Vol. IX (April, 1957), pp. 318-24.

[40] Strange, Susan, "Suez and After," in *The Yearbook of World Affairs, 1957,* London Institute of World Affairs, Stevens and Sons (London, 1957): Frederick A. Praeger (New York, 1957), pp. 82 and 84.

absolved from responsibility for the unfortunate chain of events which led to the *débâcle* of November, 1956. Paul-Henri Spaak, shortly before becoming the Secretary-General of NATO, gave some sage advice and admonished all the major allies with a simple question: "Let us not inquire who is to blame. Are not all the great powers equally guilty through letting themselves get into this situation?"[41] Perhaps there was a compensatory unifying effect upon an otherwise divided NATO in the heroic resistance of the Hungarians to Soviet oppression. Whereas NATO solidarity had been seriously damaged by a crisis arising outside the NATO area, the original spirit of the Alliance as a guarantee of liberty was rekindled by the nature of the Soviet response to a people's gallant struggle for national independence not far from NATO's eastern boundaries.

The Aftermath of Suez

By a fortuitous coincidence, the NATO Council Meeting which opened in Paris on 11 December, 1956 was scheduled to hear a report by a Committee of Three (the so-called "Three Wise Men") on non-military co-operation among the allies. This report placed great emphasis upon the need for closer political consultation within the Alliance, but it contained no recommendations for changes in the structure or the operating procedures of the North Atlantic Council. "There is a pressing requirement," said the Three, "for all members to make consultation in NATO an integral part of the making of national policy. Without this the very existence of the North Atlantic Community may be in jeopardy."[42]

---

[41] Paul-Henri Spaak, "The West in Disarray," *Foreign Affairs*, Vol. 35 (January, 1957), p. 187.

[42] Report of the Committee of Three on Non-Military Co-operation in NATO, reprinted from *The Department of State Bulletin* (7 January, 1957), Department of State Publication No. 6449.

The report included the following specific recommendations:

(a) Members should inform the Council of any development which significantly affects the Alliance. . . .

(b) Both individual member governments and the Secretary-General should have the right to raise for discussion in the Council any subject which is of common NATO interest and not of purely domestic character.

(c) A member government should not, without adequate advance consultation, adopt firm policies or make major political pronouncements on matters which significantly affect the Alliance or any of its members, unless circumstances make such prior consultation obviously and demonstrably impossible.

(d) In developing their national policies, members should take into consideration the interest and views of other governments, particularly those most directly concerned, as expressed in NATO consultation, even where no community of view or consensus has been reached in the Council.

(e) Where a consensus has been reached, it should be reflected in the formation of national policies. When for national reasons the consensus is not followed, the government concerned should offer an explanation to the Council.[43]

The US Secretary of State pointed out that the United States would not be able to bind itself rigidly with a promise to consult its Atlantic partners in the formulation of basic policy towards regions outside the NATO area. The United States, said Mr Dulles, had assumed obligations under treaties with thirty countries outside NATO and, in times of crisis, might have to move quickly to meet those commitments before it could explain its policy to the European

[43] Ibid., p. 6.

allies and seek their advice. "Implicit in the Secretary's remarks was an apparent assumption that the concern of NATO was limited to the geographic area defined by the treaty, a view not shared by other NATO members with overseas responsibilities."[44] Against a background of such reservations, the recommendations of the Three Wise Men were accepted in principle by the Council. Among these was a set of suggestions pertaining to efforts to settle inter-member disputes within the NATO framework before resorting to any other international agency and authorising the Secretary-General to tender his good offices in any internal alliance dispute.[45]

Fortunately for the West, NATO survived that grave crisis. The statesmen of the Atlantic nations seemed to realise that dangerous mistakes had been made and that the Alliance could not afford their repetition. On all sides, observers friendly to NATO warned against recriminatory arguments and tried to draw salutary lessons for the Alliance. The *Manchester Guardian Weekly*, for example, wrote as follows:

"What the crisis does show in high relief is, first, the deficiencies in NATO's conventional forces, and secondly the kind of new flanking threats which they might be called upon to meet. As the situation becomes more fluid on what used to be the frontiers of the Cold War, so the potential danger grows, and with it the need to strengthen the alliance. . . . But the crisis has done nothing to mend the gaps in NATO's defensive screen on the ground. . . . France's troops are still heavily committed in Algeria, while Western Germany's are now almost bound to come into being later than had been foreseen, with their usefulness impaired, besides, by smaller numbers and an inadequate term of service. . . . Events since July have made still more plain

[44] Stebbins, Richard P., *The United States in World Affairs, 1956*, Harper (New York, 1957), p. 374.

[45] Report . . . on Non-Military Co-operation, op. cit., pp. 6-7.

the need for mobile forces ready for action at the shortest notice. It is not just Britain and France who were caught unprepared, but NATO itself which needs to keep its forces ready and in trim."[46]

After the retirement of the British Prime Minister, Sir Anthony Eden in 1957, Washington undertook an attempt to restore cordial relations with London and Paris. The US government took steps to alleviate the fuel shortage of Western Europe which had resulted from the Suez crisis. The visits of Mr Duncan Sandys, the British Defence Minister, and Premier Guy Mollet to the United States aided in the healing process, and it seemed that complete frankness of communication was achieved in March at the Bermuda meeting of President Eisenhower and the new British Prime Minister, Mr Harold Macmillan. The Anglo-American co-operation which had long been the cornerstone of the Alliance was reinstated. But at the same time, the British were carrying out a fundamental reassessment of their strategic defence planning, and it can hardly be denied that this reassessment was a result not only of budgetary considerations but also of the humiliation felt by Britain at not being able to shape her own policy *vis-à-vis* the Middle East, where her interests were substantial. Instead of following the advice of those who concluded from the Suez crisis that the Western powers should increase their conventional capabilities, the British government, in the Defence White Paper of April, 1957, announced that it would reduce its troop commitments on the Continent and rely more heavily henceforth upon a nuclear deterrent. The British decided upon this change of policy without consulting either the NATO Council or the Western European Union Council. Within both bodies the omission gave rise to a certain amount of criticism.

[46] "European Command," *Manchester Guardian Weekly*, 22 November, 1956.

To placate her WEU partners, Britain agreed to defer half of her intended ground troop reductions until NATO could study the whole problem of nuclear and conventional defence strategies in view of prevailing economic factors. Despite disappointment over the fact that the British decision would make it more difficult than ever for NATO to achieve the Lisbon goals for conventional forces, the United States was not displeased with the British White Paper. Perhaps one reason for the tolerant American attitude was that the revision of strategic policy, which involved cuts in the size not only of the Army of the Rhine but also of the Royal Navy in the Atlantic, would bind the British more closely to the United States through NATO for the achievement of certain aspects of their security. But at the same time, the reorientation of British thinking was bound to cause misgivings among the Continental allies. It had already proved necessary to appoint a German general, Hans Speidel, onetime Chief-of-Staff to Rommel, to command the NATO forces along the central front. Now, in view of the British announcement, Chancellor Adenauer began to cite the need of West Germany for tactical nuclear weapons to assure her own defence in an environment of reduced conventional strength. These developments were to generate political attitudes which would cause headaches for the NATO leaders in the years ahead.

Disengagement Proposals

The Hungarian uprising in the autumn of 1956 led the Atlantic allies to re-examine their conception of the military threat posed by the presence of the Soviet Union in Eastern Europe. Heretofore, the Western powers had looked upon Soviet forces in Eastern Europe as a potential spearhead for a westward attack into Europe. After October, 1956, however, some in the West began to suspect that the Soviets' conventional strength in Eastern Europe had been overestimated. It was now clear that the divisions of the East European satellites could not be added to Soviet divisional strength in the event of an attack, but might actually have to be subtracted from the latter, since the USSR would have to divert some of its forces to holding national separatism in check, and to protect its own communications against hostile elements in the satellite populations.[47] The new situation raised a hope in certain Western quarters that a mutual withdrawal or thinning out of Soviet and NATO forces in Central Europe might be negotiated.

The suggestion of disengagement had been made officially by Sir Anthony Eden, at the Geneva Summit Conference on 18 July, 1955, when he said: "We should be ready to examine the possibility of a demilitarised area between East and West. . . . There is the prospect of an agreement about the total forces and armaments of the two groups both in Germany and in the countries neighbouring Germany. This would be subject to reciprocal supervision."[48] But nothing had come of Eden's suggestion. While the Soviets had shown some interest in disengagement as far back as 1947, the most significant indication of their official interest in such an arrangement (so far as alliance politics has been concerned) came in a note from the Soviet Premier, Mr Bulganin, to President Eisenhower on 17 November, 1956, just two weeks after the Soviets had dispatched their tanks to re-establish control over Budapest. The Soviets proposed that the Big Four, during 1957, should significantly reduce the armed forces which they maintained in other European countries, including one-third of their forces on German soil. Mr Bulganin said that the USSR was "prepared to consider"

[47] Cf. Cottrell, Alvin J., and Hahn, Walter F., "A New Strategy for Europe," *The Yale Review* (Autumn, 1957), Vol. 47, pp. 36-7.

[48] Text in *The Geneva Conference of Heads of Government*, 18-23 July, 1955, Department of State Publication 6044, p. 34

the possibility of permitting inspection by aerial photography up to a depth of 800 kilometres on either side of the line dividing East from West Germany.[49] This seemed to represent a partial acceptance of President Eisenhower's summit proposal for "open skies", although the aerial inspection would not cover Soviet territory. The concept of disengagement elicited considerable interest throughout the Western world. The most noteworthy disengagement proposal debated in the Atlantic Community was the one advanced by a former diplomatist, George F. Kennan, who had returned to private life during the Eisenhower Administration. In a series of lectures over the British Broadcasting Corporation (BBC), Mr Kennan suggested that he favoured the withdrawal of all American forces at least to areas west of Germany and Soviet forces to the USSR. The Kennan Plan was based on the assumption that the United States would continue to guarantee European security with its strategic nuclear deterrent which could be activated if the Soviets made any effort to re-enter Europe militarily.[50] In support of his proposal, Mr Kennan argued that disengagement offered the best hope for the evolution of Eastern Europe "towards institutions and social systems most suited to their own needs."[51] In fact one of the main arguments advanced by the proponents of disengagement was that it might re-establish the independence of the Eastern European states. Mr Kennan's proposals met stiff opposition from influential leaders within the Atlantic Community.

Some of the strongest arguments advanced against disengagement were those put forth by one of the founders of the NATO Alliance, former US Secretary of State Dean Acheson, who feared that even a partial pull-back would

[49] *New York Times,* 18 November, 1956.
[50] Cf. Howard, Michael, *Disengagement in Europe,* Penguin Books (London and Baltimore, 1958), pp. 32-3.
[51] *Russia, the Atom, and the West,* Harper (New York, 1958), p. 37.

lead inexorably to total US military withdrawal from Europe. Mr Acheson sharply attacked the assumption that the disengagement of Soviet and US troops in Europe would lead to freedom for Eastern Europe. He wrote: "There would be no power in Europe capable of opposing Russian will after the departure of the United States from the continent. . . . I cannot for the life of me see how the movement towards a greater degree of national identity in Eastern Europe is furthered by removing from the continent the only power capable of opposing the Soviet Union. . . . If the experience of 1956 had produced only the development in Poland or if the Hungarians had acted with as much restraint, it would be plain to all that the attraction of the power of the West, of the possibilities which its system opens to all, was proving very strong indeed."[52]

The year 1957 witnessed the beginning of a great debate on disengagement carried on against the background of a mounting Soviet propaganda campaign against NATO, against American bases and military presence in Europe, against the reappearance of Germany as a military power, and against the assertion by the Council in May that NATO had the right to possess whatever modern arms should be needed for its defence, meaning, of course, nuclear weapons.

In October, the Polish Foreign Minister, Adam Rapacki, unfolded before the United Nations General Assembly a plan for a denuclearised zone in Central Europe and spelt out the details in a memorandum to the powers concerned on 15 February, 1958. The Rapacki proposal referred to the territory of Poland, Czecho-Slovakia and East and West Germany. Within this zone nuclear weapons should be neither manufactured nor stockpiled, neither by the states named nor by the Four Powers. The latter powers would

[52] "The Illusion of Disengagement," *Foreign Affairs* (April, 1958), pp. 377-8.

promise not to transfer nuclear weapons to governments or other organs within the area, and would also promise not to use nuclear weapons against the territory of the zone. The states concerned would "undertake to create a system of broad and effective control in the area of the proposed zone. . . ."[53] This plan, broached by a government which had recently made friendly overtures towards the West, was immediately attractive to some Europeans as well as some Americans. For one thing it was not as vulnerable to criticism as the various schemes for disengagement. One of the most convincing arguments against disengagement was that it would remove the US military presence from the European continent whereas denuclearisation would not have this immediate effect, although conceivably it could set a precedent for more comprehensive demilitarisation proposals. Many were willing to examine the idea because it appeared much less ambitious than the more sweeping proposals for total disengagement. There can be little doubt that the view of many within the Atlantic Community was summed up succinctly by Michael Howard's statement: "Measures of local demilitarisation such as those proposed by Sir Anthony Eden in 1955 or Adam Rapacki in 1957, perhaps offer more immediate hopes of relaxing world tension than does disengagement which will raise immense political difficulties even in its most modest form."[54] Nevertheless, denuclearisation was not, in the view of many others, free from a number of serious political and military flaws. It appeared calculated, among other things, to forestall the execution of the decision made at the December, 1957, meeting of the North Atlantic Council to establish stocks of nuclear warheads in Europe and to place intermediate-range ballistic missiles at the disposal of the Supreme Allied Com-

[53] Hinterhoff, Eugène, *Disengagement,* Stevens and Sons, Ltd. (London, 1959), p. 235.
[54] *Disengagement in Europe,* op. cit., pp. 90-1.

mander.[55] The United States, in replying to the Polish Note on 3 May, 1958, rejected the Rapacki Plan for a number of reasons, including the following: (1) The plan failed to deal with the question of continued production of nuclear weapons by the existing nuclear powers and did not take into account the inadequacy of known scientific techniques for detecting the location of existing nuclear weapons. (2) Even if inspection were possible, such an agreement would endanger the security of the Western European countries, especially Germany, in view of the larger Soviet conventional forces deployed in the East. The United States feared that any denuclearisation of Central Europe might lead eventually to the weakening and perhaps the eventual disintegration of NATO, for it would greatly contract the defence-in-depth of the zone in which a nuclear strategy could be employed without violating the agreement. Denuclearisation, moreover, could conceivably bring on the neutralisation of West Germany. For the Federal Republic has been one of the staunchest supporters of NATO's tactical nuclear forward strategy and all suggestions for denuclearisation along the lines of the Rapacki Plan in Central Europe have thus far met adamant opposition from the West German government. In fact, there has been some suspicion that the leaders of the Soviet government became more interested in denuclearisation when they became fully aware of strong West German opposition to it. Furthermore, the idea of denuclearisation, although ostensibly a rather limited arms control proposal, was not entirely immune to the most serious criticism of disengagement, based upon concern over the implications of the withdrawal of US military forces from Europe. Henry A. Kissinger noted: "Once a

[55] See the text of the *Declaration and Communiqué of the December 1957 Ministerial Meeting* (Heads of Government), Appendix 5 in the *NATO Handbook, 1959*, especially p. 78.

denuclearised zone was established, it would be difficult to deal with Soviet pressures to expand it to include eventually the entire continent."[56] This, it was feared in some quarters, might lead in turn to the complete withdrawal of the US military presence from the European continent.[57]

While negotiations on disengagement and denuclearisation have thus far failed to obtain official approval within the Alliance, there can be little doubt that some support for these ideas still remains in Western Europe. It seemed inevitable that NATO would have to anticipate at some time in the future a resumption of the debate on the advisability of negotiating such arrangements with the Soviets. (See below, pp. 234-5, and pp. 239-41.)

INTRA-NATO DISPUTES

The latter half of the 1950s witnessed the emergence of three rather bitter and lengthy periods of international wrangling among members of the Alliance. The first of these centred on Iceland, and involved that country's relations with the United States and Britain. The second centred on Cyprus, and poisoned the relations of Great Britain, Greece and Turkey. The third centred on Algeria, and contributed to the alienation of France from American leadership within the Alliance. All three disputes, in varying degrees, took their toll of NATO solidarity.

[56] *The Necessity for Choice*, op. cit. (see p. 104, note), p. 155.

[57] On the other hand, the proponents of disengagement strongly favoured some form of limited disengagement plan. They hoped that such an arrangement would set a precedent. For example, Hugh Gaitskell, leader of the British Labour Party, regretted the West's complete rejection of the Rapacki Plan. He wrote: "One can hope that, despite the rejection of the Rapacki Plan, the West will be prepared to reconsider its attitude on this ['limited form of disengagement'] if and when the summit conference takes place." *Foreign Affairs* (July, 1958), Vol. 36, p. 556.

Iceland

Although Iceland maintains no armed establishment, it could justly lay claim to the title of being the "most north Atlantic country". Its major contribution to the strength of the Alliance was the air base at Keflavik, built by the United States at a cost of $200,000,000. But the activities of the base and of the 4,000 American troops stationed in Iceland came to be looked upon by many as an intrusion and an inconvenience, since they gave rise to overcrowded conditions, an upward price spiral and minor cultural irritations. On top of this, the country's exports of fish to Britain and the United States were declining. All of these unfavourable factors were exploited by nationalist, neutralist and communist elements within the body politic. The mounting national resentment, both real and artificially aggravated, resulted in an official act of protest in March, 1956, when the parliament of Iceland adopted a resolution calling for the withdrawal of all NATO forces from the national territory. The critical events in Hungary and the Middle East, however, as well as direct negotiations between the United States and Iceland, induced the government at Reykjavik to modify its stand. An agreement was reached on 6 December, 1956, under which the NATO base at Keflavik, an important source of income for the maintenance of Iceland's balance of payments, would continue to be operated as before.

Less than two years later, Iceland became seriously embroiled with Britain over the question of fishing rights. Forced to depend excessively upon the fishing industry for national livelihood, Iceland thought that an extension of her territorial waters for fishing purposes would enable her to exclude her European competitors from the fishing grounds off her own coasts and at the same time to improve her marketing position in such countries as Belgium, Germany and Britain. When the Geneva Conference on the Law of the

Sea, held from February to April, 1958, failed to produce an international agreement on the twelve-mile limit for fishing rights,[58] Iceland unilaterally extended her territorial waters jurisdiction on 1 September of that same year. Britain refused to recognise the validity of this act, and feelings between the two countries ran high. Moreover, the fact that the USSR supported the twelve-mile rule at Geneva, combined with the readiness of the Soviets to rescue Iceland's foundering export economy through the increased purchase of fish, rendered the island republic vulnerable to communist bloc political-economic influence. Once again, anti-NATO sentiments were rampant in Iceland. The legal and political issues dividing Britain and Iceland were never formally settled, but the tensions of the fishing war gradually subsided as the two countries continued to seek mutually satisfactory arrangements through diplomatic channels. One of the beneficial results of the dispute was a heightened awareness within the Alliance of the need for policies which would protect individual members such as Iceland against economic forays of the Soviet state trading monopoly.

Cyprus

More serious still than the problems of relations with Iceland was the dispute over Cyprus. At the time the British concluded the Suez Canal Base Agreement with Egypt in 1954, it was widely assumed that Cyprus would be built up into the major British military base in the Middle East. But the 400,000 Greek Cypriots, who made up four-fifths of the island's total population, had long aspired to *enosis*

[58] An account of the legal and political issues involved is presented by Johnson, D. H. N., "The Geneva Conference on the Law of the Sea," *The Yearbook of World Affairs, 1959,* London Institute of World Affairs, Stevens and Sons (London, 1959): Frederick A. Praeger (New York, 1959), especially pp. 79-85.

(union with Greece);[59] in 1954 they began to denounce British rule. The situation was further complicated by the presence on the island of 100,000 Turks, a minority whose fate was naturally a matter of concern to the government of Turkey. Turkey was also interested in the strategic aspects of the problem. As George Lenczowski writes: "The Turks were most anxious to have in their hinterland a strong allied base, from which, in case of emergency, aid and supplies could be rushed. Needless to say, the British . . . fully shared their views."[60]

By mid-1955, life on the island was marked by the terrorism of a guerrilla war carried on by the National Organisation of Cypriot Fighters (EOKA).[61] The three NATO Allies involved—Britain, Greece and Turkey—held a conference in London in September, 1955, but were unable to reach any agreement. When Archbishop Makarios, Ethnarch of Cyprus, and the recognised leader of the Cypriot movement, refused to call for the cessation of terrorist activity, the British deported him to the Seychelles in March, 1956. At this juncture, Greece recalled her ambassador to London and thereby created one of the most

[59] In ancient times Cyprus had been extensively colonised by Greece without ever becoming a constituent part of Hellenic Greece. Later, Cyprus was incorporated in the Byzantine Empire separately from Greece. Later still, in medieval times, it was part of the Ottoman Empire. It passed under British rule as a crown colony as a result of the Berlin Congress of 1878. The ostensible purpose of this transfer was to enable Great Britain to provide close strategic support to the "sick man of Europe," i.e., the Sultan, against rising pan-Slavic pressures from Russia. For a history of the Cypriot *enosis* movement in the twentieth century, see *Cyprus: Background to Enosis,* Memorandum of the Royal Institute of International Affairs (London, April, 1957).

[60] Lenczowski, George, *The Middle East in World Affairs,* Cornell University Press, 3rd ed. (Ithaca, 1962), p. 158.

[61] For an excellent discussion of guerrilla strategy and tactics in Cyprus see Alastos, Doros, *Cyprus Guerrilla,* Heinemann (London, 1960).

awkward diplomatic crises in the history of the Alliance.[62] Indeed, there were fears that Greece was in the process of reappraising her entire foreign policy, including her membership in NATO. The Secretary-General of NATO attempted in vain to persuade the parties that they should seek a solution to their differences within NATO; Britain and Turkey were willing, but Greece was not, probably because she feared that within NATO she would be at a disadvantage for three reasons: (1) there would be two NATO Allies against one; (2) the United States was likely to assign greater weight to British and Turkish interests than to those of Greece; and (3) a NATO solution would probably be worked out along the lines of strategic principles rather than according to the principle of national self-determination. The Greeks, therefore, preferred to carry their case to the United Nations General Assembly, where struggles for national causes were more popular. For the next two years, the issue of Cyprus arose intermittently within the United Nations. The British generally favoured tripartite administration of the island; the Greeks demanded independence; the Turks were not opposed to the British proposal but insisted that if the island were to be granted independence it should undergo partition.[63] In the UN debate, the British and Turkish resolutions called for negotiations, the Greek resolution for self-determination. The United States, caught in the web of conflicting interests among the three allies, usually abstained from voting in the General Assembly, much to the chagrin of the Greeks.

[62] Normal diplomatic relations were restored a year later, after the British released the Archbishop.

[63] There were at the time some unofficial suggestions to the effect that Cyprus might be made a "NATO trust territory." This solution, however, probably would have been rejected by the Cypriots and by Greece. Furthermore, many NATO statesmen would have been reluctant to embark upon a significant experiment in what hostile critics might call "NATO colonialism."

The impasse was broken at the December, 1958, meeting of the NATO Council, held at Paris. The Council members undoubtedly realised that the political difficulties generated by the Cyprus dispute were delaying agreements on the deployment of intermediate-range missiles which were then deemed essential to the security of Europe in view of the asserted Soviet ICBM (Inter-Continental Ballistic Missile) capability. During and after the Council meeting, the Secretary-General, M. Spaak, tendered his "good offices" and induced the three allies concerned to resume informal discussions in a quest for an amicable settlement "within the NATO family," as it were.[64] The Greeks apparently realised that they were losing their campaign to win American public support for *enosis*.[65] Greece and Turkey effected a rapprochement in the Zurich Agreement of 11 February, 1959, and a week later the British government, Archbishop Makarios and the leaders of the Turkish minority on Cyprus accepted the compromise plan. The Greek Cypriots renounced their demand for reunion with Greece, while the Turks renounced partition. Cyprus would become an independent republic with a Greek President and a Turkish Vice-President and the three powers would guarantee the independence of the former crown colony. Turkish minority rights were assured and both Greek and Turkish military units were invited to be stationed on the island. Britain acquired full and permanent sovereignty over two zones at Pergamos and Episcopi to be used as military bases, as well as the rights to use the port

[64] M. Spaak and the Council had done a good deal of prior diplomatic "spadework." See *Discussion on Cyprus in the North Atlantic Treaty Organisation, September-October 1958*, Command Paper 566, H.M.S.O. (London, 1959).

[65] "A newspaper interview with Makarios in which he was reported to have claimed that his independence proposal had the support of the United States government evoked a swift denial from the State Department."— "Cyprus: Conflict and Reconciliation," *The World Today*, Vol. 15 (April, 1959), p. 146.

facilities at Famagusta and the airport at Nicosia and to overfly the territory of Cyprus without restriction.[66] The Cyprus settlement, declared President Eisenhower, represented not only "a victory of common sense," but also "an imaginative and courageous act of statesmanship which cannot fail to strengthen and encourage the whole NATO alliance."[67] The agreement brought to an end four years of bitter and enervating recriminations and paved the way for the repair of NATO's defence posture in the eastern Mediterranean.

Algeria

Algeria was in many respects the most complex of the international conflict situations to confront the Western coalition during the latter 1950s. With Morocco and Tunisia having been converted from French protectorates into independent states, Algeria was France's last remaining gateway to her possessions in Equatorial Africa. It was also the last European territorial foothold on the southern shores of the Mediterranean, once Britain had withdrawn from the Canal Zone. Furthermore, France had always looked upon Algeria as *sui generis*—being in an entirely different category from Tunisia and Morocco. When the latter areas had been protectorates, their external relations, defence and trade policies had been regulated by Paris as foreign matters, primarily through the Foreign Ministry. But internally their social structures always remained essentially Arabic. Algeria, on the other hand, was always taken to be an integral part of metropolitan France, and its departments along the coast came under the jurisdiction of the Minister of the Interior.

---

[66] Text of British White Paper of 23 February, 1959, Setting Forth Agreements Ending Dispute Over Cyprus, in *New York Times*, 24 February, 1959.

[67] Quoted in Stebbins, Richard P., *The United States in World Affairs 1959*, for the Council on Foreign Relations, Harper (New York, 1960), p. 191

At the time the Algerian rebellion broke out, there were about a million *colons* in the country, mostly of French extraction, compared to a population of eight million Arabs. Under both the Third and Fourth Republics, Algeria sent deputies to the French parliament. However imperfect this representative system may have been, the French regarded it as symbolic of the fact that all Algerians were French citizens. Until well after the Second World War, neither Left nor Right in France had ever been willing to admit a distinction between the soil of France and the soil of Algeria. Prior to colonisation by the French in 1830, Algeria had no boundaries, no history, no organised population, no legal-administrative order, not even a name. The French *colons* had brought their own national consciousness with them; later, the Moslems who were educated in the metropolitan country imbibed French political and legal ideas and developed a sense of nationality which they had not known before. Hence, in one way or another, the French were the real architects of Algerian nationalism.[68]

In order to contend with the guerrilla threat posed by an estimated 20,000 *fellaghas* of the Algerian National Liberation Front (FLN), the French were compelled to siphon off some 400,000 of their troops from the NATO structure on the Continent for duty in North Africa, leaving little more than cadres along the French sector of the Central Front. Just at that time, the Western allies were trying to achieve an adequate level of ground forces to permit greater defensive flexibility as to the choice of nuclear or conventional strategies in the event of a Soviet challenge. The Algerian rebellion, to the extent that it caused the diversion of French forces from NATO's European theatre, redounded to the

---

[68] The authors have analysed the historical background in "Algeria: A Case Study in the Evolution of a Colonial Problem," in Strausz-Hupé, Robert, and Hazard, Harry W., editors, *The Idea of Colonialism,* Frederick A. Praeger, (New York, 1958).

strategic advantage of the Soviet Union. It was to the Soviets' interest to see prolonged a guerrilla war for national liberation which served to immobilise a large Western conventional force, to furnish grist not only for communist propaganda mills but for neutralists and anticolonialists everywhere, and to keep the Western Alliance in a state of diplomatic turmoil. Although the Soviet Union refrained from formally intervening in French affairs by overtly supplying arms to the FLN, the latter was indirectly assisted by Radio Moscow, by Soviet diplomacy at the United Nations and by the shipment of arms from the Soviet bloc to Egypt, which in turn made at least some military equipment available to the Algerian rebels.

The United States, which had been very pleased with the French decision to guide Tunisia and Morocco towards independent status, was troubled over the dilemmas which the Algerian War raised for NATO and for American policy in the Arab world. In the eyes of many Americans, the French appeared to be denying patently the very ideals of "Liberty, Equality and Fraternity" which *la mission civilisatrice* was supposed to have brought to Algeria. French officials, for their part, frequently accused the United States of failing to understand the rationale of France's Algerian policy. In their view, the American anti-colonial tradition prevented many US policy makers from examining the Algerian problem in the light of cold strategic realities, without the colouration of emotion and sentiment. Some Frenchmen suspected the United States of trying to curry favour with Arab nationalists for the purpose of replacing France as the major outside power in North Africa. In an effort to allay such suspicions, the US Ambassador to Paris, C. Douglas Dillon, declared that the French quest for "liberal solutions" to the Algerian problem would receive the diplomatic support of the Eisenhower Administration.[69] But the ensuing years found the

[69] *New York Times*, 21 March, 1957.

United States frequently caught in a vice between its allegiance to a major ally and its attempts to maintain cordial relations with the Arabs. At times, the United States seemed relatively sympathetic to the French argument that North Africa was the southern flank of NATO and that if this region were allowed to fall under the pro-Soviet form of Arab nationalism which Nasser appeared to espouse in the years from 1955 to 1958, the Atlantic allies would sooner or later lose every one of their bases in Morocco, Libya and Tunisia and conceivably might some day confront a network of Soviet bases along the southern and eastern shores of the Mediterranean. At other times, the United States was bothered by actions which the French took against such pro-Western Arab states as Tunisia. For a while, President Habib Bourguiba of Tunisia apparently entertained hopes of building a North African Federation of Morocco, Tunisia and an autonomous Algeria which might undertake an association with NATO and a partnership for economic development based upon the French franc.[70] The US Department of State was deeply disturbed by the French military attack, in February, 1958, upon the Tunisian village of Sakiet near the frontier, which the French believed Algerian rebels were using as a sanctuary. When it appeared that the United States might furnish arms to Tunisia, it was France's turn to be upset. And so it went on, with American policy seeming to oscillate between the exigencies of Alliance solidarity and the desire to remain on good terms with the emergent nations. President Eisenhower summed it up when he said: "We do have a NATO ally, and we also are great friends of the North African area, and so it is a very hard

[70] See the article by Anthony Nutting, former British Minister of State for Foreign Affairs, in the *New York Herald Tribune,* 17 February, 1958; and Hahn, Lorna, "Last Chance in North Africa," *Foreign Affairs,* Vol. XXXVIII (January, 1958).

problem and one that holds the attention of the Administration, each day."[71]

A nadir in Franco-American relations on this issue was reached in December, 1958, when the United States abstained from voting on a General Assembly resolution which would have recognised the right of the Algerian people to independence. The newly installed French government of President de Gaulle looked upon this as tantamount to a betrayal. Yet, in the same year, the United States helped France to obtain more than half a billion dollars in financial assistance in order to overcome the economic troubles which had been caused in large part by prosecuting the war in Algeria. The effect of this policy was not lost upon the Arabs, who charged the United States with extending half-hearted symbolic support to the Arab cause while furnishing tangible support to the French. In August, 1959, the Conference of Independent African States meeting in Monrovia, Liberia, appealed formally to NATO "with a view to urging France to desist from using in Algeria arms supplied by that organisation for defensive purposes."[72] The French government rejoined that NATO furnished no support except "incidentally", in so far as French troops were withdrawn from NATO and dispatched to Algeria with equipment previously issued to them as NATO forces. The Arabs, of course, were not able to appreciate the subtlety of this distinction, but in support of it the French were able to point to the fact that the metropolitan departments of Algeria were specifically named in the NATO Treaty as part of the area to be defended against attack.

The US attitude towards French objectives in Algeria

[71] Quoted in Stebbins, Richard P., *The United States in World Affairs 1958,* for the Council on Foreign Relations, Harper (New York, 1959), p. 245.

[72] Cited in *Algerian Developments 1959,* ed. by A. G. Mezerik, International Review Service, Vol. VI, No. 55, p. 17.

became more benevolent following President de Gaulle's speech of 16 September, 1959, in which he promised that within four years the Algerian people would be allowed to choose freely from three alternatives : (1) complete secession from France and the severance of all economic ties; (2) complete political integration with the metropolitan country; and (3) a locally autonomous Algeria, closely associated with France in regard to economic development, education, defence and foreign policy.[73] The US government gave its tacit support to the French policy of employing military power to bring about a "pacification" of the country prior to, or simultaneously with, the conduct of negotiations concerning Algeria's political future. The Evian Accord of March, 1962, embodied essentially the third alternative listed above.[74] The agreement concluded between the French government and the FLN did not settle all the questions pertaining to the future orientation of North Africa. But at least it offered hope that some French forces would again become available for the defence of continental Europe. Meanwhile, however, the Algerian conflict had contributed to a rather serious scarring of NATO's political face and gave impetus to French particularist tendencies which would long trouble the Atlantic Alliance.

THE ALLIANCE IN THE SIXTIES

The early years of NATO's second decade found the Western Alliance, like all voluntary coalitions of independent states since the time of the ancient Greeks, plagued with certain recurring political difficulties. With pacifist and neutralist tendencies growing within the bodies politic of many states outside the Sino-Soviet alliance system, it was to be expected that the direct criticism and suspicion of NATO's policies

[73] The *New York Times*, 17 September, 1959.
[74] Ibid., 11 March, 1962.

and motivations would become more noticeable, especially in view of an increasingly sophisticated communist propaganda campaign against the West's joint military defence efforts. Not a few of those who demanded less emphasis upon military programmes and greater stress upon such devices of competitive co-existence as foreign aid, information programmes and cultural exchanges often seemed to overlook the fundamental fact that it was NATO's stance of preparedness-with-restraint which had compelled the leading communist powers to eschew military provocations in favour of more subtle methods of presenting their international challenges. Perhaps more serious than pacifist demands for unilateral disarmament was the basic disagreement between "nuclearists" and "non-nuclearists" over the optimum strategies to be pursued for the defence of Europe; this particular argument was not merely a technical one, since it had far-reaching political implications for Alliance solidarity in dealing with such questions as the proper response to a Soviet move against West Berlin.

These were not by any means the only bones of contention. The Atlantic Allies were divided on several other important issues as well. The efforts of Britain to negotiate entry into the European Economic Community encountered an obstacle in the policy of France. French attitudes towards both European integration and the relationship of Europe to the United States were a cause of concern to European federalists and Washington policy-makers alike. The conflicting claims on the hearts of many of the West German people of allegiance to NATO and the desire for the restoration of national unity further complicated NATO's existential situation. Other members of the Alliance experienced, in their continued adherence to NATO, political difficulties peculiar to themselves. Outside the area of common defence concerns defined in the North Atlantic Treaty, the Allies encountered political misunderstandings and conflicts of interest which not infrequently led to bitter internal recriminations. Finally, the Allies were not always agreed as to the best approach to be made towards the adversary whose behaviour had called NATO into being as an historic entity on the international scene. Since it is impossible to analyse in detail all of the political problems confronting NATO in this decade, only a few of the more important ones can be selected for discussion.

During the years 1960-2, Britain remained, as in the past, an intimate partner of the United States. Mr Macmillan's government continued the policy of maintaining an independent contribution to the Western nuclear deterrent and sought to co-ordinate closely the planning of Bomber Command operations with that of the US Strategic Air Command. At the same time, Britain of all the NATO Allies seemed more openly anxious to promote an understanding between the Soviet Union and NATO on a slowing down of the arms race and the achievement of stability in the European theatre. Generally speaking, the British government appeared to be more interested than most other NATO governments in the quest for a nuclear test ban, in "summit diplomacy" as a means of resolving some if not all East-West political differences, and in negotiations with the Soviets on Berlin as a logical first step towards the reduction of tensions in Europe. The British and the United States did not always see eye-to-eye, however, on the formulation of their international policies. They agreed to differ, for example, over the important question of the proper policy to be adopted towards China. They also came to a slight parting of the ways over the best method of handling the crisis which arose in the Congo in the summer of 1960. Nevertheless, NATO's two major English-speaking partners kept their lines of political communication fully open and made a steady effort to co-ordinate their foreign policies as closely as possible, after comparing the losses suffered at Suez with the gains reaped from the joint Anglo-American intervention in the Middle East in the summer of 1958. The

United States was quite pleased with Whitehall's application for admission to the European Economic Community in 1961. American policy-makers apparently hoped that a closer political and economic relationship between Britain and the Continent would provide a steadying influence upon a Western Europe which had fluctuated rather unsteadily between ideological extremes in recent decades. There was also reason to believe that the forging of more intimate ties between the Six and the country whose political institutions were the most closely related to those of the United States would help to guarantee the permanence of the transatlantic union against all temptations towards a European Third Force.

Meanwhile, the opening years of this decade found France pursuing policies which prompted some observers to wonder whether there was any diminution in her enthusiasm for the Atlantic Alliance as now constituted. President de Gaulle strove to restore his country's prestige as a power to be reckoned with in world affairs. Although France, throughout the postwar period, had been included as one of the four principal participants in international disarmament negotiations, de Gaulle expressed the conviction of many of his countrymen that no nation could hope to wield substantial influence in the international arena unless it possessed its own nuclear arsenal. French officials apparently were convinced that one of the main reasons why Britain had long enjoyed a privileged position within the Alliance was the fact that she possessed such capabilities. A few months after coming to power in the summer of 1958, de Gaulle had made overtures towards a co-ordinated Anglo-French-US global strategic policy, but his bid had met a poor reception in Washington and London. Hence the French President pressed forward the national policy of building an independent *force de frappe* (later officially renamed the *force de dissuasion*). The United States, fearful that further nuclear proliferation would render even more complex the already difficult task of achieving workable arms control, continued to withhold atomic information from France. The French interpreted this US policy as a deliberate effort to delay the accomplishment of the objective on which they had fixed their sights which would compel them to waste their resources needlessly. In 1959, they had shown their displeasure by withdrawing French ships from assignment to the Allied Naval Forces in the Mediterranean, by vetoing the integration of French fighter planes in NATO's air defence system, and by refusing to permit the United States to emplace medium-range missiles and atomic stockpiles on French territory. As the year 1962 drew to a close, these policies of holding back on NATO co-operation—symbols of official French pique—were still in force. France, moreover, was still boycotting the Eighteen-Nation Disarmament Conference at Geneva, in whose success the United States and Britain were keenly interested. Within Europe, France appeared to be stiffening her position in the Brussels negotiations regarding the terms for Britain's entry into the Common Market, while trying to lay the foundations of a Franco-German political partnership within Western Europe and within NATO. But few observers doubted that, when crucial issues arose involving the fundamental defence interests of the Atlantic Community, France would stand loyally with her allies, as she did during the Cuban blockade in October, 1962. At the same time, it was widely recognised that some political adjustments would have to be made, perhaps in the direction of a European nuclear deterrent, in order to reduce the disparities in the status of Britain and France within the Alliance and to provide the conditions for further progress towards European integration within a NATO framework.

The future of Germany remains one of the most critical questions in international relations. Within recent years, the Soviets have carried on intensive propaganda against what they call "neo-fascist militarism" in the Federal Republic. The emergence of General Adolf Heusinger as head of the NATO Military Committee in Washington in 1960 was the occasion for an especially vituperative outburst. The communist propaganda campaign was clearly designed to arouse suspicions among the NATO allies of a German desire to dominate the alliance, to forestall a settlement of the Berlin question, to acquire atomic arms and even to provoke a war with the USSR for the purpose of bringing about a reunification of the country. As indicated previously in Chapter 2, the separation of West Germany from NATO ranks as a major Soviet objective in Europe. In pursuit of this objective, the Soviets seek to promote anti-American feelings among the Germans, and anti-German feelings among the NATO allies, especially the United States and Britain. The Soviets undoubtedly would like to induce the Federal Republic to seek national unification through such proposals for demilitarisation in Central Europe as nuclear disengagement and eventual neutralisation.

Yet, in spite of persistent Soviet efforts, the Federal Republic has displayed an unswerving loyalty to the Alliance. To be sure, Dr Adenauer was not always in full agreement with the approach taken by the United States and Britain towards Berlin negotiations with the Soviets. Some Germans have at times undoubtedly feared that Washington and London might be contemplating an accommodation with Moscow at their country's expense. But, for the most part, the Federal Republic has reposed its trust in the solidarity of the coalition on basic issues. True, there have been occasions when official German behaviour has appeared to the allies to be imprudent, e.g., Bonn's efforts to acquire military training bases in Spain, Ambassador Kroll's private conversations with Mr Khrushchev and the manner in which the government handled the *Der Spiegel* affair in the autumn of 1962. But these were relatively minor squalls on what has been an otherwise tranquil sea. Germany, over the course of nearly a decade, has been a responsible and stable ally, despite the fact that the decision to integrate the Federal Republic into the military, economic and political structures of the Six and of the Atlantic Community has contributed towards a deepening and a hardening of the nation's division. If *der Alte* was attracted to the idea of a German-French political alliance, perhaps largely to please President de Gaulle in his desire to offset what he deemed the special Anglo-American relationship, it should be remembered that Adenauer for many years had also proved himself the staunchest advocate of NATO military integration. During 1962, the German leader tended to side with de Gaulle in his sceptical attitude towards the British application for entry into EEC. But there was little reason to doubt that if and when British admission could be arranged on mutually satisfactory terms, Adenauer and the great majority of the people of the Federal Republic would welcome the new member. Finally, there were grounds for expecting that if a European nuclear deterrent under multilateral control should eventually come into existence, the Bonn government, whether it be under Christian Democratic or Socialist leadership, would insist that such a deterrent be organised in such a way as would not weaken the mutual security ties which now bind West Germany to the United States through NATO.

Not only the major powers, but other NATO allies had their share of political problems which gave rise in the early 1960s to resentments, misgivings and troubled relations within the Alliance. Italy's "opening to the left," for example, i.e., the coalition between the Italian Christian Democrats under Amintore Fanfani and the Socialists of Pietro Nenni, caused observers in other capitals to wonder whether Italian policy might shift perceptibly away from commitment to the

Atlantic Community towards neutralism.[75] In addition to
this possibility, Italy and Austria from 1960 onwards were
involved in a bitter local dispute over the Alto Adige region
in Northern Italy. Austria, of course, was not a member of
NATO, but she was a member of the OECD and an applicant
for associated status with the EEC. The Alto Adige controversy, which was tantamount to a revival of nineteenth-
century nationalist rivalry, was bound to be a source of
embarrassment to NATO in its efforts to promote closer
economic and political co-operation within the West.

Belgium experienced a major political-economic crisis
during the early 1960s as a result of events in the Congo
and these events had repercussions throughout the entire
Alliance. The Belgian grant of independence to the Congo
on 30 June, 1960, was premature in so far as the Belgians
themselves had failed to prepare the Congolese for the sudden
assumption of responsibilities, and the result was political
chaos. Here was an excellent example of dismal consequences flowing from a reluctance on the part of the NATO
Council, during the 1950s, to discuss frankly the question
of European colonial policies and objectives. Admittedly,
the subject was a delicate one, in view of the divergence of
opinion which prevailed between Europe and the United
States, but the Council's discreet silence paid poor dividends.
In the diplomatic imbroglio which accompanied the Congo
crisis, it was sometimes hinted vaguely that Belgium had
acted precipitately in granting independence partly because
she had felt herself to be under the increasing pressure of
anti-colonial sentiment in the United States, but there was
no concrete evidence that American policy had figured in

---

[75] In the late spring of 1963, following the publication of
the Papal Encyclical, *Pacem in Terris,* there were some fears
that Italian Socialists and leftist Christian Democrats might
be drifting into a coalition with the Communists on the disarmament issue that would jeopardise NATO. See Edmond
Taylor, "A New Popular Front?" *The Reporter,* 20 June, 1963.

Belgium's decision. Once developments in the Congo were catapulted into the centre of the world's stage, however, they did provide occasions for political controversies among the Allies. The Belgians complained that the United States abandoned them in the United Nations debates and voting. France and Portugal sided with the Belgians in attempting to limit narrowly the role of the United Nations Emergency Force as a reunifier of the fragmented Congo. In time, even the British began to draw away from the US policy of relying almost exclusively upon the resolutions of the General Assembly for the purpose of solving the Congo's troubles. In the eyes of many Europeans, the United States showed greater solicitude over the political opinion of the neutralists than it did over the interests of Europeans in Africa. The Congo crisis showed that, although the Western powers had made considerable progress towards completely liquidating their former colonial empires, the process of decolonisation could still cause a good deal of difficulty within NATO. On this score, the Portuguese experience left no doubt whatsoever.

One of the bitterest political disputes to rend NATO in recent years arose between Portugal and the United States. The Portuguese, virtually the last Europeans to hold out in the struggle to preserve overseas possessions, were extremely disappointed over the lack of diplomatic support and sympathetic understanding accorded them by their principal NATO ally. The dispute originated in January, 1961, not over a colonial question but over a bizarre episode involving the seizure on the high seas of the Portuguese ship *Santa Maria* by political opponents of President Salazar's regime. The Portuguese government was irked that the United States Navy, acting under instructions from Washington, exhibited greater concern for the welfare of the ship's passengers than for Portugal's sovereign right to retrieve the vessel and punish

the "pirates". Lisbon's resentment mounted when, after
the outbreak of an insurrection in Portuguese Angola on
15 March, 1961, the United States voted against Portugal on
a UN resolution proposing an inquiry into the latest African
case of anti-colonial troubles. The United States obviously
felt it necessary to dissociate itself from Portugal and other
European powers which were pressing overseas territorial
claims[76] because of its traditional sympathy for independence
movements and in order to be able to meet the USSR on the
propaganda battleground of anti-colonialism. But for striking
a pro-African posture at Portugal's expense, the United States
had to bear many weeks of vehement denunciation in the
Portuguese press and in Portugal's foreign radio broadcasts.
Portuguese disaffection with the Alliance was further aggravated by the Western reaction to the Indian attack on Goa.
The Portuguese government's anger was in no way assuaged
by the "charterial scolding" administered to India in the
United Nations by the US delegate, Adlai Stevenson. Nor
was Portugal able to derive any comfort from the attitude
of her oldest ally: the British government had made it clear
in advance that it would take no action against another member of the Commonwealth. During the years 1961 and 1962,
the Salazar government took a second hard look at the
Alliance. Portugal's principal contribution to NATO, apart
from a modest force commitment and the advantages of her
geographical location, took the form of a grant of base rights
to the United States in the Azores, and the Angola and Goan
crises prompted hints that these rights might not be renewed
at all or, at least, only after hard bargaining. At one point,
there was even some fear that Portugal might withdraw from
NATO. Although her departure might not materially weaken

[76] The Netherlands government was far from satisfied
with US policy in the Dutch-Indonesian dispute over
West Irian, i.e., the area of New Guinea administered by
the Dutch but claimed as part of the national territory by
the Sukarno government in Indonesia.

the military position of NATO, it would nevertheless represent a distinct political and psychological loss in terms of the dynamic image of the Alliance, much as a single national defection from the Soviet bloc would mar the dynamism of the communist camp, or the expulsion or resignation of a member of the United Nations would be taken as a bad omen, as though the organisation had passed its historic peak.

Alliance problems have not been confined to the European side of the Atlantic. Within recent years, many Canadians have become critical of the close political and military relationship prevailing between their country and the United States. There seems to be a growing fear that Canadian policy is so dominated by Washington that the nation's independence may be jeopardised. This fear, to a large extent, springs from a certain amount of Canadian resentment against the cultural standardisation which the peoples of North America are experiencing; against expanding American investment in Canada and the inescapable dependence of the latter upon the US market; and against the system of North American air defence (NORAD) which, in the view of some Canadian observers, may some day unnecessarily implicate their own territory in a Soviet-American nuclear war.[77] But, in spite of these misgivings, the overwhelming majority of the Canadian people and their leaders remain firmly committed to the Atlantic Alliance. "The necessity for the nuclear deterrent and joint defence," writes a political scientist from the University of Western Ontario, "has long been accepted by most Canadians; indeed they take considerable pride in having suggested NATO. . . . If independence is thought to be the right to control one's own destiny, it is hard to see

[77] Lyon, Peyton V., "Problems of Canadian Independence," *International Journal*, Vol. XVI (Summer, 1961), pp. 250-4.

how Canada's independence could be enhanced by a withdrawal from either NATO or NORAD. Rather it would
mean the abandonment of whatever influence we now
possess over the most vital decisions having to do with
Canada's defence."[78] Early in 1963, when criticism of
Canada's nuclear defence policy by the United States Department of State helped to precipitate the downfall of the
Diefenbaker government, it was clear that US-Canadian
relations were henceforth likely to be characterised by
increasingly subtle and sometimes tension-ridden difficulties.

Despite its intramural political tensions, NATO has proceeded, year after year, to provide for the defence of the
West. On the eve of 1963, American military forces were
still deployed in strength on the soil of the European allies.
The Benelux countries were still among the most ardent
advocates of a joint Atlantic defence effort, as were Norway
and Denmark, notwithstanding the sporadic temptations of
some groups within the latter countries to replace their
NATO ties with a form of Scandinavian regional defence
system.[79]

The Cuban crisis evoked from NATO a rather remarkable
degree of political unity, even though the allies were not consulted in advance concerning President Kennedy's decision
to institute a naval blockade for the purpose of interdicting
Soviet or Soviet-chartered ships bearing missiles and other
offensive weapons to Cuba. It was only a matter of hours
before the President announced his intentions to the
American public that Dean Acheson, the original designer

[78] Lyon, Peyton V., op. cit., p. 254. Melvin Conant has
written a thorough account of Canada's strategic role in
NATO, entitled *The Long Polar Watch: Canada and the
Defense of North America*, for the Council on Foreign
Relations, Harper (New York, 1962).
[79] See Lindgren, Raymond E., "International Co-operation
in Scandinavia," *The Yearbook of World Affairs 1959*,
London Institute of World Affairs, Stevens and Sons
(London, 1959): Frederick A. Praeger (New York, 1959).

of the US commitment under NATO, arrived in Europe to explain the impending action. Perhaps the US government had concluded that unilateral measures were necessary in view of at least two factors: (1) its patchy success in the efforts several weeks earlier to enlist the co-operation of the allies on the question of Cuban shipping; and (2) the unexpected speed with which the USSR had carried out the missile build-up in Cuba.[80] If some allied statesmen felt disappointed at the lack of advance consultation, they refrained from making acrimonious public statements. Within a surprisingly short time, they pledged unreserved support for the US move. Some could scarcely conceal their satisfaction upon learning that the United States recognised the unavoidable necessity, under certain circumstances, of resorting to unilateral strategic initiatives. Within twenty-four hours, all the NATO member delegations in the United Nations had received their instructions to vote for the US resolution which was to be introduced that evening.[81] Generally speaking, the reaction in Western Europe reflected a widespread consensus that, whatever risks were posed by President Kennedy's decision, they would have to be faced sooner or later and were the less grave for having been

[80] Walter Lippman gave the following reason for US failure to consult its NATO allies prior to taking action in the crisis: "As I understand what went on, our allies were not consulted in the Cuban crisis because of the belief that the risk of war would have been much increased. The American intention was to react sharply, but react for a limited aim and limited means. . . . Had this intention become known there was a probability that the Soviet government would take the initiative either by proclaiming defiantly the presence of the missiles or by denouncing the proposed quarantine as an act of 'piracy'." Mr. Lippmann stated that had this happened, both the United States and the USSR "would have been committed to a collision course." —*Washington Post Outlook*, 2 December, 1962, p. 31.

[81] "Cuban Crisis: A Step-by-Step Review," *New York Times,* 3 November, 1962.

faced sooner. On 27 October, 1962, Mr Khrushchev attached
a condition to the Soviet evacuation of missiles from Cuba,
viz., a corresponding liquidation of the US missile bases
in Turkey. But NATO representatives in Paris, as well as
US policy-makers in Washington, immediately recognised
the Soviet proposal as an attempt to appeal to world opinion
and sow discord within the ranks of the allies. Max Frankel
gave the following incisive account: "It was pointed out that
the United States missile-bases in Turkey were put there on
the openly proclaimed decision of the heads of government
of the NATO states in December, 1957. Further, it was
recalled, this was in direct response to repeated threats of
employment of Soviet missiles against the West. It would be
intolerable, in the opinion of some Western diplomats, to
equate this action with the clandestine installation of Soviet
missiles in Cuba at a time when the highest Soviet officials
were proclaiming that none but defensive arms were being
supplied to Cuba."[82]

There was a widespread expectation, following the sub-
sidence of international tensions in the Cuban crisis, that
conditions were ripening for working out a comprehensive
understanding on a number of disputed issues between the
United States and the Soviet Union, or between NATO and
the Warsaw Pact countries. Perhaps some important lessons
had been learned from the dangerous strategic confrontation which occurred in the Atlantic waters around Cuba.
But it must be remembered that Cuba may have highlighted
the profound risks of international politics in the thermo-
nuclear age; it contributed little, however, by way of an

[82] *New York Times,* 28 October, 1962. [*Editor's note:*
Following the crisis, and despite its unwillingness to appear
to be involved in a "trade" with the Soviets, the United
States did announce that, in keeping with a programme of
modernisation decided upon before Cuba, it was, with the
concurrence of Turkey and Italy, substituting Polaris missiles
for the intermediate-range Thors and Jupiters previously
based in those countries.]

answer to the complexities of the problem of armaments and national security, or regional security, confronting the world in the 1960s.

The three major Western powers—the United States, Britain and France—have participated in thousands of disarmament negotiating sessions with the Soviet Union during the last decade-and-a-half. All four governments have accumulated vast experience through the lengthly discussions of the technical problems posed by plans for general and complete disarmament. The three NATO allies are fully aware that the wide-sweeping disarmament plans now resting on the international conference table at Geneva would, if accepted, mean the end of NATO as a defence organisation. Sir Winston Churchill once said: "We arm to parley." The parley has gone on for many years, and may continue for many more, for, as the NATO governments recognise only too clearly, the problem of disarmament is not in the first instance a technical problem of devising the proper international control organisation, inspection systems, sanctions against violation, and effective world police forces. The arms problem is primarily a political problem. The critical question is not whether general and complete disarmament is possible, but whether the political and ideological differences which currently divide the world into two hostile systems can be composed in a mutually acceptable manner which does not raise the issue of survival for the most deeply cherished human values of either side. Such a question may require many years or decades to answer. And, until it can be answered in the affirmative, responsible Western leaders are in little doubt that NATO, as the shield of the West, will endure.

The question of US policy with respect to nuclear sharing became the most pressing political issue within the Alliance as 1962 gave way to 1963. The basic position of the Kennedy Administration was that, since the American nuclear guarantee was sufficient for the defence of Europe, there was no real military necessity for creating a separate Western European deterrent. But the United States also recognised that the Europeans, for political reasons, were bent upon acquiring a significant voice in the control of the West's nuclear power and strategy. The Europeans looked upon the development of indigenous nuclear capabilities as the only sure way of being admitted to the inner sanctum where nuclear policies are made. The United States, for its part, regarded independent national deterrents across the Atlantic as posing a threat to the "indivisibility of the nuclear deterrent" and increasing the dangers of nuclear war.

President Kennedy, therefore, made an effort to meet the political desires of the Europeans and at the same time to head off the proliferation of national deterrents. In his "Declaration of Interdependence" on 4 July, 1962, he said that the United States was prepared to assist in the creation of a European deterrent provided that the Europeans could agree among themselves on a system of unified controls.[83] The one fear of many American policy-makers stemmed from the possibility, however remote, that the creation of a European deterrent might set the stage for the eventual emergence of a Third Force which would seek to play the role of balancer between the United States and the Soviet Union. To prevent such a schism within the Atlantic Community, the Kennedy Administration seemed to prefer a NATO multilateral deterrent rather than a purely European deterrent. Furthermore, in the first half of 1963, there was little evidence that the Europeans were close to political unity. Hence the fulfilment of President Kennedy's conditions did not appear to be in sight.

The issue came to a head in December, 1962, when the United States cut from the defence budget appropriations for the development of Skybolt, a 1,200-mile air-to-ground missile on the purchase of which the Macmillan government

[83] *New York Times*, 5 July, 1962.

had staked the future (for at least five or six years) of Britain's V-bomber force. There is no need to examine the details of the Skybolt controversy except to say that this particular weapons-project gave rise to strategic, technical and economic difficulties which, if not insuperable, were nevertheless substantial enough to warrant a thorough reassessment. But there is little doubt that the whole affair could have been handled better, both in Washington and in London. The episode demonstrated vividly how policy decisions which may be necessitated in a rapidly changing technological-strategic environment can place severe strains upon the NATO Alliance. The British were made to feel, at least for a brief time, that they were being unceremoniously expelled from the "nuclear club" as the result of a unilateral American decision which, assuming its necessity, should have been a joint Anglo-American decision.

Fortunately for the Anglo-American bond, efforts were immediately made to correct the damage done. President Kennedy and the British Prime Minister, Mr Macmillan, meeting at Nassau in December, 1962, reached agreement on a plan where the United States would furnish to Britain Polaris missiles which would, within five years, be integrated into a multinational NATO submarine force. According to the Nassau Pact, the United States would furnish only the delivery vehicle, i.e., the Polaris missile. The submarines and the nuclear warheads would be furnished by the British. A similar offer was made by the United States to France. Perhaps the most significant aspect of this plan for a NATO Polaris force is the provision which allows the components contributed by member nations to be withdrawn at times when the "supreme national interest" requires it. Such a formula was intended to enable the British to continue their "independent contribution to the deterrent", which would remain under the constitutional control of the government. The formula undoubtedly was devised also to appeal to President de Gaulle, who was not expected to agree to the irrevocable integration of national forces. The French President seemed at first to be interested in the plan, but in January, 1963 he rejected it, perhaps in part because it did not go far enough in meeting his demands for French participation in the control of the West's nuclear strategy. De Gaulle at the time appeared more interested in immediate acquisition of nuclear warheads than in obtaining a delivery vehicle half-a-decade later. Furthermore, as Raymond Aron suggested, the Nassau Agreement was interpreted by de Gaulle as another example of Britain's reluctance to place her commitment to Europe before her special relationship with the United States. According to Aron, in December, 1962, the British had several possibilities open to them: "There was the possibility of going to America and asking for a substitute for Skybolt. There was the possibility of dropping the British deterrent completely. But there was—in de Gaulle's mind, at least—a third possibility. That was to go to the French and say: 'Let's produce ballistic missiles together.' Nobody in Britain mentioned the third possibility. The British reaction was to ask the United States for something else. And this was at the exact time when Britain was trying to get into the Common Market."[84]

The year 1963 found NATO at the crossroads. The differences between the United States and France appeared to be widening. Many observers were unable to escape the conclusion that at the root of the disagreement between President de Gaulle and US officials over the problem of nuclear sharing and the conduct of Alliance policy lay the question of Britain's future relationship to the Continent. The United States still favoured the further economic and political integration of Western Europe and the inclusion of Britain in the European Community. President de Gaulle, however, who had long been critical of American leadership

[84] "Size-Up of de Gaulle," *US News and World Report*, 22 April, 1963.

of NATO, made little effort to conceal his suspicion that the entry of Britain into the EEC would serve Anglo-American interests more than it would serve those of France as he perceived them. In the meantime, British and American leaders had misgivings that de Gaulle's attempt, over the objections of Italy and the Benelux countries, to forge a special Franco-German relationship might lead to deleterious consequences both for European unity and for the solidarity of the Atlantic Alliance. And when, in January, de Gaulle vetoed British membership in the Common Market on political grounds, the signs were clear that the "permanent alliance" was in some trouble. It was passing through a period of significant structural change. The Soviets were undoubtedly watching events with keen interest, hoping that in an unexpected way Stalin's "last thesis" might be validated and the Western allies have a serious falling out among themselves. The advocates of NATO, on the other hand, preferred to view the vigorous airing of transatlantic differences as evidence that the Atlantic Community, far from disintegrating, was passing through a great "constitutional debate" concerning the form of its next and higher phase of existence.

The summer of 1963 witnessed what appeared to all observers to be a major development in East-West relations. Speaking in June at the commencement exercises of American University in Washington, President Kennedy announced that special representatives of Britain, the United States and the Soviet Union would meet in Moscow in July to try again to reach agreement on a test ban treaty, after hundreds of sessions at Geneva since 1958 had failed to produce such an agreement. President Kennedy's speech, in which he suggested a "strategy of peace" to lead the Powers out of the Cold War, was well received in the USSR. Premier Khrushchev, while visiting East Berlin on 2 July, offered to accept something which had frequently been sought by the

American government under both Eisenhower and Kennedy, and by the Macmillan government as an alternative to an agreement requiring on-site inspections, viz., a partial and nationally policed ban on nuclear tests in the atmosphere, under the seas, and in outer space. But Khrushchev at first linked the conclusion of a test ban with the signing of a non-aggression treaty between NATO and the Warsaw Pact countries. The Western Powers were extremely wary of the proposal for a European non-aggression pact, which had long been an objective of Soviet diplomacy. Most Western statesmen were not opposed to a non-aggression pact as such, apart from the fact that they could see no necessity for such a pact, in view of the defensive nature of NATO and the pledges already undertaken in the United Nations Charter. They feared, however, that the Soviets might exploit such a pact either to secure formal Western recognition of East Germany or to bring about a weakening of NATO solidarity, or both.

Averell Harriman and Viscount Hailsham led the American and British delegations, respectively, in the Moscow talks which culminated, on 18 July, 1963, in the initialling of a treaty banning tests in the three environments mentioned above. Except for the treaty of 1959 which demilitarised Antarctica, this was the first formal arms agreement ever reached between the Soviets and the West. Western analysts were not agreed on the political, economic and strategic motivations which may have been behind the Soviet decision to enter the treaty. Some attributed the Soviets' *démarche* to a desire to mend their fences with the West as their dispute with Peking over ideology and strategy became more acrimonious. Others traced it to a concern over domestic pressures for raising the standard of living and sustaining the economic growth rate. Still others were inclined to think that the Soviet leaders, recognising the strategic nuclear superiority of the United States (as manifested in the Cuban confrontation), may have decided that it would be to their advantage to damp the rate of military-technological competition and to lessen Soviet-Western tensions. Finally, there were some who interpreted the shift in terms of a Soviet desire to join the United States in halting the further proliferation of nuclear weapons to nations not already possessing them. It was doubtful, however, that the test ban would serve to inhibit the Chinese, who vehemently denounced it. Whether or not France would eventually adhere to the treaty depended to a considerable extent upon the policy which the United States and Britain would adopt with respect to French nuclear aspirations. President de Gaulle, in his press conference of 29 July, 1963, declared that France could not possibly adhere to the treaty under existing circumstances. Whether or not the existing circumstances could be altered remained to be seen. There were straws in the wind, lofted by President Kennedy himself, that the United States and Britain were contemplating an offer of closer military co-operation with France in the form of shared knowledge and weaponry, contingent upon the modification of France's official attitudes towards the organisation of NATO.[85] The French President, however, was reported to have turned down the American offer of nuclear assistance in exchange for a French signature on the partial test ban treaty.[86] In August, 1963, de Gaulle appeared to be committed to a "do-it-yourself" policy so far as his country's nuclear capabilities were concerned. No one could predict with any degree of assurance whether France might be persuaded to take a second look at NATO as well as her own rôle within it, and to participate in the reunification of the Western deterrent.

In the latter half of 1963, the Atlantic Alliance found itself entering upon a period in which it would face new opportunities, some of them quite promising, and new challenges,

[85] *New York Times*, 2 August, 1963.
[86] *Ibid.*, 7 August, 1963.

some of them not a little dangerous. Throughout history, democratic coalitions have found it difficult to maintain their cohesion whenever the particular external threats which have brought them into existence began to show signs, either actual or apparent, of diminishing. The Soviets, irrespective of what their real purposes happened to be in concluding a test ban agreement, could be expected to exploit the *détente* to make political inroads against NATO and Western Europe. They were certain to encourage the formation of "united front" governments wherever possible, while at the same time promoting schemes for disengagement, denuclearisation, a settlement in Berlin, and German reunification on terms beneficial to themselves and disadvantageous to NATO. Western governments felt obliged to maintain an open, probing mind towards whatever arms control measures might genuinely help to improve the safety of the international environment against the outbreak and the damages of war. But they also had to remember two other important facts. First, totalitarian systems, even assuming that they wish to change (which is itself a rare phenomenon), take a very long time to modify their essential character by evolving towards less oppressive institutions and processes. Second—and more important—the Atlantic Alliance, in the hearts of its founders and supporters, was always intended to be more than a mere military defence organisation. From the very beginning there was a hope that co-operation in military matters would lay the groundwork for a closer political unity—for a restoration of a cultural region which had, somewhere along its historic route, experienced a tragic fragmentation. No matter what the Soviets did, no matter how much they mellowed, the progressive growth of the Atlantic Community and of its institutions would continue to strike many thoughtful men as an eminently worthwhile task.

Chapter 6

CONCLUSIONS

Within recent years, and especially since the disruption of alliance solidarity during the Suez crisis, the charge has often been heard that NATO is in disarray. Undoubtedly, many of the recent and current criticisms are quite justifiable. But the disarrayal theme has not always been justified. Actually, the Atlantic allies have accomplished a great deal within the last twelve years, and their achievements should not be depreciated. Compared with the precarious situation which prevailed in 1949, Europe today presents a picture of stability and prodigious development in all dimensions. It has been under the protective shield of NATO that Europe has been able to register the remarkable economic, technological, social and political gains of the last decade. Indeed, some of the key policy problems confronting the Alliance in recent years arise more out of the successes rather than the failures of the NATO coalition.

The Soviets themselves cannot but deem NATO to be of the utmost historic importance. As they gaze westwards, the Soviet leaders must at times wonder about the wisdom of the USSR's postwar foreign policy towards Western Europe. If it had been their objective to keep Europe disunited and separated from the United States, it is difficult to envisage a policy less calculated to achieve this goal than the one which they have pursued since 1945. Their postwar policy in Eastern and Central Europe (exemplified by the Czech coup of 1948) was based professedly upon fear of a threat to their security from a rearmed Germany, but led paradoxically to the formation of NATO, the rearmament of West Germany and the integration of that country into the Western Alliance as a key military partner.

The NATO bulwark on the Soviets' western flank, which represents a total military investment of well over $100 billion, has brought the "flow period" of Soviet expansion to an end, at least along the European sector of the world front. This centre of military and economic power is thwarting the smooth operation of the Marxist dialectic. It has slowed "the inevitable march of history" by forcing the communist bloc to be extremely cautious in its direct confrontation with the West. The Soviets, in their desire to avoid a frontal clash with NATO, have sought to outflank it in Asia, Africa and Latin America. They have also been forced to manoeuvre more subtly, employing diplomatic, economic and psycho-political techniques, as well as "safer" and more controllable forms of organised violence. But even in the peripheral or "gray" areas, the existence of NATO presents a deterrent effect, since a Soviet attack upon a region not protected by the North Atlantic Treaty may lead to increased efforts of preparedness on the part of the Atlantic Allies (as the communist aggression in Korea most certainly did).

The United States as the premier NATO ally is frequently criticised for the emphasis which it places upon military defence. An increasing number of observers, pointing to what they regard as the failure of military containment, have urged that Western efforts be shifted to the economic and psycho-political fields. But if the social struggle between communism and the Western world has been raised in recent years to a higher level of rational competition, this is not because the communists disdain military power. Rather it is because they respect it. There can be little doubt that the NATO countries must increase their efforts in the non-military fields and the volume of resources devoted thereto. But this will require an increase in the West's total strategic output. It should not be accomplished by diverting resources from the vital area of military defence, or the day may come when the violence which is now deterred will be calculatedly unleashed, once the Soviets have gained a decisive margin of superiority in military technology and deployment. The West most assuredly must strive to parry and out-perform the Soviets on the more subtle manoeuvring ground of "competitive coexistence" which they have chosen in the Khrushchev era. By all means the West must look to its flanks—in Asia, Africa and Latin America—lest they be turned. But under no circumstances should the central front be neglected. And on the global strategic battlefield, NATO is still the central front.

Even along the NATO central front, the problems of military defence are far from having been solved. Within recent years, and especially since the address of the US Defence Secretary, Mr McNamara, at the University of Michigan in June, 1962, there has been an open disagreement between the United States and some of its principal NATO partners over the relative roles to be accorded nuclear and non-nuclear forces in the local defence of Europe. Although NATO statesmen regularly pay lip service to the solidarity of the Allies in their determination to resist Soviet aggression, NATO has yet to arrive at a consensus regarding a strategic rationale for the defence of Europe. The argument comes down to the issue of deterrence versus operational military planning. Whereas many Europeans appear to be primarily interested in keeping a Soviet attack "unthinkable", and in relying heavily on the deterrent functions of nuclear weapons for this purpose, American policy-makers have urged greater emphasis upon non-nuclear capabilities for coping with

Soviet military challenges in the intermediate range. Hence the NATO problem today, as it has been for many years, is to reach a basic understanding on the essential *raison d'être* of the Alliance: Is NATO a sort of tripwire, designed to trigger strategic nuclear retaliation, should deterrence fail, or is the Alliance an organisation for the local and relatively limited defence of Europe? The problem is an urgent one. Its settlement cannot be postponed pending the resolution of NATO's other dilemmas.

One of these other dilemmas—since the latter part of 1962 perhaps the major dilemma—concerns independent European nuclear forces. Many Europeans who are unenthusiastic about raising their contribution to NATO's conventional forces have become increasingly interested in achieving a certain degree of strategic nuclear self-sufficiency, both to enhance their deterrent against Soviet aggression and to give them greater political-strategic leverage within the Alliance as well as in the world arena. It is not likely that those Europeans who aspire to the creation of national or European multilateral nuclear deterrents will be in full agreement with the American proposals for a so-called NATO deterrent, since many of them are convinced that such a deterrent would remain substantially under US control. It has often been suggested that these aspirations are a phenomenon associated with the policy of President de Gaulle. But these aspirations antedated de Gaulle's ascendancy to power in France. There can be little doubt that they will endure beyond his rule, and will be likely to grow more widespread throughout the European NATO community. In fact, as 1963 drew to a close, some Europeans were speaking more and more confidently of Europe's ability, based on the success of the Common Market, to establish its own nuclear deterrent, with or without US assistance, within a period of five to ten years.

In the economic realm, the Atlantic nations possess capabilities not only for defending themselves against the threat of communist aggression but also for projecting their political and economic influence throughout the developing regions of the world. The Soviets must realise that the Atlantic nations at the present time possess a much larger productive base with which to carry out the process of international development, if only they can manage to co-ordinate their economic policies. This is one reason why Mr Khrushchev has led the communist bloc attack upon the Common Market as a grave neo-imperialist threat to the independence of the emergent nations. It is obvious that the communist leaders are deeply concerned over the long-range implications of the integration which has been carried out in Europe under the mantle of NATO. If the course of events in Western Europe has carried the states of that region "beyond redemption" so far as the Soviets are concerned, then the Soviets cannot but conclude that their policy in Europe has failed and that the tide is running against them. As they look to the future, Soviet strategists have reason to despair over their ability to match the combined economic and political resources of the Atlantic Community. Barring a major breakthrough in military technology, their chances of achieving world hegemony are likely to diminish with each passing year.

A continuing objective of Soviet strategy, therefore, will be to work for the dissolution of the Atlantic Alliance before the latter can bring its full power to bear upon the international environment. It is no mere coincidence that practically every serious Soviet disarmament proposal in the last six years has called, in one way or another, for the withdrawal of United States military power from Western Europe. The Soviets apparently look upon the American military presence in Europe as the "cement" of the Alliance, and doubt that cultural, economic and political factors alone would be sufficient to hold it together for long. Whether such analysis is correct is beside the point. The main point is that the Soviets can be expected during the 1960s to work towards creating an international situation which will be unfavourable to the continuation of the North Atlantic Treaty beyond 1969, the year in which the member states may reconsider their adherence. The Soviets may be encouraged to think that their chances of eventually dismantling NATO have been enhanced by the divisions which de Gaulle's opposition to British entry into the Common Market provoked among the Atlantic Allies.

The early months of 1963 indeed seemed to be a time of troubles for the Western Alliance. It seemed clear that, if NATO was to retain its cohesion, compromise was necessary on both sides of the Atlantic. Perhaps there is no more appropriate way to conclude this modest volume on the Atlantic Alliance than to repeat a discreetly optimistic statement made by one of NATO's principal founders. The former US Secretary of State, Dean Acheson, speaking at the University of California on 13 March, 1963, said: "The writer of Ecclesiastes has told us that there is 'a time to every purpose . . . a time to break down and a time to build up'. January last was, apparently, a time to break down in the midst of a long time of building up. It did some damage. It is now time to repair that and get on again with building up."

WORKS REFERRED TO IN TEXT

BOOKS AND DOCUMENTS

ABRAHAMSEN, SAMUEL, *Sweden's Foreign Policy*, Public Affairs Press, Washington, 1957.

ACHESON, DEAN G., *Sketches from the Life of Men I Have Known*, Harper, New York, 1961.

ALASTOS, DOROS, *Cyprus Guerrilla*, Heinemann, London, 1960.

American Diplomacy 1900-50, University of Chicago Press. 1951.

American Foreign Policy 1950-1955, Basic Documents, US Department of State Publication 6446.

BALL, M. MARGARET, *NATO and the European Union Movement*, Stevens, London, 1959, and Praeger, New York, 1959.

BAUMANN, CAROL ELDER, *Political Co-operation in NATO*, University of Wisconsin, 1960.

BROWN, W. A., Jr., and OPIE, R., *American Foreign Assistance*, Brookings Institution, Washington, 1953.

BRZEZINSKI, ZBIGNIEW K., *The Soviet Bloc: Unity and Conflict*, Harvard University Press, 1960 (also in Praeger Paperback series, revised edition 1961).

BUCHAN, ALASTAIR, *NATO in the 1960s*, Chatto and Windus, London, 1960 ; Praeger, New York, 1960.

CONANT, MELVIN, *The Long Polar Watch: Canada and the Defense of North America*, Harper, New York, 1962.

Control and Reduction of Armaments, US Senate Hearings, Part II, 1957.

The Council of Europe and the Schuman Plan, Council of Europe Directorate of Information, Strasburg, 1952.

Cyprus: Background to Enosis, Royal Institute of International Affairs, London, 1957.

DALLIN, DAVID J., *Soviet Foreign Policy after Stalin*, Lippincott, Philadelphia, 1961.

DAVISON, W. PHILLIPS, *The Berlin Blockade* (A Rand Study), Princeton University Press, 1958.

The Declaration of Paris, NATO Letter, Vol. X, Paris, 1962.

DIEBOLD, WILLIAM, Jr., *The Schuman Plan*, Praeger, New York, 1959.

DINERSTEIN, H. S., *Military Force and Soviet Goals*, The Rand Corporation, RM-2771, 1961.

——, *Soviet Strategic Ideas*, The Rand Corporation, RM-2532, 1960.

Discussion on Cyprus in the North Atlantic Treaty Organisation, September-October 1958, Cmnd. 566, HMSO, London, 1959.

DONOVAN, ROBERT J., *Eisenhower: The Inside Story*, Harper, New York, 1956.

Economic Problems and NATO, Aspects of NATO series, NATO Information Service, Paris, 1961.

The European Common Market, American Management Association, New York, 1958.

The European Community: The Facts (2nd Edn.), European Community Information Service, 1960.

FINLETTER, THOMAS K., *Foreign Policy: The Next Phase*, Harper, New York, 1960.

Foreign Aid Appropriations for 1951, Hearings before the Subcommittee of the House Committee on Appropriations, 81st Congress.

FRANK, ISAIAH, *The European Common Market: An Analysis of Commercial Policy*, Praeger, New York, 1961.

GARTHOFF, RAYMOND L., *The Soviet Image of Future War*, Public Affairs Press, Washington, 1959.

The Geneva Conference of Heads of Government, US Department of State Publication, 6044, 1955.

GOERLITZ, WALTER, *History of the German General Staff*, Praeger, New York, 1953.

HAAS, ERNEST B., *The Uniting of Europe: Political, Social and Economic Forces 1950-7*, Stevens, London, 1958.

HAAS, ERNEST B., and WHITING, ALLEN S., *Dynamics of International Relations*, McGraw-Hill, New York, 1956.

HINTERHOFF, EUGENE, *Disengagement*, Stevens, London, 1959.

HOWARD, MICHAEL, *Disengagement in Europe*, Penguin, London and Baltimore, 1958.

ISMAY, Lord, *NATO, The First Five Years, 1949-1954*, The North Atlantic Treaty Organisation, Paris, 1955.

KEATING, KENNETH B., *Survey of Trade Relations Between the United States and Common Market Nations*, Government Printing Office, Washington, 1962.

KENNAN, GEORGE F., *Russia and the West Under Lenin and Stalin*, Atlantic-Little Brown, Boston, 1961.

——, *Russia, the Atom and the West*, Harper, New York, 1958.

KISSINGER, HENRY A., *Nuclear Weapons and Foreign Policy*, Harper, New York, 1957.

——, *The Necessity for Choice*, Harper, New York, 1961.

KNIGHT-PATTERSON, W. M., *Germany from Defeat to Conquest, 1913-33*, G. Allen, London, 1945.

KNORR, KLAUS (Ed.) *NATO and American Security*, Princeton University Press, 1959.

LANCASTER, DONALD, *The Emancipation of French Indo-China*, Oxford University Press, 1961.

LENIN, V. I., "Left-Wing Childishness and Petty Bourgeois Mentality", *Selected Works*, New York.

LENKZOWSKI, GEORGE, *The Middle East in World Affairs*, Cornell University Press, 1962.

LERNER, DANIEL MAX, and ARON, RAYMOND, *France Defeats EDC*, Praeger, New York, 1957.

LINDSAY, KENNETH, *European Assemblies: The Experimental Period 1949-59*, Stevens, London, 1959 ; Praeger, New York, 1959.

LISKA, GEORGE, *Nations in Alliance: The Limits of Interdependence*, The Johns Hopkins University Press, 1962.

LONDON, KURT, *The Permanent Crisis*, Walker, New York, 1962.

MACKINTOSH, J. M., *Strategy and Tactics of Soviet Foreign Policy*, Oxford University Press, 1962.

MAGER and KATEL, *Conquest Without War: An Analytical Anthology of the Speeches, Interviews and Remarks of N. S. Khrushchev, with Commentary by Lenin, Stalin and others*, Simon and Schuster, New York, 1961.

MARLOWE, J., *Arab Nationalism and British Imperialism*, Cresset Press, London, 1961 ; Praeger, New York, 1961.

MARSHALL, C. B., *Two Communist Manifestos*, The Washington Center of Foreign Policy Research, 1961.

MIKSCHE, F. O., *The Failure of Atomic Strategy*, Praeger, New York, 1958.

MOORE, BEN T., *NATO and the Future of Europe*, Harper, New York, 1958.

MULLEY, F. W., *The Politics of Western Defence*, Thames and Hudson, London, 1962 ; Praeger, New York, 1962.

MURRAY, T. E., *Nuclear Energy for War and Peace*, World Publishing Co., New York, 1960.

NOEL-BAKER, PHILIP, *The Arms Race*, Stevens, London, 1959; Oceana Press, New York, 1960.
The NATO Handbook, NATO Information Service, Paris.

Organisation for Economic Co-operation and Development, Hearings before the Senate Committee on Foreign Relations, 87th Congress.
OSANKA, FRANKLIN M. (Ed.), *Modern Guerrilla Warfare*, Free Press of Glencoe, 1962.
OSGOOD, ROBERT, *NATO: The Entangling Alliance*, University of Chicago Press, 1962.

PRICE, H. B., *The Marshall Plan and its Meaning*, Cornell University Press, 1955.
PURCELL, VICTOR, *Malaya: Communist or Free*, Stanford University Press, 1954.
PYE, LUCIEN W., *Guerrilla Communism in Malaya*, Princeton University Press, 1957.

Report of the Committee of Three on Non-Military Co-operation in NATO, US Department cf State Publication 6449.
Reports and Recommendations adopted by the Seventh Annual NATO Parliamentarians' Conference, 1961.
RIDGWAY, M. B., *Soldier: Memoirs of Matthew B. Ridgway*, Harper, New York, 1956.
ROBERTSON, A. H., *European Institutions*, Stevens, London, 1958; Praeger, New York, 1958.
ROSTOW, W. W., *The United States in the World Arena*, Harper, New York, 1960.

SALVADORI, MASSIMO, *NATO: A Twentieth Century Community of Nations*, Von Nostrand, Princeton, 1957.
SNYDER, GLENN H., *Deterrence and Defense*, Princeton University Press, 1961.
STEBBINS, RICHARD P., *The United States in World Affairs, 1959*, Harper, New York, 1960.
STRAUSZ-HUPE, R., DOUGHERTY, J. E. and KINTNER, W. R., *Building the Atlantic World*, Harper, New York, 1963.
STRAUSZ-HUPE, R., and HAZARD, H. W. (Eds.), *The Idea of Colonialism*, Praeger, New York, 1958.
STRAUSZ-HUPE, R., KINTNER, W. R., DOUGHERTY, J. E., and COTTRELL, A. J., *Protracted Conflict*, Harper, New York, 1959.
The Suez Canal Problem, US Department of State Publication 6392, 1956.

Survey of Trade Relations between the United States and Common Market Nations, Government Printing Office, Washington, 1962.

TAYLOR, MAXWELL D., *The Uncertain Trumpet*, Harper, New York, 1959.
TRUMAN, HARRY S., *Memoirs*, Vol. II, *Years of Trial and Hope*, Doubleday, New York, 1956.

The United States and the Sino-Soviet Bloc in South-East Asia, The Brookings Institution, Washington, 1962.
United States Policy in the Middle East, US Department of State Publication 6505, 1957.
United States Policy: Western Europe, a report prepared at the request of the US Senate Foreign Relations Committee by the Foreign Policy Research Institute, University of Pennsylvania, 1960.

WEIR, SIR CECIL, *The First Step in European Integration*, The Federal Trust for Education and Research, London, 1957.
WHITAKER, ARTHUR P., *Spain and Defense of the West: Ally and Liability*, Harper, New York, 1961 (also in Praeger Paperback Series).
WOLFERS, ARNOLD (Ed.), *Alliance Policy and the Cold War*, Johns Hopkins University Press, 1959.

ESSAYS AND ARTICLES

ACHESON, DEAN G., "Fifty Years After", *The Yale Review*, Autumn, 1961.
——, "The Illusion of Disengagement", *Foreign Affairs*, April, 1958.
——, "The Premises of American Policy", *Orbis*, Autumn, 1959.
AMME, CAPT. CARL H., "Psychological Effects of Nuclear Weapons", *US Naval Institute Proceedings*, Vol. 86, April, 1960.
ARON, RAYMOND, "The Future of Western Deterrent Power", *Bulletin of the Atomic Scientists*, Vol. XVI, September, 1960.
ASCHINGER, F. E., "The United States and the Common Market", *Swiss Review of World Affairs*, Zürich, March, 1962.
BLACK, C. E. and YEAGER, F. J., "The USSR and NATO", in *NATO and the European Movement*, Margaret M. Ball (Ed.), Stevens, London, 1959 ; Praeger, New York, 1959.

BUCHAN, ALASTAIR, "Refashioning NATO: A Partnership Puzzle", *The Washington Post*, August 12, 1962.
——, "The Reform of NATO", *Foreign Affairs*, January, 1962.

BURNS, A. L., "NATO and Nuclear Sharing" in *NATO and American Security*, Klaus Knorr (Ed.), Princeton University Press, 1959.

"Common Market on the Move", *Manchester Guardian Weekly*, January 18, 1962.

"Commonwealth Ministers Are Apprehensive", *EFTA Reporter*, October 9, 1961.

COTTRELL, A. J., "Nuclear Weapons, Policy and Strategy", *Orbis*, Summer, 1957.

COTTRELL, A. J. and DOUGHERTY, J. E., "Algeria: A Case Study in the Evolution of a Colonial Problem", in *The Idea of Colonialism*, Robert Strausz-Hupé and Harry W. Hazard (Eds.), Praeger, New York, 1958; "The Lessons of Korea", *Orbis*, Spring, 1958; "Cyprus: Conflict and Reconciliation", *The World Today*, April, 1959.

COTTRELL, A. J., and HAHN, W. F., "A New Strategy for Europe", *The Yale Review*, Autumn, 1959.

"Cuban Crisis: A Step-by-Step Review", *New York Times*, November 3, 1962.

DOUGHERTY, J. E., "The Aswan Decision in Perspective", *Political Science Quarterly*, March, 1959.

——, "The Guerrilla War in Malaya", in *Modern Guerrilla Warfare*, Franklin M. Osanka (Ed.), Free Press of Glencoe, 1962.

DUPUY, T. N., "Can America Fight a Limited Nuclear War?", *Orbis*, Spring, 1961.

EDEN, SIR ANTHONY, "The Slender Margin of Safety", *Foreign Affairs*, January, 1961.

"EEC Farm Policy", *Bulletin from the European Community*, No. 52, March-April, 1962.

"EEC Ministers Agree at Last", *Manchester Guardian Weekly*, January 18, 1962.

"European Command", *Manchester Guardian Weekly*, November 22, 1956.

FURNISS, E. S., Jr., "De Gaulle's France and NATO: An Interpretation", *International Organisation*, Summer, 1961.

FORBATH, PETER, "Coming to Terms with the Common Market", *The Reporter*, June 20, 1963.

GAITSKELL, HUGH, Article in *Foreign Affairs*, July, 1958.

GASS, OSCAR, "Crusade for Trade", *The New Republic*, March 19 and 26, 1962.

GINIGER, HENRY, "De Gaulle Still Tough", *New York Times*, June 9, 1963.

HAHN, LORNA, "Last Chance in North Africa", *Foreign Affairs*, ✓ January, 1958.

HALPERIN, M. H., "The Dilemma of the Western Alliance", *The New Republic*, May 7, 1962.

HEALEY, DENIS, "NATO and the Cold War", *Confluence*, Autumn, 1957.

"Highlights of the Agricultural Agreement", *Bulletin from the European Community*, No. 52, March-April, 1962.

HILSMAN, ROGER, "NATO: The Developing Strategic Concept", in *NATO and American Security*, Klaus Knorr (Ed.), Princeton University Press, 1959.

——, "On NATO Strategy", in *Alliance Policy and the Cold War*, Arnold Wolfers (Ed.), Johns Hopkins University Press, 1959.

HOAG, M. W., "Interdependence for NATO", *World Politics*, Vol. 12, April, 1960.

——, "NATO's Strategy and Limited War", in *NATO and American Security*, Klaus Knorr (Ed.), Princeton University Press, 1959.

JOHNSON, D. H. N., "The Geneva Conference on the Law of the Sea", *The Year Book of World Affairs, 1959*, Stevens, London ; Praeger, New York.

JOHNSTON, ERIC, "We Must Join the Common Market", *New York Times Magazine*, November 12, 1961.

KAHN, HERMAN, "The Arms Race and Some of its Hazards", *Daedalus*, Autumn, 1960.

KALB, MADELAINE and MARVIN, "The Communist Dread of the Common Market", *The Reporter*, July 14, 1962.

KARCH, JOHN T., "Oder-Neisse: Anachronism of World War II", *World Affairs*, Winter, 1960.

KENNAN, GEORGE F., "The Sources of Soviet Conduct", Appendix 1, *American Diplomacy 1900-50*, University of Chicago Press, 1951.

LAWSON, RUTH, "Concerting Policies in the North Atlantic Community", *International Organisation*, Spring, 1958.

LINCOLN, GORDON, "The Organisation for European Economic Co-operation", *International Organisation*, 1956.

LINDGREN, RAYMOND E., "International Co-operation in Scandinavia", *The Yearbook of World Affairs, 1959,* Stevens, London ; Praeger, New York.

LIPPMAN, WALTER, Article in the *Washington Post Outlook*, December 2, 1962.

LYON, PEYTON V., "Problems of Canadian Independence", *International Journal*, Summer, 1961.

MCKESSON, JOHN A., "The Schuman Plan", *Political Science Quarterly*, March, 1952.

MAY, JOHN ALLEN, "Common Market Bars Loan", *Christian Science Monitor*, January 11, 1962.

——, "Mirror on Commonwealth", *Christian Science Monitor*, January 11, 1962.

MERRY, HENRY J., "The European Coal and Steel Community: Operations of the High Authority", *Western Political Quarterly*, June, 1955.

MORGENTHAU, HANS, "Beleaguered Bastion", *The Washington Post*, July 2, 1961.

NOVE, ALEC, "Communists and the Common Market", *The New Republic*, September 17, 1962.

NUTTING, ANTHONY, Article in the *New York Herald Tribune*, February 17, 1958.

"OEEC into OECD", *The World Today*, May, 1961.

PADELFORD, NORMAN J., "Political Co-operation in the North Atlantic Community", *International Organisation*, Summer, 1955.

PETERSEN, HOWARD, "The Common Market: Opportunity Knocks", *Christian Science Monitor*, January 11, 1962.

"Reflections on the Quarter", *Orbis*, Spring, 1962.

REYNAUD, PAUL, "The Unifying Force for Europe", *Foreign Affairs*, January, 1950.

"Right Decision: Wrong Route", *Manchester Guardian Weekly*, August 3, 1961.

SCHUMAN, ROBERT, "France and Europe", *Foreign Affairs*, April, 1953.

SCHWARZ, HARRY, "Soviet is Pressing Hard on Economic and Political Fronts: The Economic Front", *New York Times*, September 2, 1962.

SETHUR, FREDERICK, "The Schuman Plan and Ruhr Coal", *Political Science Quarterly*, December, 1952.

"Size-up of de Gaulle", *US News and World Report*, April 22, 1963.

SPAAK, PAUL-HENRI, "The West in Disarray", *Foreign Affairs*, January, 1957.

SPEIER, HANS, "Soviet Atomic Blackmail and the North Atlantic Alliance", *World Politics*, April, 1957.

STRANG, LORD, "Germany Between East and West", *Foreign Affairs*, April, 1955.

STRANGE, SUSAN, "Suez and After", *The Yearbook of World Affairs, 1957*, Stevens, London ; Praeger, New York.

STRAUSS, FRANZ-JOSEF, "Soviet Aims and German Unity", *Foreign Affairs*, April, 1939.

TAYLOR, EDMOND, "A New Popular Front?", *The Reporter*, June 20, 1963.

WALTON, CLARENCE C., "Background for the European Defence Community", *Political Science Quarterly*, March, 1953.

WAUTERS, ARTHUR, "Four Constants of Stalinism", *Western World*, August, 1958.

WELCH, WILLIAM, "Soviet Commitments to Collective Action", in *Alliance Policy and the Cold War*, Arnold Wolfers (Ed.), Johns Hopkins University Press, 1959.

WOHLSTETTER, ALBERT, "NATO and the N + 1 Country", *Foreign Affairs*, April, 1961.

WORSWICK, G. D. N., "Britain, the Common Market, and a Free Trade Area", *Year Book of World Affairs, 1958*, Stevens, London ; Praeger, New York.

YEAGER, F. J., *The USSR and NATO: A Study in the Implications of Soviet Foreign Policy* (unpublished dissertation, Princeton University, 1959).

INDEX